TRANSACTIONS

OF THE

AMERICAN PHILOSOPHICAL SOCIETY

HELD AT PHILADELPHIA
FOR PROMOTING USEFUL KNOWLEDGE

NEW SERIES—VOLUME 65, PART 2
1975

DISTRACTIONS OF PEACE DURING WAR:

The Lloyd George Government's Reactions to Woodrow Wilson
December, 1916—November, 1918

STERLING J. KERNEK

Department of History, Western Illinois University

THE AMERICAN PHILOSOPHICAL SOCIETY

INDEPENDENCE SQUARE

PHILADELPHIA

April, 1975

To

F. H. HINSLEY

Library of Congress Catalog
Card Number 75-2608
International Standard Book Number 0-87169-652-5
US ISSN 0065-9746

PREFACE

This book examines the reactions of Lloyd George's wartime government to Woodrow Wilson in relation to peace moves and war aims. The general theme of the work is that, in their handling of the president, the British easily achieved their major goals. During the latter stages of Wilson's neutrality, they readily parried his attempts to stop the war short of a victory for either side. After the United States entered the conflict, the British leaders were able to exploit the president's determination to win the war while avoiding commitments to carry out any American aims which they considered hostile to British interests.

Research on this project began at Cambridge University in 1967 soon after some important British collections of documents were opened to scholars. Numerous debts of gratitude have been incurred since then. Dr. Jonathan Steinberg helped to define the topic. Professor F. H. Hinsley provided invaluable supervision and encouragement. Helpful suggestions were made by Arthur S. Link, Henry Pelling, and A. J. P. Taylor. The work also profited by the criticism of Christopher M. Mason, John D. Leslie, C. T. Stannage, and Charles G. Sadler. I am responsible for any defects which remain.

The Penrose Fund of the American Philosophical Society provided a grant which enabled me to examine relevant documents in the United States. The Research Council of Western Illinois University also extended financial assistance.

In addition, I must thank the following for access to and/or permission to quote documents in which they hold the copyright: Cambridge University Library; Yale University Library; the University of Birmingham; the Princeton University Library; the Houghton Library, Harvard University; the Warden and Fellows of New College, Oxford; A. J. P. Taylor and the First Beaverbrook Foundation; the Manuscript Division, Library of Congress; the Marquess of Lothian and the Scottish Record Office; the Trustees of the British Museum; and the Public Record Office in London. Extracts from Crown-copyright records in the Public Record Office appear by permission of the Controller of H. M. Stationery Office.

S.J.K.

NOTE ON REFERENCES

The British Cabinet and Foreign Office papers are the most important primary sources in this work. The references to these documents appear in a somewhat unconventional form, but the system is both specific and easy to use.

All citations beginning with CAB or F.O. can be found in the Public Record Office. The first two numbers following the letters CAB and F.O. can be used in the Public Record Office to request the volume of documents required—for example, CAB 23/1 or F.O. 371/2806. Once the reader has the correct volume, he merely needs to remember that the remaining number or numbers refer to increasingly specific classifications. With the correct volume in hand, the classifications should be readily apparent. For instance, CAB 23/1 is a volume of Cabinet minutes. In the reference CAB 23/1/10/3, the number 10 refers to the tenth meeting; the number 3 refers to the third minute. CAB 24/32 is a volume of various documents submitted to the Cabinet. In the reference CAB 24/32/2648, the number 2648 refers to the number of the document.

The Foreign Office references are used in a similar way. That is, each subsequent number refers to an increasingly specific classification. For the reader who is familiar with the F.O. documents of the period, it is sufficient to mention that the file number precedes the number of the paper. For example, in the footnote reference F.O. 371/2806/252387/265104, the number 252387 is the file number; the so-called number of the paper is 265104. The latter number will be stamped upon the "minuting jacket," which is attached to the document. A particular "minuting jacket" will often cover a small group of related documents, but the specific document being cited can readily be found within that group.

Some series of F.O. documents do not have file numbers and paper numbers. In such cases additional information has been noted to indicate the document cited.

A frequently cited published source is the Department of State's series entitled *Papers Relating to the Foreign Relations of the United States*. This will be referred to as *Foreign Relations*.

DISTRACTIONS OF PEACE DURING WAR: THE LLOYD GEORGE GOVERNMENT'S REACTIONS TO WOODROW WILSON, DECEMBER, 1916—NOVEMBER, 1918

STERLING J. KERNEK

CONTENTS

I. INTRODUCTION

Peace is the perpetual alternative to war, and questions of peace frequently complicate the lives of war leaders. When and how should the war be ended? Could any of the enemy powers be drawn into a separate peace? What should the territorial peace terms be? How can the need for security be met after the war? What economic terms are necessary or desirable? What statements about peace should be made public? David Lloyd George's wartime government dealt with many such questions and one of the key figures in their calculations was the president of the United States.

1. THE WOULD-BE PEACEMAKER

Woodrow Wilson dominated the foreign policy decisions of the young, *nouveau riche* power of enormous potential across the Atlantic. Moreover, during the first two years of the war he had developed a strong and increasing desire to play a great role in arranging peace. Wilson's office and his ambitions made the problem of handling him persistent and potentially dangerous to Britain's war efforts.

In their relations with the American president, the British were dealing with a skillful and successful politician. The fact that his name has been popularly associated with a kind of moralistic, liberal idealism is a tribute to his brilliant political rhetoric. Wilson had a flair for rationalizing his political decisions in glittering rhetorical terms. Indeed, he displayed great virtuosity in shaping essentially the same oratorical themes to fit a variety of political purposes and dramatic changes in policy.

This is not to suggest that he was cynical and insincere. On the contrary, he believed virtually every idealistic thing he said. It was his evident sincerity which earned for him the criticism that he was naïve. Actually, as historians have increasingly realized over the last twenty years, he was far from unrealistic about his political interests. He believed his idealism, but he also used it for shrewd political reasons. There is no contradiction here. As Professor Arthur S. Link once remarked, Wilson's process of rationalization was "unconscious, automatic, and completely satisfying."[1] He brought idealism to the support of expediency as spontaneously as he used English to express ideas. The president's mastery of political rhetoric also

---

[1] Link, 1956: p. 393.

helped him to keep his options open. He used eloquent generalities to create an impression of adventurous commitment when he was, in fact, being quite cautious.[2] His famous "Fourteen Points" address, for example, initially seemed specific and bold, but eventually proved to be vague and wide open to divergent interpretations. It was, of course, fortunate for the British that Wilson's great ambitions were usually tempered by considerable prudence. Indeed, he frequently seemed to abhor trouble, and sometimes his actions were only a pale reflection of his original intentions.

One of the dangers that Wilson might venture beyond the bounds of his usual prudence stemmed from a flaw in his character. He was prone to wishful thinking when an intense ambition was involved. This trait has probably been exaggerated by his critics, but he could be unduly optimistic when abundant evidence suggested that his cherished goals were futile. If facts were inconvenient, he could quite easily ignore them, because he characteristically relied on intuition rather than careful reasoning. Indeed, he tended to be impatient with rational arguments when they contradicted his intuition.

The president was open to suggestions when he was still making up his mind and he could even be critical of his own prejudices, but he was intolerant of opposing advice once he had reached a decision. This was the reason that his chief advisers remained silent when they had misgivings. If they disagreed openly, they might not remain chief advisers.

Much—perhaps too much—has been written about Wilson's Presbyterian faith. Being the eldest son of a Presbyterian minister and of a devout mother, he was imbued with Calvinistic religious beliefs which he put at the service of his restless ambition. He believed that God had established a moral law which men should follow, and he tended to assume that his own opinions harmonized with the divine rules. He felt that the Creator had foreordained the course of history and that he himself was destined to perform great works. These notions may have contributed to the president's irritating air of self-righteousness.

A characteristically American sense of mission was another source of his self-righteousness. Like his religious beliefs, a sense of America's mission was used to promote his own interests. He was wonderfully adept at showing that it was America's mission to pursue whatever goals he wanted to achieve. In the field of international affairs he assumed that a system of nation states was analogous to a society of individuals. What they both needed was what had made America

great: law, democracy, commerce and respect for inalienable rights. Just as America had led the world in creating a good domestic society, she should take the lead in improving the society of nations. Those who followed were friends of mankind; those who disagreed were selfish and reactionary.

Wilson often took political opposition personally. Moreover, he was not only sensitive to criticism on important issues, but he also tended to bear prolonged grudges. It was easy to offend him and difficult to make amends.

These striking aspects of Wilson's character were potentially threatening to friendly Anglo-American relations in 1916. The two governments had radically different perspectives, and the British were sorely tempted to make statements which offended the president. The government in London was totally engaged in waging war; Wilson was leading a "neutral" nation which wanted to remain at peace. The British were determined to win the war; Wilson sought a negotiated settlement without victory for either side. What appeared as dedication to a just cause in Britain, Wilson interpreted as intransigence. What the president thought was a reasonable defense of neutral rights, the British regarded as moral obtuseness, cheap politics, and despicable meddling. Self-righteousness was frequently reciprocal.

The British had one further source of resentment. The American economy was prospering while the British were making enormous sacrifices. In his less irrational moments, Ambassador Spring Rice tried to explain to his countrymen the difference in outlook between a nation at war and one at peace. "The obvious fact is," he wrote, "that if we had the choice of making war or making money, as the U. S. have it, we should probably do the same." He went on, "We should also say, as they do, that we do it in order to serve humanity with the proceeds." Yet Spring Rice's unusually temperate mood did not prevent an expression of irritation. Recalling a famous remark about Gladstone, he added that "one can forgive a man having an ace up his sleeve, but not for saying that God Almighty put it there."[3]

2. LLOYD GEORGE AND THE INCREASE OF BRITISH–AMERICAN ANTAGONISM IN 1916

Lloyd George became prime minister in December, 1916. Before that he served in Asquith's coalitions as minister of munitions and secretary of state for war. His rise in politics was phenomenal. Without powerful family connections, wealth, or a degree from a famous university, he climbed to the summit of British political life.

Critics abound but few doubt his extraordinary abilities. He often spoke eloquently and pungently. In

---

[2] Sir Cecil Spring Rice, British ambassador to Washington, observed in Feb., 1916, that the character of Wilson's "language, while very elevated and convincing, does not lead to any definite practical conclusions." The British were familiar with this kind of style. Spring Rice added that the president had been "likened to Mr. Gladstone" in this respect. See Gwynn, 1929: 2: p. 313.

[3] Spring Rice to Lord Newton, 20 Oct., 1916, *ibid.* 2: p. 322.

debate he could be devastating. He was a shrewd judge of character and in negotiation he adroitly tailored his persuasion to suit his listeners. Lloyd George often succeeded in charming opponents and disarming women.

The most frequent criticism of him is that he was untrustworthy, but to those who supported his move to No. 10 Downing Street, Lloyd George's devious political style seemed much less important than his qualities which could help win the war. He had tremendous energy and he usually began working in the early morning. His methods were unsystematic but he had a forceful way of administering. Though he was not physically brave, he displayed political courage, and he exhibited an imaginative approach to intractable problems.

Undoubtedly he could be an irritating colleague. He preferred circuitous maneuvers to straightforward approaches. Woodrow Wilson was once described as "a man of high ideals and no principles." Even after every allowance is made for the president's expediency, the remark seems more appropriate for Lloyd George. His political pragmatism was relatively unencumbered by moral qualms or genteel social conventions. The chief result of his childhood religious training was a love of hymn singing. It was difficult to predict his tactics or even to discern his real goals. He voraciously gathered information and advice from innumerable sources, but he was inclined to act impulsively on intuition and to rely afterwards on his agile mind to devise facile justifications. His penchant for secrecy further aggravated the mistrust which dogged him. As far as Anglo-American relations are concerned, Lloyd George's devious and volatile political style was a potential source of trouble which added to the manifold anxieties of the British Foreign Office.

Before Lloyd George became prime minister at the end of 1916, Anglo-American relations had become seriously strained. One of the sorest points between the two governments was the question of American mediation. This was the principal result of the famous House-Grey Memorandum. The British helped to raise Wilson's hopes and then proceeded to frustrate them.

The House-Grey Memorandum was an understanding worked out in February, 1916, by Sir Edward Grey,[4] the British foreign secretary in Asquith's government, and Colonel Edward M. House, the president's unofficial adviser and diplomatic agent. They agreed upon conditions for mediation by the president. On a cue from Britain and France, Wilson would propose a peace conference. If Germany refused, the United States would probably enter the war against Germany. If the Germans consented to a peace conference, but proved unreasonable about peace terms, the U. S. "would leave the conference as a belligerent"

on the Allied side. The U. S., according to the memorandum, was decidedly favorable to the restoration of Belgium, the transfer of Alsace-Lorraine to France, an outlet to the sea for Russia, and compensation for Germany's loss of territory by concessions outside Europe. The president approved the agreement in March after making only one amendment. He inserted the word "probably" in the line about leaving the peace conference as a belligerent.[5]

Colonel House was the Foreign Office's best channel of communication with Wilson. He was the president's closest adviser and in his various trips to England he had developed a sympathetic relationship with Sir Edward Grey. House was vainglorious, ambitious, and discreet. Having little chance of wielding great power on his own, he knew that he must work through Wilson and that the greater the role for the president, the greater his own role would be. To ensure his immortality, he faithfully kept a detailed diary which remains an invaluable but not completely trustworthy historical source.

Grey had encouraged House's belief that Wilson's mediation could be arranged, and House, in turn, helped mislead the president. The British foreign secretary was, in fact, seriously interested in the president's mediation, but chiefly as an option which could be used in case the Allies' military prospects worsened.[6] That is, if defeat seemed likely, Wilson's mediation might be called upon to soften the peace terms. Meanwhile, Grey did not want to invite Wilson to move for peace as long as an Allied victory seemed feasible to British military and naval authorities.

When the foreign secretary brought the proposal before a meeting of the War Committee on 21 March, the response of his colleagues was more decisively negative. Bonar Law, the colonial secretary and leader of the Tory party, said that

at the present time the only result of peace negotiations must be based on the *status quo* before the war, and in the present state of public opinion the Government could not enter into negotiations on such a basis, which would be equivalent to defeat for the allies.[7]

Arthur Balfour, the first lord of the admiralty and an ex-prime minister, was uncharacteristically emphatic and decisive on this occasion. "At present," he said, "the proposal was not worth five minutes thought." He went on to remark that, if the proposal were carried out, it would greatly enhance the president's prestige in the United States and get him out of his political difficulties. The British were acutely aware that 1916 was an American presidential election year.

---

[4] Later, in July, 1916, he became Viscount Grey of Fallodon.

[5] For a more detailed account, see Link, 1964: pp. 101–138.

[6] Secret addendum to the proceedings of the War Committee on 21 Mar., 1916, CAB 42/11/16.

[7] *Ibid.* For a new published source on the British rejection, see Cooper, 1973: pp. 958–971. Dr. Cooper suggests that Grey may have actually favored American mediation during the spring of 1916.

With mounting frustration, Wilson and House repeatedly tried to induce the British to accept American mediation. They not only prodded Grey with confidential messages, but the president also publicly fulfilled one of his apparent conditions for American mediation. In earlier correspondence the British foreign secretary had linked the question of accepting Wilson's mediation with the question of America's readiness to join a postwar League of Nations. Thus, on 27 May, in an address to a group known as the League to Enforce Peace, the president declared that the United States was willing to become a partner in an association of nations which would guarantee peace and security. Wilson and House eventually became disillusioned as the British continued to withhold consent to mediation, but their hopes died hard. House persisted with his importunate correspondence into the summer.[8]

The president's disillusionment had an important corollary. Once he realized that he could not achieve mediation by cooperating with Britain, he began considering an independent peace move. If the Allies could not be coaxed, perhaps they should be forced to accept mediation. Wilson knew that he could exert tremendous pressure upon Britain without resorting to arms. He could interfere with her essential supplies from America. Even a mere threat of such action would be frightening in London.

Securing legislation which empowered him to interfere with British supplies was not difficult. During the spring and summer of 1916, anti-British sentiment in America had increased. The harsh suppression of the Easter Rebellion and the execution of Irish rebels produced a predictable outcry. The British continued their interference with the mails despite protests, and they aggravated their unpopularity by intensifying their efforts to stop trade with Germany. In July the British blacklisted American firms which were suspected of trading with the Central Powers. British subjects were not allowed to have any dealings with these American companies. Wilson was furious and actively promoted retaliatory legislation. Early in September, the president was authorized by Congress to prohibit imports from any country which discriminated against American products. He was also given the power to close American ports to the ships of any nation which denied port services to American ships.[9] The implications for Allied supplies from America were, to say the least, ominous. Moreover, the retaliatory legislation was admirably suited to the president's ambitions to stop the war. It could be invoked at his discretion to press the British to accept American mediation.

Meanwhile, Wilson's relations with the German government were at a stage which made the idea of an independent peace move increasingly attractive. The dangerous problem was submarine warfare. The president had hedged and procrastinated on the issue, but he was, nevertheless, deeply committed to restricting (though not prohibiting) Germany's use of her submarines even if it meant risking war. He made this clear during the spring of 1916. On 24 March, a German submarine torpedoed a Channel steamer, the *Sussex,* without warning. Several Americans were injured. The ensuing crisis was particularly serious, because during the previous year Wilson had secured a promise from Germany not to sink passenger ships without warning and without providing for the safety of passengers and crew. The president's response was firm. In April, 1916, he threatened Germany with an immediate break in diplomatic relations unless she refrained from torpedoing without warning not only passenger ships but merchant ships as well. Germany yielded with her so-called *Sussex* pledge. The German promise went far enough to accommodate Wilson, but it was qualified by an ominous reservation. Germany reserved freedom of action if the president failed to compel the British to observe international law at sea. In short, unrestricted submarine warfare might be used unless Wilson breached the British "blockade" of Germany. Thus, America still faced a real threat of war with Germany, despite the improvement in German-American relations after the *Sussex* crisis.

This danger looming in the future made an independent peace move seem all the more imperative. Moreover, early in May, the German chancellor, Bethmann-Hollweg, encouraged the president "to take up peace." The German government had strong second thoughts several weeks later, but they were still willing to maintain a moderate pose as long as the British were manifestly against the president's mediation.[10]

Opposition in London to an American peace move showed clear signs of continued strength. Indeed, Wilson was publicly warned not to interfere. At the end of September, Lloyd George, then secretary of state for war, gave an extraordinary interview to a prominent American journalist, Roy Howard. Lloyd George asserted that Britain had just reached her stride militarily and was suspicious of any suggestion that Wilson should "butt in" to stop the war before victory could be achieved. "The fight," he said, "must be to a finish—to a knockout." He wanted the "whole world, including neutrals of the highest purposes," to know that there could be "no outside interference at this stage."[11]

Lloyd George had not consulted the foreign secretary about the interview. Grey was angry and dismayed, but he could do nothing more than protest in a personal letter to his mercurial colleague. He did not disagree that Wilsonian mediation was undesirable at that time,

[8] Link, 1965: pp. 18–26, 32–38.
[9] *Ibid.,* pp. 65–71.

[10] *Ibid.,* pp. 16–17, 30–31; Birnbaum, 1958: pp. 96–97, 103–106.
[11] *New York Times,* 29 Sept., 1916.

but he felt that the public warning was unnecessary and probably harmful.[12] Lloyd George replied to Grey with the following justification for his brash action:

If the hands of Wilson had been forced—and there is every indication that the Germans and Irish in cooperation could do so—then we should be in a very tight place. Any cessation of hostilities now would be a disaster; and although we could always refuse or put up impossible terms, it is much better that we should not be placed in that predicament. You could not have warned off the United States without doing it formally. I could commit a serviceable indiscretion; you could not. It would ruin you: I am inoculated!

The Welsh politician neglected to mention that a stiff public warning to Wilson would be very popular in Britain. It undoubtedly helped promote his image as a vigorous champion of victory.

Lloyd George did not admit that his press interview involved serious risks, though he did try to reassure Grey:

You will find that it will work out all right. I know the American politician. He has no international conscience. He thinks of nothing but the ticket, and he has not given the least thought to the effect of his action upon European affairs.[13]

The logic of Lloyd George's remark implied that the British would have less to fear after the election in November. In fact, the opposite was true.

The president had decided to wait until after the election before launching a peace move. In the meantime he adopted the peace issue as one of his most effective themes. The desire to avoid war seemed to be increasing dramatically, and the slogan "He kept us out of war" quickly became a favorite among Democrats.

The German chancellor tried to capitalize on this trend in American sentiment. Late in the summer he had returned to the policy of actively encouraging Wilson's mediation. Pressure for an all-out submarine campaign was building up again, and an American peace move might, in Bethmann-Hollweg's view, be the only way to prevent the United States from entering the war against Germany. If Wilson could force the Allies to the peace table, a satisfactory peace might be negotiated without resorting to the submarine gamble. Moreover, even if the Allies were recalcitrant, Germany could blame them for prolonging the war. This would help Germany justify unrestricted submarine warfare and might help keep the United States neutral. Thus, in September and October Bethmann-Hollweg encouraged the president to act. Wilson was warned at the same time that the German government was considering all-out submarine warfare, though the chancellor did his best to play down the explicit threats

which the Kaiser insisted upon conveying to the president.[14]

In fact, the Germans promptly intensified their submarine activity in mid-October. Their campaign was not yet unrestricted. The U-boat commanders were ordered to give warnings before they attacked and to spare passenger ships, but it was difficult to stay within the limits. Violations of Germany's *Sussex* pledge soon occurred, which reminded Wilson that he would probably have to choose between war and diplomatic humiliation unless the war were stopped quickly.

The president stuck to his decision to wait until after the election, but soon after his narrow victory at the polls, he began preparing his most sensational peace move of the war. By late November, Wilson had produced the first draft of his famous peace note to the belligerents. It not only called for the warring powers to state their war aims, but also proposed a peace conference, which the neutrals "most directly involved" would attend.[15] At the same time, he found another way to exert pressure on the Allies to accept his mediation. On 27 November, the Federal Reserve Board issued a public warning against investment in renewable short-term British treasury bills and recommended caution about unsecured loans. The immediate result was a dramatic slump in the price of Allied bonds and American war stocks. The Morgan firm, acting for the British, had to spend nearly $20,000,000 to support the pound's exchange rate. Moreover, Britain's financial plans were seriously damaged. The House of Morgan had decided to use renewable short-term treasury notes as well as unsecured long-term loans to meet Britain's enormous financial commitments. The implication was that the British would have to find collateral acceptable to American investors.[16]

Wilson had threatened the British jugular vein. Large quantities of essential war supplies depended upon adequate financing. This was not a matter of over-all balance of trade. It was a question of raising large amounts of United States dollars at a rapid rate. The British were very vulnerable on this point and they knew it. During October, 1916, an interdepartmental government committee had carefully assessed Britain's ability to cope with American interference with supplies and credit. Their fears centered upon possible threats to their loans in the United States. They were much less worried about the president invoking the retaliatory legislation to impose general restrictions upon American trade with Britain. One reason was that such a policy would have "disastrous" effects upon the United States itself. Those weapons were, in Grey's words, "too big for them to use." But Britain's credit in America was a different matter.

[12] Grey to Lloyd George, 29 Sept., 1916, published in Lloyd George, 1933: 2: pp. 282–283.
[13] Lloyd George to Grey, 2 Oct., 1916, Lloyd George Papers, E/2/13/6. Lloyd George did not publish this remark about Wilson's lack of "international conscience" in his *War Memoirs*.

[14] Link, 1965: pp. 165–175; Birnbaum, 1958: pp. 129–130, 151–169.
[15] Baker, 1937: 6: pp. 380–386.
[16] Link, 1965: pp. 201–203.

Her loans could conceivably be threatened even if Wilson did nothing to exacerbate the situation. Indeed, Grey wrongly thought that it was not a question of relations with the United States government, "but of the feeling of American financial and business interests and of the whole lending public towards Britain."[17] This was clearly open to doubt, and the danger of action by the president was not overlooked.

On 24 October, Reginald McKenna, the chancellor of the exchequer, ventured an unpleasant prophecy when he submitted a gloomy financial report to the Cabinet. "If things go on as at present," he warned, "I venture to say with certainty that by next June or earlier, the President of the American Republic will be in a position, if he wishes, to dictate his own terms to us."[18] As we have seen, Wilson encouraged the Federal Reserve announcement in November which showed that he could rock Britain's financial plans with a minimum of risk to himself. In fact, he did not even have to admit his support for the action.

The British Treasury panicked after the Federal Reserve Board's announcement and advised that Britain should go off of the gold standard, but the Cabinet rejected the idea.[19] Perhaps there was some feeling that the Treasury had made false prophecies of doom in the past and could, thus, be ignored.[20] But the main factor in the Cabinet's steadiness was their determination not to alarm their allies or drastically curtail their war effort.[21] They were deeply committed to a headlong pursuit of military victory.

The government's desire to win the war was clearly evident in its study of questions of peace. At the end of August, 1916, Prime Minister Asquith formally invited members of the War Committee as well as the president of the board of trade to consider and report on questions which were likely to arise in negotiations at the end of the war.[22] The ministers who responded to Asquith's request usually assumed that decisive victory should be the basis for any discussion of peace terms. When an "inconclusive" peace was mentioned, its undesirable implications were emphasized.[23] The same attitude was reflected in public speeches. Shortly after Lloyd George's "knock-out blow" interview, Prime Minister Asquith declared in the House of Commons that the strain of war, which admittedly involved neutrals, "cannot be allowed to end in some patched-up, precarious, dishonouring compromise, masquerading under the name of Peace."[24]

This kind of determination persisted despite worsening conditions. An extensive government review of the situation produced some ominous memoranda. Germany's intensified submarine campaign was having alarming success even though it was not unrestricted. Walter Runciman, the president of the board of trade, reported a growing shortage of shipping on 26 October, and on 9 November, he forecast a "complete breakdown in shipping" by June, 1917. His experts thought it would come much sooner.[25] The president of the board of agriculture and fisheries forecast a food shortage if the war continued much longer.[26] Britain's financial burdens have already been mentioned. It was obvious that supplies of manpower were also declining. Reports of casualties from the battle of the Somme were appalling. Furthermore, during the autumn, Rumania, Britain's new ally, was overrun and the prospects for effective Russian participation in the war grew increasingly dubious.

Lord Lansdowne cited much of this ominous information in his memorandum of mid-November, 1916, which urged the Cabinet to consider peace negotiations. His arguments were disturbing. Foreboding about the course of the war was increasing. A few days earlier Lloyd George himself had remarked to Sir Maurice Hankey, "we are going to lose this war."[27] He had just drafted a stinging, even bitter memorandum criticizing many aspects of the Allies' war effort. Yet Lloyd George's dismal comment did not necessarily imply any willingness to consider making peace at that stage of the war. Circumstantial evidence suggests that it may have merely expressed a moment of dismay and dejection. Perhaps it was also part of his personal campaign for power—the implication of his words being that the war would be lost if Asquith's government were allowed to continue as before. Soon afterwards Lloyd George set about trying to reshape the government. This effort would soon gain for him not only greater influence, but the office of prime minister as well. In the meantime he agitated for a more effective prosecution of the war.

His gloomy memorandum, which was intended for an imminent conference in Paris, exemplified this theme. Certainly it revealed no readiness to consider a negotiated peace. The main purpose of his paper was to encourage the development of an Eastern strategy as a shorter path to victory. He argued that military successes could cure some of the serious ailments in the Allied war effort. To support his case, Lloyd George mentioned the problem of finance caused by

[17] Grey's memorandum, dated 20 Oct., 1916, published in *ibid.*, pp. 180–182. For the views of the interdepartmental committee, see CAB 37/158/3.

[18] Quoted in Link, 1965: p. 184.

[19] CAB 1/24/13b; CAB 37/160/30.

[20] Lloyd George, 1933: 2: pp. 134–137.

[21] See Bonar Law's statement on finance to the Imperial War Cabinet, 3 Apr., 1917, CAB 1/24/13b.

[22] CAB 37/154/33.

[23] See CAB 29/1/3, 5, 6, 8, 12; CAB 37/157/7.

[24] *Parliamentary Debates*, Commons **86**: col. 103 (11 Oct., 1916).

[25] CAB 37/158/10; CAB 37/159/24, 26.

[26] CAB 37/158/21; CAB 37/159/22.

[27] Hankey, 1961: 2: p. 557.

growing Allied dependence upon American supplies. "If victory shone on our banners," he declared, "our difficulties would disappear. Success means credit: financiers never hesitate to lend to a prosperous concern. . . . The problem of finance is the problem of victory. . . ." Lloyd George also related his argument directly to the question of peace without victory. He pointed out that the Western strategy of attrition would prolong the war and lead to increased burdens. This made his short-cut to victory imperative for the following reason:

Efforts will be made perhaps by powerful neutrals to patch up peace on what would appear to be specious terms, and there is a real danger that large masses of people, worn out by the constant strain, may listen to well-intentioned but mistaken pacificators. . . .[28]

This attitude toward peace negotiations was not merely a bold front for the benefit of anxious allies. In a War Committee meeting on 13 November, the day on which Lansdowne completed his memorandum, Lloyd George urged the great importance of handling the food situation boldly, lest Britain's internal situation should become difficult and "give the opportunity for peace propagandists and agitators."[29] Nor was the government seriously divided on the peace question. Lansdowne's admirable document has received considerable historical attention, but as far as the attitude of the British government is concerned, it is most notable for its eccentricity. Lansdowne himself observed that Lloyd George's formula of the "knock-out blow" held the field. His memorandum was a desperate plea that the Cabinet should think again.[30]

It is true that in Asquith's government, prominent men like Reginald McKenna and Walter Runciman were very pessimistic about the war. When Grey replied to the Lansdowne memorandum late in November, he almost seemed to be wondering whether the time had come for peace negotiations through the medium of "not-unsympathetic mediation."[31] On the one hand, he acknowledged—even agreed with—recent military assurances that prospects were good, and he stated that as long as the naval and military leaders believed in victory, peace was premature; yet, on the other hand, Grey felt that the submarine problem was "getting more and more beyond our control." He also knew that the Admiralty felt helpless against the menace.[32] These were serious doubts but they did not lead to powerful support for Lansdowne's attitude. Furthermore, early in December, McKenna, Runciman, and Grey went out of office with Asquith.

The predominant response to Lansdowne's point of view was reflected in a memorandum by Lord Robert Cecil, the minister of blockade and parliamentary under-secretary for foreign affairs. Though he was a devoted admirer of Grey, Cecil was much more emphatic and resolute in his opposition to peace negotiations at that stage of the war. He agreed that the situation was grave, but he concluded that "a peace now could only be disastrous." Cecil explained: "At best we could not hope for more than the *status quo* with a great increase in the German power in Eastern Europe." He also pointed out that, since the Germans would realize that peace had been forced upon Britain by their submarines, her insular position would increase instead of diminish her vulnerability. Thus, Britain was, he felt, "bound to continue the war."[33]

In advocating perseverance, Cecil added a warning. To carry on, he wrote, "without drastic changes in our civil life would be to court disaster." This remark expressed another widespread attitude. The gravity of the Allies' position had produced serious anxiety in government circles, but the prevailing demand was not for a peace without victory; it was for a more vigorous war effort. The talk was of tighter import restrictions, rationing, turning ships around more quickly in port, of using more machinery and female labor to produce food, of avoiding waste, introducing industrial conscription, and of the need to reorganize the government. Fear of defeat was one of the main reasons why Lloyd George was able to supplant Asquith as prime minister. Asquith was against peace negotiations, but his leadership lacked vigor. In contrast, Lloyd George's image as the boldest and most energetic champion of victory fitted the political demand perfectly, and he was given, as Paul Guinn phrased it, a "mandate to win the war."[34]

Pessimists about victory in an all-out war are often correct in their predictions of burdens to be born or worsening trends, but they tend to underestimate the resourcefulness and determination of embattled nations. The British were in a pell-mell, irrational state of belligerency. They were willing to run colossal risks not only of worse defeat, but also (as conservatives like Lansdowne feared) of drastic changes in the social order. Yet, there were also some apparently rational reasons behind their intransigence. For example, the British felt that with the Germans entrenched on a large part of Allied territory, the Allies' bargaining position was weak. Peace negotiations at that stage of the war offered little chance of gaining much of what they wanted or much of what the Allies had promised each other. To revise their secret agreements was to risk dangerous divisions in Allied unity. At the same time, the British felt that they were just reaching their stride militarily. To attempt peace from a weak position before their greatest efforts had been exerted did not seem sensible. Not only was it emotionally unbearable to think that the appalling costs

[28] Lloyd George, 1933: **2**: pp. 330–343.
[29] CAB 37/159/33.
[30] CAB 37/159/32. Published in Lloyd George, 1933: **2**: pp. 288–296.
[31] CAB 37/160/20.
[32] Guinn, 1965: pp. 176–177.

[33] CAB 37/160/21.
[34] Guinn, 1965: p. 177.

and casualties which had already been incurred were in vain, but there was also a notion that Britain's alliances comprised a relatively favorable situation for fighting Germany. After an "inconclusive" peace, the enemy would be in a stronger relative position than before August, 1914. Unless Germany were defeated in the present war, Britain would be, as Cecil suggested, less secure in the future. In short, December, 1916, seemed a bad time for peace initiatives.

II. THE PEACE MOVES OF DECEMBER, 1916

Soon after Lloyd George attained the office of prime minister as the most vigorous champion of victory, his life was complicated by two major peace moves. On 12 December, 1916, Germany and her allies proposed peace negotiations. The offer was made public during the course of a speech in which Bethmann-Hollweg read the note which he was sending to enemy governments. The United States had been asked to transmit the note to Britain.[1] About a week later the American president launched his own peace move. In a note dated 18 December, he asked the belligerents to state their peace terms.

1. THE GERMAN OVERTURE

Even before Wilson made this dramatic request, the British were acutely concerned about their relations with America. The Foreign Office perceived that one of the German government's principal motives was, in the words of the permanent under-secretary, "to put the Allies wrong with the neutral world, and especially the Americans."[2] The British government's main problem was how to turn the Germans down without offending the United States.

In shaping Britain's response to the peace moves of December, 1916, Lord Robert Cecil was probably the figure who mattered most in the Foreign Office. Indeed, he was in charge of the Foreign Office during the crucial early days of the Lloyd George government while Balfour, the new foreign secretary, recuperated from an illness. Cecil is not yet as well known to historians as some of his colleagues. He was a prominent Conservative with excellent connections. The third Marquess of Salisbury was his father. Balfour was his cousin. He received his education at Eton and University College, Oxford. High Church convictions had been instilled in him during childhood and he remained emotionally devoted to religious and moral principles. Cecil developed enthusiastic commitments on some issues. This led several times to an independent stance, and it occasionally distorted his political

judgment. He frequently threatened to resign from Lloyd George's government, and at one time wanted to force Balfour out of the Foreign Office. Were it not for the opposition and lethargy of his colleagues, Cecil's activism about the League of Nations and intervention in Russia might have caused trouble with Wilson late in the war. Yet, his advice with regard to Anglo-American relations was more often sensible and prudent. Fortunately he was not burdened by one of his policy fixations during the early days of the Lloyd George government.

In a memorandum dated 15 December, Cecil emphatically expressed his anxiety about British-American relations.[3] After assuming that British policy was "to avoid being forced into peace negotiations at the present time," he asserted that there were "only two events which could defeat this policy: (1) the defection of one of the principal Allies; (2) the active intervention of the United States by cutting off supplies of money and munitions." Cecil did not think that the danger of the former was imminent; however, the danger from America was different. Pacifist sentiment in America appeared to be very strong. Cecil also noted that the German ambassador in Washington seemed to be hoping that Wilson could be induced to intervene, and he warned that Wilson's intervention was "not intrinsically improbable." Repeating what Spring Rice had written from Washington, Cecil explained that "he [Wilson] has nothing to hope for in domestic politics; he is known to be a genuine and ardent lover of peace; and the role of mediator in the greatest war in European history may well be attractive to him."[4]

The British minister undoubtedly took this danger of the president's intervention very seriously. "It must further be recognized," Cecil asserted, "that, if he desired to put a stop to the war, and was prepared to pay the price for doing so, such an achievement is in his power." Cecil thought that the recent Federal Reserve Board warning to American investors may have been intended "to remind us of that fact, since it seems to be clear that it was due to the President's own intervention that the Federal Reserve Board took their action. . . ."[5] He felt certain that Wilson could pre-

[1] *Foreign Relations, 1916, Supplement:* pp. 87–89. This chapter is a revised version of an article in *The Historical Journal* **13** (1970): pp. 721–766. The author is grateful to the Cambridge University Press for permission to reprint it.

[2] Lord Hardinge to Sir George Buchanan, about 16 or 17 Dec., 1916, Hardinge Papers 28.

[3] CAB 23/1/10/Appendix IV.

[4] For Spring Rice's views, see CAB 37/160/28; CAB 37/161/3, 4.

[5] The Foreign Office had accumulated some convincing information about the president's role in the affair. On 3 Dec., Spring Rice transmitted confidential information from the governor of the Federal Reserve Board, who had intimated that the "highest authority" had intervened in the preparation of the statement and advised a careful watch on "the foreign policy of the President in relation to H. M. Government." Spring Rice also stated that he had had similar warnings from another quarter. "Object is," he observed, "of course to force us to accept the President's mediation by cutting off supplies." Telegram from Spring Rice, 3 Dec., 1916, Balfour Papers, Add. MSS. 49740. Also, Lord Robert Cecil's minute to this paper suggests that he "understood" that the British Naval Attaché

vent "the raising of Allied loans in America, not to speak of interference with the export of munitions and other necessaries." Cecil did not expect that the president would take such action because of a quarrel with Britain (presumably over maritime and commercial measures), but he added: ". . . unless I misread his character, it is not impossible that he might take even very violent action to enforce what he regarded as a just peace."

Cecil concluded that a "contemptuous rejection" of the German note would be unwise, especially if Britain acted alone. He also suggested that Britain should "not take the lead in the matter" but should contrive to put France "in the first place." This kind of suggestion was virtually automatic. Since early in the war the Foreign Office had frequently tried to keep the French between America and themselves when something contentious was being handled. As Cecil explained: "Her [France's] sacrifices have been far greater than ours; she cannot, by any stretch of imagination, be regarded as the aggressor in this war; and she has a very special position in the United States."

On 16 December, the British War Cabinet decided to consult the French government, and a telegram was promptly sent to Paris. The British had not yet officially received the German note, but on the basis of newspaper reports they had concluded that it could only be regarded as a political maneuver. The telegram to Paris went on to state that the prime minister "would be glad" to learn the French view on the matter before speaking publicly on the subject.

Actually the War Cabinet was already certain of the French government's opposition to peace negotiations. Premier Aristide Briand had reaffirmed it in a bombastic speech several days earlier, but as the Foreign Office explained: "It is of great importance that for the sake of the effect on America, England should not be represented as forcing the Allies to continue the war." Therefore, the British suggested that the French send the prime minister "some message which he could read out." [6]

Meanwhile, Spring Rice sent a flurry of cables on the American problem. The essence of his advice was summarized as follows for the War Cabinet:

Sir C. Spring Rice reports that general feeling is that Allies should not refuse to receive from the Germans authentic terms of peace. Refusal would much strengthen the German position in the United States of America.

His Excellency advises expressing strong desire for peace, but stating that the action of His Majesty's Government must be guided by the nature of the terms offered, and by agreement with our Allies. It should be added that, in the meanwhile, war would be continued with all means in our power until a secure peace is restored. If the President should make any suggestions on his own account, His Majesty's Government should express ap-

preciation for his friendly action in a non-committal way. The German party in the United States of America are clearly hoping for a direct refusal.

. . . The United States Administration is anxious to end the war, fearing that submarine campaign will be intensified, and that the war will spread to America. [7]

These summaries together with Robert Cecil's memorandum and other relevant papers were before the Cabinet meeting of 18 December. By then the American ambassador in London had officially transmitted the German note.

The War Cabinet debated whether to hold an Allied conference to consider the reply to Germany, but this procedure was rejected. It was decided that the "best plan would be for the Allies to concert an identic note, which should be signed by the representatives in Paris, of all the Allies . . . and handed by the representative of France, in the presence of his colleagues, to the American Ambassador in Paris." [8]

Lord Robert Cecil informed the War Cabinet that M. Briand was preparing for consideration a draft reply to Germany. As far as the British were concerned, one of the key aspects of the German note was that it did not state Germany's conditions for peace. The War Cabinet readily agreed that the Allied reply should state that "a general offer of peace, without defining terms, was useless." However, the secretary recorded that "the question as to whether the Allies should ask the Germans to state their terms was more controversial. . . ." This particular issue was left undecided until the Cabinet could consider M. Briand's draft. [9] Meanwhile, the War Cabinet went on to confer about "the general principles on which the statement to be made in both Houses of Parliament on the following day should be based." [10]

During this meeting, Cecil also reported that in transmitting the note on Germany's behalf, Walter Hines Page, the American ambassador, had conveyed an additional message from Washington. Page had indicated that his government would appreciate a confidential intimation of the reply which the British proposed to make to the German note. Furthermore, Page revealed "that his Government itself intended to make representations on the subject at the appropriate moment, and had for some time had such intention independently of the German Note." [11]

By making this revelation, Wilson was obviously trying to ameliorate one of the difficulties raised by the German move. It had been widely known that the Ger-

in Washington was "certain" of the president's intervention in the matter.

[6] F.O. 371/2805/252387/254952.

[7] CAB 23/1/10/Appendix II. The respective dates when the dispatches were received together with their Foreign Office references are as follows: F.O. 371/2805/252387/253643 (15 Dec.), 254012 (15 Dec.), 254641 (16 Dec.).

[8] CAB 23/1/10/2.

[9] CAB 23/1/10/3.

[10] CAB 23/10/4. The statement in the House of Lords was made by Lord Curzon. See *Parliamentary Debates: Lords* 23: cols. 936–939.

[11] CAB 23/1/10/1.

mans had wanted the president to propose peace negotiations. Even if Berlin had not made an overture, the president could have expected that his move would be widely construed as supporting German wishes. Obviously the British government would be offended if he appeared to propose what Germany wanted. Hence, when his note was preceded by the German chancellor's proposal, Wilson readily anticipated that he should do something to offset the embarrassing impression that he was supporting the German move.

To the British government, on the other hand, the declaration of independence which Page conveyed was primarily important as another clear warning of an impending American peace move. Yet, even without this message, the British would have known that a peace move was imminent. Arthur S. Link has noted that Wilson was at first depressed by Berlin's overture, but that he was soon "immensely encouraged—and spurred to action"—by messages from the German government indicating its continued desire for his peacemaking services.[12] Unknown to Wilson, the British government had intercepted one of these communications, as well as an earlier one of his own messages to Germany soliciting "practical co-operation" in creating a favorable opportunity for his peace move.[13] This served as dramatic evidence of Wilson's preparations.

Another difficulty for Wilson which had been raised by Germany's overture was the possibility that in responding to it the Allies would commit themselves completely against peace negotiations. Reports from the Allied capitals were very unfavorable. Moreover, it had been announced in London on 16 December that Lloyd George would make a statement in the House of Commons on the nineteenth. Fearing that the door to negotiations might be slammed, Wilson had hastily revised his note.[14] It was sent by wire during the evening of 18 December, but was not delivered by Ambassador Page to the British Foreign Office until the afternoon of 20 December. By that time Lloyd George had publicly taken up a good defensive position, which he developed with America and her president specifically in mind.[15]

Lloyd George's task had been further complicated by advice from Paris. In response to the British request of the sixteenth, the French did not supply the prime minister with a statement. Briand referred him to his recent uncompromising statement to the Chamber of Deputies and gave Lloyd George the following warning:

It is manifestly essential for us not to admit any modification of our position as "defendants" vis-à-vis the German demands nor to allow ourselves to become involved, in the present general state of affairs, in highly dangerous negotiations by returning a reply which might either have the appearance of asking Germany to specify more precisely her conditions or might seem to indicate that we would be willing to allow ourselves to be led into formulating our own conditions.[16]

This advice reflects an important difference of opinion which confronted Lloyd George with a sticky problem. The French were adamantly against appearing in any way to ask the Germans to state their peace terms, but the advice with regard to America was that Britain must avoid appearing to refuse to listen to precise terms. Furthermore, the War Cabinet was undecided on the question.

The British government's indecision on this issue was not due to a general loss of determination to pursue victory. Indeed, the particular suggestions in government circles that the Germans be asked to state their terms probably do not signify any receptivity to peace negotiations.[17] The disagreements which the British had with the French over the German move were not about acceptance or rejection. They were about tactics. The main problem was to avoid peace negotiations but at the same time to avoid appearing guilty of slamming the door to peace and thus of prolonging the war. Lloyd George came up with a very interesting response.

Early in his speech of 19 December, the prime minister cited France's and Russia's negative reactions to the enemy peace move. He said that they had given the first answer as they had the "unquestionable right" to do and that his purpose was "to give clear and definite support to the statement which they have already made."

Lloyd George skillfully defined the peace issue in moral terms as follows:

Any man or set of men who wantonly, or without sufficient cause, prolonged a terrible conflict like this would have on their soul a crime that oceans could not cleanse. On the other hand, it is equally true that any man or set of men who out of a sense of weariness or despair abandoned the struggle without achieving the high purpose for which we had entered into it being nearly fulfilled would have been guilty of the costliest act of poltroonery ever perpetrated by any statesman.

Clearly framing his answer for American ears, the prime minister invoked the aid of Abraham Lincoln. According to Lloyd George, the revered American statesman had, "under similar conditions," uttered the following words: "'We accepted this war for an object, and a worthy object, and the war will end when that

---

[12] Link, 1965: pp. 214–215.

[13] Lloyd George Papers, F/3/2/2, F/3/2/1.

[14] Link, 1965: p. 217.

[15] A minor but well-known diplomatic move should be mentioned here. Charles Seymour has described an attempt by Colonel House and Sir William Wiseman to delay Lloyd George's speech until House could unofficially find out Germany's terms. House was told on 18 Dec. that London could not postpone the prime minister's statement. See Seymour, 1926: 2: pp. 400–402. I have not been able to locate any reference to this move by House and Wiseman in the British documents.

---

[16] Telegram dated 18 Dec., 1916, F.O. 371/2805/252387/256076.

[17] Cf. Link, 1965: pp. 230–231.

object is attained. Under God I hope it will never end until that time.'" Having declared his official attitude in this agile fashion, the British prime minister then posed some rhetorical questions:

Are we likely to achieve that object by accepting the invitation of the German Chancellor? That is the only question we have to put to ourselves. There has been some talk about proposals of peace. What are the proposals? There are none. To enter at the invitation of Germany, proclaiming herself victorious, without any knowledge of the proposals she proposes to make, into a conference, is to put our head into a noose with the rope end in the hands of Germany.

Thus, Lloyd George conveyed the War Cabinet decision of the previous day that a peace offer without defined terms was useless. But what of the question of challenging Germany to state her terms? Essentially the prime minister tried to put *useful* German peace proposals beyond the pale of possibility. "This is not the first time we have fought a great military despotism that was overshadowing Europe," he said, "and it will not be the first time we shall have helped to overthrow military despotism." This was, of course, a moralistic declaration that Germany must and would be defeated. Lloyd George cited Asquith's formula for peace and stiffened it. "Let me repeat again," he stated, "complete restitution, full reparation, effectual guarantees." He suggested that Britain had already begun exacting reparation and that "we must exact it now so as not to leave such a grim inheritance to our children." This commitment to victory was emphasized over and over again. He said:

The Allies entered the war to defend themselves against the aggression of the Prussian military dominator, and having begun it, they must insist that it can only end with the most complete and effective guarantee against the possibility of that caste ever again disturbing the peace of Europe.

To argue the necessity of this victory, Lloyd George employed a popular interpretation of German history, which argued essentially that Germany (or Prussia) had a disreputable past. The prime minister's rather oratorical and unrestrained version was as follows:

Prussia since she got into the hands of that caste, has been a bad neighbour, arrogant, threatening, bullying, litigious, shifting boundaries at her will, taking one fair field after another from weaker neighbours, and adding them to her own domain, with her belt ostentatiously full of weapons of offence, and ready at a moment's notice to use them. . . . There was no peace where she dwelt.

In a special appeal to America, Lloyd George added: "It is difficult for those who were fortunate enough to live thousands of miles away to understand what it has meant to those who lived near their boundaries." After this long introduction, he concluded by stating, very rhetorically to be sure, the essence of Britain's position as follows:

Now that this great War has been forced by the Prussian military leaders upon France, Russia, Italy, and ourselves,

it would be folly, it would be cruel folly, not to see to it that this [Prussia's] swashbuckling through the streets of Europe to the disturbance of all harmless and peaceful citizens shall be dealt with now as an offence against the law of nations. The mere word that lead [sic] Belgium to her own destruction will not satisfy Europe any more. We all believed it. We all trusted it. It gave way at the first pressure of temptation, and Europe has been plunged into this vortex of blood. We will therefore, wait until we hear what terms and guarantees the German government offer other than those, surer than those which she so lightly broke, and meanwhile we shall put our trust in an unbroken Army rather than in a broken faith.[18]

Thus, Lloyd George answered Germany by stating, in effect, that Britain would not negotiate without hearing Germany's terms, that Germany was dangerous and not to be trusted, and that any terms would have to be more unfavorable to Germany than the *status quo ante bellum*. Largely for the benefit of America, Lloyd George had merely chosen a round about way of stating that he would make peace with Germany when she accepted defeat.

His speech protected his victory policy from untimely peace talks in various ways. It had advantages which went well beyond avoiding an appearance of complete intransigence. In the first place, there was a possibility that Germany could be placed in an unfavorable light. The German government seemed likely to want considerable gains from the war. If so, they might not state their terms for fear of appearing bellicose and immoderate. On the other hand, if they did venture to announce immoderate terms, they might expose the spurious character of the Central Powers' peace move.[19] The danger was, of course, that Germany might announce fairly moderate terms, particularly regarding France and Belgium. Hence, the prime minister's statement in the House of Commons staked out a defensive position against this possibility by stating, as we have seen, that any terms Germany announced would be fruitless unless they left the Allies in a stronger position than they had enjoyed before the war. Other advantages in his having made such a reply arose from the fact that Great Britain could not prevent the president from requesting the belligerents to state their terms, as he was about to do. It would have been more difficult for Lloyd George to make such a stern reply to Germany's overture if he had had to reply to President Wilson at the same time. Moreover, having publicly committed itself before the president had intervened, the new British government could argue that changing its position would be very difficult, and that it could only elucidate the same views in future statements. Lloyd George's speech was, of course,

---

[18] *Parliamentary Debates:* Commons **88**: cols. 1333–1338.

[19] Sir Eric Drummond, private secretary to the foreign secretary, suggested forcing Germany to state her terms precisely for this reason. See his memorandum entitled "German Peace Proposals," dated 14 Dec., 1916, F.O. 800/197 or Lloyd George Papers, F/231.

timely, since the president's famous note was already on its way.

2. THE PRESIDENT'S INITIATIVE AND THE SECRETARY OF STATE'S "CLARIFICATIONS"

When Woodrow Wilson asked the belligerents merely to state their peace terms, he evidently hoped that they would announce moderate demands because of their fear of appearing intransigent and aggressive. Presumably he felt that once the belligerents had committed themselves to moderate terms, negotiations could be started. Thus his note was undoubtedly a peace move in spite of his assertion that he was not proposing peace.

The president's note also stressed that he was not offering to mediate, though he clearly coveted this role and made a special effort to maintain an impartial position. He denied any desire to determine how peace should be settled. Moreover, the note stated that the objects of both sides, as stated in general terms by their leaders, were (or seemed to be) virtually the same. No doubt the latter statement was also an attempt to constrain the belligerents to be moderate. Wilson even tried to summarize the apparently harmonious objects of both parties. The note mentioned each side's desire to secure the rights and privileges of weak peoples and small states, the desire for lasting peace and security against aggression or "selfish interference," and the desire of each side for a "league of nations to insure peace and justice." He expressed his eagerness to cooperate in accomplishing these ends when the war was over, but he insisted that the war must first be concluded. The United States government was "not at liberty" to suggest peace terms, but the president felt it was his duty to declare their intimate interest in an end to the war,

lest it should presently be too late to accomplish the greater things which lie beyond its conclusion, lest the situation of neutral nations, now exceedingly hard to endure, be rendered altogether intolerable, and lest, more than all, an injury be done to civilization itself which can never be atoned for or repaired.[20]

This line of argument was similar to the one that the president would use in his "Peace Without Victory" address a month later. If the terrible attrition proceeded until one side collapsed, the injuries, resentments, and despair incurred would make the "ultimate arrangements" of peace futile.

On 21 December, the day after Ambassador Page delivered the president's note, Secretary of State Lansing made a sensational statement to the press about the reasons behind the note. He said that the note had been sent because America was drawing nearer to the verge of war and needed to know what each

belligerent sought in order to regulate her future conduct accordingly. He also stated that the president did not regard the document as a peace note, but merely as an effort to get the belligerents to define their war aims. Since the expectation that Germany would further intensify her submarine campaign was very much in the air at this time, the statement was widely interpreted as being menacing to Germany. Not surprisingly, the president promptly insisted that Lansing attempt to nullify this impression by stating that he had not intended to intimate that the government was considering any change in its policy of neutrality. Wilson no doubt felt that Lansing's press conference had damaged his chances to start peace negotiations, and Lansing was perhaps fortunate not to have been dismissed.[21]

Lansing also had confidential conversations with the French ambassador, J. J. Jusserand, and with Spring Rice about the president's note. According to Jusserand's reports, the secretary of state intimated that the president's preferences were with the democracies, that he intended no harm to their interests, that Wilson only wanted to know the belligerents' terms, and that they could state their extreme demands as they saw fit. Lansing added that "speaking personally," he thought the Allies could rightfully demand the return of Alsace-Lorraine to France and indemnities for France, Belgium, and Serbia. The secretary of state said he had little faith in the president's league to maintain peace, which only liberalization of the autocracies could guarantee. When he spoke to Spring Rice, Lansing added that the Allies should demand an autonomous Poland under Russian sovereignty, transfer of the Trentino from Austria to Italy, and expulsion of Turkey from Europe.[22]

The secretary of state's various commentaries on Wilson's peace note provoke curiosity and even suspicion about his motives. There are at least two plausible interpretations. The more benign one is that Lansing was primarily trying to avoid trouble with the Allies. He himself gave this explanation when he tried to justify his "verge of war" statement. In his memoirs, he revealed a memorandum on the subject which he claimed was written shortly after the event.[23] The document deserves careful consideration. Evidence in the House Diary suggests that Lansing did, in fact, compose his justification when he said he did. House's entry for 4 January, 1917, contains the follow-

---

[20] *Foreign Relations, 1916, Supplement:* pp. 97–99.

[21] Link, 1965: p. 222.

[22] *Ibid.,* pp. 223–224. After summarizing Lansing's comments, Link cited French documents used in Hoelzle, 1962: pp. 477–478. As he mentioned in his preface, Link also had access to a secret French diplomatic archive which he was not allowed to cite. Lansing's conversations with the French and British ambassadors probably took place respectively on 20 and 21 Dec. See footnote 28 below.

[23] Lansing, 1935: pp. 188–190. There is a copy of the memorandum in the Lansing Papers, Box 2, File II (Princeton University Library).

ing record:

I was with Lansing for more than an hour. His first concern was to put himself straight regarding the two statements he had made the morning the peace note was published. He has written a careful statement of his purposes and has made a good argument in favor of them.[24]

Lansing's memorandum explained that in the circumstances in which the "verge of war" statement was issued, he believed that the American note would be construed as being in support of the German overture.[25] He was convinced that "if such an opinion became fixed . . . the Allies would be deeply offended . . . and in all probability send a curt refusal to the request for a statement of terms." The Germans, on the other hand, would believe that the note "was not actually intended to draw out the Central Powers on terms of peace." To prevent the general interpretation of the American note from "becoming rigid," Lansing therefore "determined . . . to give another reason for the issuance of the note than the one furnished by conjecture from the circumstances."

The credibility of this memorandum is not contradicted by the terms which Lansing mentioned to Jusserand and Spring Rice. He may have suggested attractive terms to the Allies in an effort to encourage them to fulfill the president's request. That is, a friendly, positive answer to the president may have been his first priority. Before Wilson had launched his peace move, Lansing had, in fact, warned him about the danger of the Allies returning an answer which was less acceptable than the Germans. It might be asked why Lansing would suggest announcing such extreme demands. He may have been so worried that the Allies would return a negative reply that he was willing to suggest extremely attractive terms in order to prevent it, in spite of the risk of the Allies sounding more unreasonable than Germany. There was still the possibility that the German government would decline to announce their terms. Another consideration is that Lansing probably believed that the Allies were legitimately entitled to the terms he suggested, that it was in the interests of the United States for the Allies to have them, and that they were publicly defensible in America. As will be shown later, the men who mattered in London were inclined to feel the same way.

A more incriminating interpretation of Lansing's motives has been advanced by Professor Link in his major biography of Wilson. He has suggested that the "verge of war" statement was intended to intimate to the Allies "that the American government would stand behind them even to the point of entering the war on their side." Furthermore, he argues that Lan-

sing's conversations with Jusserand and Spring Rice reinforce the impression that the secretary of state was trying to sabotage Wilson's peace move. Lansing may have reasoned that, if the French and British announced terms which implied an Allied victory, the war would be prolonged. This, in turn, would increase the chances of all-out German submarine warfare, which would probably provoke American belligerency.[26]

Such reasoning is not necessarily consistent with the "verge of war" statement. It can, for example, be read as a notice to Germany about intensified submarine warfare. If this was Lansing's intention, he had chosen an odd way to promote war with that country. Germany was unlikely to be encouraged to resort to all-out submarine warfare by a warning that the result would be war with the United States. Yet, Link's case is persuasive. We know that Lansing was strongly pro-Ally and that he repeatedly urged Wilson to take firm action against Germany on the submarine issue. He had little faith in the president's peace move. He considered his own ability to handle foreign policy superior to Wilson's, and he profoundly resented the president's autocratic ways. Perhaps Lansing actually did try to undermine the most important policies of his chief.

As far as this study is concerned, there is a more important question about Lansing's actions. What was the secretary of state's impact upon the British government's response to the president's note? Speculation on this matter can now be cleared up.[27] The available British documents suggest that no statement by Lansing had a significant effect upon the British position. In fact, it is doubtful that the British paid much attention to Lansing's suggestion of peace terms. The present author has not been able to find any evidence in the British Foreign Office papers that Spring Rice reported Lansing's suggestions in full and in detail.[28] Perhaps the reports were burned. On the other hand, the available documents make it very clear that Lansing was not Spring Rice's only source of congenial information. For example, on 21 December, he reported the opinion of "a friend of the President," who suggested that "Mr. Asquith's phrase as to reparation and

---

[24] House Diary, 4 Jan., 1917.

[25] Lansing noted in his desk diary that before he made his statement to the press, he spoke with the counselor of the State Department, Frank L. Polk, about the president's note and the "ugly British feeling." Lansing Desk Diary, 21 Dec., 1916.

[26] Link, 1965: pp. 221–225.

[27] See *ibid.*, pp. 232–239. Writing before some important British documents were opened to scholars, Link tentatively concluded that Lansing may have succeeded in his alleged attempt to sabotage the president's peace move.

[28] Actually, there is no record in the Foreign Office files on the German and American notes that Spring Rice had a conference with Lansing on 22 Dec., the date given by Link; however, there are reports about a meeting with Lansing on the twenty-first. This may be the interview to which Link refers. See dispatch from Spring Rice, 22 Dec., 1916, F.O. 371/3075/2/583. Spring Rice also sent a telegram on 21 Dec. in which he wrote: "A high official speaking most confidentially and in his own person thought statement should be made to the effect that only adequate security for permanent peace would be a popular and responsible Government in Germany." F.O. 371/2805/252387/259910.

security was considered a satisfactory statement." [29]
Moreover, the British ambassador did not take the
secretary of state's comments as the last word. A
week later he was still reporting on the terms America
wanted to hear.[30] Further, even if Lansing's comments
reached the Foreign Office in the same form as Jusserand reported them, it is unlikely that Spring Rice
or the Foreign Office would base their recommendations on Lansing's opinion alone. Lansing said he was
speaking personally. It may, of course, have been
thought that Lansing was loyal to his chief. On the
other hand, Spring Rice very much doubted Lansing's
knowledge of the presidential mind, and he would probably have been inclined to view his confidential remarks as an agreeable expression of sympathy. The
British ambassador had often noted that the president
kept his own counsel. Indeed, he wrote a letter to
Balfour on 22 December, complaining about precisely
this presidential trait.[31]

The second reason for believing Lansing's statements
to be an insignificant factor is that the British leaders
who may have learned of Lansing's suggestions of
peace terms retained the quite accurate conviction that
Wilson was pursuing an end to the war. For instance,
in a telegram received by the Foreign Office on the
twenty-fourth, Spring Rice reiterated his long-standing
belief that Wilson's object was peace "quite irrespec-
tive of terms." [32] As will be shown later, Balfour
stressed the same conclusion. Indeed, it was an essential theme of the note which he sent as a supplement
to the Allied reply to Wilson. British leaders would
be likely to conclude from Lansing's suggestions of
peace terms merely that the American administration
knew what the Allied terms were and that Wilson was
primarily interested in learning the German terms. In
fact, when the French and British conferred on the
Allied reply, M. Berthelot, who represented Briand,
expressed essentially this interpretation, which he used
to support the French proposal of an evasive response.[33]
This was the worst damage that Lansing's advice could
have done to Wilson's peace move, and in the end the
proposed evasive reply was rejected.

If Lansing did cause any British leaders to believe
that Wilson was slyly maneuvering to prepare the
American public for war in case his hand should be
forced by the Germans, the conclusion would have been
based not upon Lansing's statements to Jusserand and
Spring Rice about peace terms but upon his "verge of
war" statement to the press. Some British leaders
actually considered this idea. Indeed, various versions

of it appeared in the press, in messages to the prime
minister, as well as in Foreign Office papers. Eric
Drummond, formerly Grey's private secretary, now
Balfour's, sent a memorandum to Lord Robert Cecil
which recalled that letters from Colonel House had
emphasized that President Wilson felt that he could
not get the American people to go to war over the submarine issue, but that, if it came to a "really big" issue,
such as peace, the people of America would support him
in using armed force against Germany if she refused
terms that the president considered just. Drummond
continued:

Personally I doubt the President's belief is true, but it is
clear he holds it himself and it is worth bearing in mind
in dealing with the present note, since there is no doubt
the submarine menace is very much in the President's
mind just now. He may feel that everything he has said
and written on submarine warfare will force him to advocate war with Germany but that as he cannot carry his
people with him, he wishes to have another issue with
Germany on which public opinion in the United States
will support him in extreme measures. The statements
of Mr. Lansing which I think must rest on conversations
with the President rather strengthen this view, in spite of
the fact that the President has, I understand, disavowed
Mr. Lansing.[34]

On 24 December, C. P. Scott, editor of the *Manchester Guardian*, informed the prime minister of a
similar analysis of the president's motives by Walter
Lippmann, then editor of the *New Republic*.[35] Several
days later, Lord Northcliffe sent a message to Lloyd
George from Roy Howard, which may have reinforced
Drummond's theory or others like it. Northcliffe reported that Colonel House had said that Lansing's *first*
statement that America was on the verge of war was
"the secret of the Note's real purpose." [36] On 28
December, the Foreign Office received from Spring
Rice another interpretation relating the president's note
to the submarine problem. By the time it arrived,
Balfour and Cecil had already decided on the line they
would take, but it is an example of what was possible.
Spring Rice stated:

From several quarters I am assured that President prepared his peace note in consequence of submarine outrages which he was convinced must lead to a break with
Germany for which he wished to prepare public opinion
by making a strong appeal for peace to both parties. It
was quite independent of German step which is thought
to have been taken to anticipate action on his part.
"World" newspaper which is inspired from White House
says to-day that Germany having flatly refused, United
States is confronted with "a manifest necessity to determine how to safeguard their interests if war is to continue."
A conciliatory answer from Allies might thus strengthen
President's hand in dealing with submarine question.

[29] F.O. 371/2805/252387/259910.
[30] Telegram received 29 Dec., 1916, F.O. 371/2806/252387/
263824 or F.O. 115/2091/Mediation/109.
[31] Published in Gwynn, 1929: 2: p. 366.
[32] F.O. 371/2806/252387/260933.
[33] Minutes of Anglo-French Conference, 26 Dec., 1916, CAB
28/2/13(a).

[34] The memorandum is dated Dec., 1916. F.O. 800/197/
Drummond.
[35] Lloyd George Papers, F/45/2/2.
[36] Lloyd George Papers, F/41/7/2.

Feeling in Congress is strongly pacific and if above is true, President Wilson may encounter very strong opposition.[37]

Perhaps Balfour and Cecil had anticipated this telegram with similar considerations. In any case, the idea that Wilson intended the peace note to strengthen his position for resisting unrestricted submarine warfare clearly had various sources. The same interpretation might have been made even if Lansing had said nothing.

A more important comment to make about this interpretation of Wilson's motives is that it did not supplant the idea that Wilson wanted first of all to start peace negotiations. In a letter written on 28 December, in which the British ambassador considered the view that the president was trying to prepare American opinion for a dangerous crisis with Germany, he made it clear that Wilson also wanted his move to lead successfully to peace.[38] On the same day, he also sent a telegram stating that Counselor Polk of the State Department had confirmed a statement in the press which indicated that the American note referred solely to outrages on United States rights and her consequent desire to see the war ended.[39] Thus, the conviction that the president was trying to bring about peace persisted in Whitehall despite the "verge of war" statement.

Actually, in one sense Lansing's famous press statement had only served to confirm what the British had long thought. Spring Rice had often pointed out that the American government was acutely worried about a crisis with Germany over the submarine issue. It was obvious that the president might face a choice between war and an embarrassing surrender. The British ambassador had repeatedly warned the Foreign Office in the past that the president was likely to try to put an end to the terrible war, and when he saw the president's note he readily assumed that Wilson was trying to promote peace talks. On the day that Lansing made his "verge of war" statement to the press, Spring Rice cabled:

> There is little doubt in minds of all Allied representatives here that although President's strong wish is to play great part as peace maker main reason for his action is fear of German submarines and of his being involved in war. . . .
> President . . . does not wish to be forced into alternative of war or ignominious surrender. . . . To avoid this alternative President is determined to arrange a peace or at any rate peace negotiations.[40]

In another cable on the same day, Spring Rice referred to the fact that the president had ordered Lansing "to issue a notice that he has no intention of departing from his attitude of perfect neutrality." Spring Rice

commented: "He evidently fears being regarded with suspicion by either party and it is plain that he hopes that his diplomatic intervention will be accepted." Earlier in the same telegram, he stated that the secretary of state had told him that Wilson had been planning to send a note for some time and had sent it when the German peace proposal "gave him cause for fearing that the Allies would return . . . [a] categorical refusal."[41]

If the British continued to believe that Wilson wanted to stop the war, they would be unlikely to believe that he wanted a statement of "extreme terms." Indeed, the fact that the leaders in London remained convinced that the president was trying to promote peace negotiations means that Lansing did not "sabotage" the president's peace move. The British leaders considered the American note a peace move from the outset and Lansing did nothing which removed that quite accurate conviction. As will be shown below, this conclusion is further borne out by their official reply to Wilson, in which the British leaders tried to defend themselves against his arguments in favor of a peace without victory.

3. THE BRITISH RESPONSE

An important key to understanding the British government's reply is to realize that the president's note was, barring rash and impulsive action, safe for all concerned. Of course, any diplomatic act related to a controversial issue involves a risk to prestige. Even silence is a risk. Most maneuvers can also be badly bungled. But the president's peace move would only be likely to incur serious damage to his prestige if he first made it into an ultimatum and then failed to carry out his threat.

Wilson was usually prudent. He coveted greater power, glory, and good works, but he abhorred troublesome complications, and he usually preserved ample room to maneuver when taking any step. Accordingly, he readily accepted Colonel House's advice to deny explicitly, if not quite ingenuously, that he was trying to mediate or demand peace.[42] Yet, even if Wilson had clearly stated that he was attempting to mediate, it is unlikely that a rebuff from all the belligerents would be fatal to his prestige.[43] As the elected head of a very powerful nation he had many options. For instance, it would be politically easy for him to put his public commitment to a postwar League of Nations on ice and move back toward a more isolationist position, complete with claims of moral superiority. This could be made very popular at home, and it was, in fact, a

[37] F.O. 371/2806/252387/263332.
[38] F.O. 371/3075/2/8779.
[39] F.O. 371/2806/252387/263818.
[40] F.O. 371/2805/252387/259525.

[41] F.O. 371/2805/252387/259890. It is possible that Spring Rice had intended to attribute the last quoted remark to Counselor Polk. He sent a dispatch by bag which seems to suggest that Polk might have been his source. F.O. 371/3075/2/583.
[42] Seymour, 1926: 2: p. 394.
[43] Cf. May, 1959: pp. 360–361.

position not very far from the one he actually occupied. His international commitments were related to a post-war world and, in any case, were more rhetorical than real. Meanwhile the great economic power and military potential of the United States would assure him of an attentive hearing around the world. If his prestige did slip he would soon have opportunities to regain it. Political prestige soon returns to the powerful.

Wilson's only major obstacle to an isolationist response would be his own international ambitions. He would probably have found it more congenial to use one of the other options. He might, for example, have stated the terms America would have favored and then apply pressure on the belligerents. He could have started protesting about Germany's treatment of the Belgians, made speeches about what the prolongation of the war was doing to Western civilization, or even have severed diplomatic relations with Germany over the submarine issue. Against the Allies he could have used his economic weapons. But these sanctions are academic in the sense that it is unlikely that Wilson would have to do anything drastic to salvage his prestige. His ability to retaliate or to give American support to the more receptive side was enough to assure that the belligerents would be very polite in rejecting any move the president made. Wilson also must have known that there was the strong possibility, particularly if he were cautious, that some of the neutrals would openly support his peace move, as several in fact did.[44]

A rebuff by both sides was not the only possible difficulty to be sure. There was obviously the chance that Germany would accept his initiative and the Allies would reject it. Certainly Wilson was aware of this possibility. Both Colonel House and Secretary of State Lansing pointed it out to him.[45]

Yet, from his point of view the risks were much less than in the House-Grey understanding. He thought that war with the Allies was practically out of the question, while he knew that the House-Grey agreement contained considerable risk of war. Perhaps Wilson would have actually preferred that Germany accept his peace move and the Allies reject it rather than that both sides turn him down. His sympathy for the Allies was at a low ebb and was probably not significantly greater than his sympathy for Germany. Moreover, it is possible that the president might well have preferred that Germany accept and the Allies reject rather than the other way around. His only feasible way to force Germany to the peace table would be war, but he had the power to force Britain and the other Allies to negotiate by measures short of war.

On the other hand, it was unlikely that the Allies would balk so completely that Wilson would have to withdraw his offer or put pressure on them. If Germany stated her terms, the Allies could be counted upon at least to come out with the proper pieties about a lasting peace, a League of Nations, the rights of small nations, and national self-determination. Upon these principles they could easily base terms that would be very unfavorable to the Central Powers. Issues such as Belgium, the Polish parts of Germany, Alsace-Lorraine, and an "end to militarism" were all readily available. It was also fairly obvious that some demands regarding *Italia irredenta,* Serbia, and reparations could be defended in moral terms. Hence, it was likely that the Allies would provide Wilson with an ample excuse for not opposing them, should he not want to risk it later. Finally, even if the Allies were to demand terms that went far beyond the principles of national self-determination and the rights of small nations (as they in fact did), they could still comply with Wilson's request for terms, and thus still let him off the hook.

Thus, Wilson had created an opportunity for Germany to do what he wanted them to do at a time when he could be fairly sure that the British government would be very unlikely to give him an abrupt rebuff. Given his ability to influence Allied credit in America, and given the fact that his note left the Allies with palatable options other than a sharp rebuff, the president probably did not risk anything more serious than a bad foreign press. Unfortunately for his peacemaking intentions, however, when he retained for himself plenty of room to maneuver, he also left ample room for the belligerents. This became clearly apparent to the British leaders when they got down to the task of formulating a reply.

Meanwhile the British government's first diplomatic task was to restrain the predictable reactions of the press. Early in the afternoon on 21 December, a telegram from Spring Rice arrived containing the following advice: ". . . I think that our Press should adopt as reserved an attitude as possible until United States public opinion has declared itself. It is most important not to offend the President personally. . . ."[46] The Foreign Office duly instructed the press to exercise some caution.

[44] The British also felt that this would happen. On 25 Dec., 1916, they sent cables to their representatives in neutral countries, authorizing them, if they thought it desirable, to give a friendly warning to the governments to which they were accredited that "they would expose themselves to a severe rebuff if they allowed themselves to come forward in support of President Wilson's note regarding peace." F.O. 371/2806/252387/261605. When some of the neutrals did support the president's move, there was considerable anger in the F.O. In a letter to his cousin in Spain, Lord Hardinge referred to "these rotten Scandinavian Powers who want to play a big role." Hardinge to Sir Arthur Hardinge (Madrid), 2 Jan., 1917, Hardinge Papers 29.

[45] House Diary, 15 Nov., 1916. Published in Link, 1965: p. 189. For Lansing's advice, see his letter to the president of 10 Dec., 1916. Published in Lansing, 1935: pp. 179–180.

[46] F.O. 371/2805/252387/258250. Wilson's reputation for vindictiveness had no doubt added to Spring Rice's fear of offending him. F.O. 371/2806/252387/260988. For a brief survey of the reactions of the British Press, see Rappaport, 1951: pp. 119–123.

Prudence was the main theme among those who mattered. Lord Hardinge wrote:

I presume that our first preoccupation must be to reply to the German note, and there needs to be no great hurry in framing a reply to the President, though we should lose no time in urging upon our Allies to give no reply until we have come to some agreement as to its nature and scope. Our reply should be firm but very cautious.[47]

The strength of this desire for restraint can be appreciated by considering what Hardinge actually felt about the American move. In a letter to Spring Rice dated 21 December, 1916, he freely expressed his exasperation. He wrote that the American peace note was "a 'slimy' mass of murkiness" and "quite impracticable." It seemed as though its intention was "to create disunion amongst the Allies, for if each Ally were to enunciate its own special demands and get those satisfied without considering the claims of others it would probably soon lead to dismemberment of the Alliance." Lord Hardinge considered this "a somewhat clumsy proceeding"—a remark which revealed the special contempt of a professional diplomat for the amateur. He also thought that it was altogether not "a friendly proceeding on the part of the President," who apparently wanted "to prejudice the reply of the Allies to the German Note by some sort of concession to meet his own views." Hardinge wondered whether the president realized that the action which he desired to take in promoting peace at that time was "nothing more than the support of Militarism in opposition to Right." He saw no mention in the president's note "of the smaller Powers or of any claims that they may have for a free and independent existence." The president should realize that, if he obtained peace within the next month, militarism would "still be rampant and . . . the right of smaller Powers to an independent existence would have been lost, or at least jeopardized." Hardinge asked rhetorically: "Would he [the president] care to have his name associated with a peace which only means giving a breathing space for the repetition of a war in a few years time which would even be more deadly and ghastly than the present one?" At the culmination of this tirade, Hardinge recalled the president's past sins, the chief one being his failure to support openly Britain's crusade against Germany. He wrote:

The President seems to me to be a man who has missed his opportunities in a very remarkable manner. His famous phrase of "Being too proud to fight" will be as memorable as Bethmann-Hollweg's "Scrap of Paper," and it almost seems deplorable to think what fine opportunities the President has had and has missed.[48]

Hardinge did not participate in the drafting of the Allies' reply to the president, because he left on the twenty-second for ten days of overdue leave. But his irritation with the American note was by no means unique.

Robert Cecil expressed his reactions to Ambassador Page on 26 December. Cecil's tone was much less violent than Hardinge's letter to Spring Rice, perhaps because he had had some time to cool off, and also because Page was, though deeply sympathetic to Britain, one of the president's representatives. Nevertheless, Cecil was quite frank. He said that "the President's message had produced a very unfortunate impression" in Britain. He particularly called Page's attention to two passages. In one, the president appeared to put Britain's war aims on the same level as Germany's.[49] In another, "he used language which almost amounted to a covert threat."[50] Cecil said that "speaking very frankly and merely as a private individual . . . if any threat was intended it would be disregarded" as the British "were determined to carry on the war to a victorious conclusion so long as . . . [they] were physically able to do so." He added that he deeply regretted "the apparent check" in the cordiality of Anglo-American relations, and he tried to dismiss any impression that he was being bellicose. Cecil declared himself a "very confirmed lover of peace," and said that he "shared to the utmost President Wilson's view that some effort should be made at the end of this war to erect a barrier against future wars." He also observed that this "could be done with any chance of success only by the close co-operation of the United States and Great Britain, with the assistance of France, and anything that made any interruption or lessening of our friendly relations was very grievous."[51]

Cecil, of course, did not suggest to the American ambassador that Britain and the United States should cooperate closely in an effort to force an end to the war. That would have meant a return to something like the House-Grey understanding of February, 1916. Actually the question of reconsidering that arrangement was raised again during December. When Grey left the Foreign Office, he gave Cecil a copy of the House-Grey understanding together with a covering memorandum which suggested that mediation should be seriously considered if the major allies should be-

---

[47] See Hardinge's minute, F.O. 371/2805/252387/258250.
[48] Hardinge to Spring Rice, 21 Dec., 1916, Hardinge Papers 28.

[49] Wilson's apologists stressed that the president referred only to the war aims as announced by the belligerents, not the actual objectives being pursued. See telegram from Spring Rice, 21 Dec., 1916, F.O. 371/2805/252387/259890; dispatch from Spring Rice, 22 Dec., 1916, F.O. 371/3075/2/583.
[50] The president had suggested that, if the war were not soon ended, the situation of neutrals might become altogether intolerable. See p. 16 above.
[51] This narrative is based on Cecil's account of the conversation. F.O. 371/2806/252387/263429. For Page's report, see *Foreign Relations, 1916, Supplement:* pp. 115–116. See also Hendrick, 1923: 2: pp. 209–211. For a report of Lloyd George's initial incensed reaction to Wilson's note, see Wilson, 1970: p. 253.

come unable to continue the war.[52] In a memorandum dated 13 December, just after the German peace move, Sir Eric Drummond urged that the British government should consider mediation by the president in case any of the Allies should make a separate peace. Cecil disagreed, stating that Britain would have warning of a separate peace by her allies and could wait to consider the president's mediation if the situation arose. Nevertheless, Cecil sent the prime minister the memoranda which Grey had given him and suggested that he ought to decide whether they should go to the Cabinet, in view of the German peace maneuver. Apparently Lloyd George thought this unnecessary; however, the arrival of Wilson's note made the documents more relevant. Drummond advised Cecil that the War Cabinet should have the House-Grey memorandum before it when considering the American note. He also suggested that a telegram should be sent to House enquiring whether the president still agreed to it.[53] Cecil promptly circulated the House-Grey memorandum to the Cabinet, mentioning that "if thought desirable," the Foreign Office could enquire of House whether the understanding still held good.[54] There is no record that this enquiry was made, nor is there any evidence that the War Cabinet discussed the memorandum. This is not surprising in view of the British government's attitude toward peace negotiations at that stage of the war.

The British leaders realized, of course, that Anglo-American differences on this issue could be very dangerous to the Allies' cause. This was the most compelling reason why the Foreign Office emphasized the need for caution. While it was tempting to return a negative reply to the president because they felt angry and insulted, it would be foolish to insult Wilson, not to mention the effect of a negative reply on neutral opinion. In an important memorandum on the American note, Lord Robert Cecil carefully considered the pros and cons of such a response.[55] He posed the negative reply as follows:

We may . . . inform the Americans that we are not prepared to make any statement as to terms of peace at present; that Germany was the aggressor, and it is for her, if she wishes to do so, to make any proposals in the direction of peace; and that we cannot admit in any way the doctrine that the aims of the belligerents are identical or similar, or that at this stage any good purpose would be served by admitting the intervention of a neutral Government.

Cecil suggested that such a reply had some possible advantages. "It would," he wrote, "emphasize the impossibility of considering any peace terms at pres-

ent . . . it would put heart into the most determined parts of the Allied populations, and . . . it might stifle the protests of those who are inclined to look for some means of putting a stop to the war." On the other hand, Cecil pointed out the disadvantages at such length that his memorandum can be considered an effort to justify a positive reply to the president. He suggested that a negative response would stiffen German resistance. It might induce Allied pacifists to demand an immediate end to the war and give them the argument that if the Allies' terms were moderate or defensible, the Allies would be glad to state them, and that the fact that they refused to state them showed that their terms were unacceptable to all moderate men. Cecil said he was afraid of the effect of this upon English public opinion. "Englishmen do not mind doing violent things," he explained, "but they like to persuade themselves that they are all the while models of moderation." Moreover, he thought the effect of a negative reply on neutral opinion must be bad. Invoking what was by then a cliché in the Foreign Office, he conceded that it might meet with the approval of people in the eastern states of America, but not in the west, and the west was politically more important. Cecil continued:

The President himself would evidently be much disappointed, to put it mildly, and though, on reflection, I think it very unlikely that he would proceed to direct hostile measures against the Allies, undoubtedly he would look about for means to make them feel his displeasure.

Cecil warned that Wilson could stir up the old trouble about the blacklist and censorship of the mails, that he might use the retaliatory legislation, that he might encourage the Swedish and Dutch governments to resist the blockade, and that once an "atmosphere of irritation had been created . . . it was not at all impossible that the President would feel himself strong enough to proceed to much more drastic measures."

Cecil's fears about Britain's vulnerability to American interference were well supported by other documents. On the morning after Wilson's note arrived, in a preliminary discussion about the president's "overtures," the War Cabinet had decided that it needed information first as to the consequences for British and Allied interests if President Wilson were to put his maximum available pressure on the Allies to stop the war, and secondly, as to what the consequences of hostile trade and financial measures would be for America. Sir Maurice Hankey, the secretary to the new War Cabinet, was told to furnish a memorandum as soon as possible. Characteristically, he had already contacted relevant government departments about the problem.[56]

The ominous replies were produced very promptly on the twenty-first and twenty-second.[57] Surviving documents indicate responses from the Ministry of

---

[52] Grey, 1925: 2: pp. 126–128.

[53] See the covering note to the prime minister from Robert Cecil, dated Dec., 1916, and memoranda by Drummond dated 13 and 21 Dec., 1916, F.O. 800/197.

[54] Lloyd George Papers, F/160/1/4.

[55] CAB 23/1/16/Appendix I. The memorandum is dated 22 Dec., 1916.

[56] CAB 23/1/13/1.

[57] Cf. Link, 1965: pp. 232–233.

Munitions, the director of army contracts, the food controller, and the director of military operations. Memoranda associated with the enquiry during October into the same basic problem were also resurrected and submitted together with a general memorandum by G. M. Young, one of Hankey's assistant secretaries.[58]

Hankey complained to his diary that in a subsequent War Cabinet discussion the enquiry was apparently "forgotten."[59] But the fact that the memoranda were seemingly neglected later was probably not related to Lansing's comments. The War Cabinet's business methods were not very systematic. Moreover, they did not need to refer specifically to the memoranda when discussing the reply to the president. The new reports did not alter the basic, long-established facts of Britain's heavy dependence upon American supplies.

The two essential aspects of the situation were as follows: (1) Britain remained undeniably vulnerable to pressure from America; (2) yet, the question of interrupted supplies remained only a dangerous possibility, not an imminent blow or a concrete fact. The importance of these considerations are worth discussing, because interfering with supplies by using retaliatory legislation or by damaging Allied credit was Wilson's trump card.

Balfour also expressed the view that the United States had the power to force peace negotiations on Britain,[60] and there is no reason to believe that anyone in the War Cabinet thought otherwise. The idea of Britain's serious vulnerability to American pressure was a long-standing assumption at Whitehall. While the Ministry of Munitions felt assured of a supply of ammunition over the next six months that compared favorably with the rate of expenditure since the commencement of the Somme offensive at the end of July, 1916, there was no doubt that America could cripple the war effort. Beyond June, 1917, the effect of America's merely cutting off supplies of nitro-cellulose would, they felt, be catastrophic. The food controller estimated that Britain depended upon America for forty per cent of its supplies of flour, and that only about four months' supply was in hand or already on passage. The director of army contracts admitted that there was no alternative supply for lubricating oil, without which Britain's machinery could not keep running. He also indicated that Britain was almost as dependent for petrol supplies. Beyond these essentials, the collected memoranda showed a large range of important commodities which would be difficult to obtain outside America in sufficient amounts.

This information does not mean that the British government felt themselves to be in a helpless position. They felt that their power of reprisal was formidable, and efforts were being made to reduce Britain's dependence. Moreover, as mentioned above, the Interdepartmental Committee which had examined the problem back in October had concluded that general restrictions by America upon supplies were improbable.

Nevertheless the situation was perilous—especially in regard to finances. As we have seen, the Committee had warned that there was a probable danger of an unfavorable American attitude toward loans and that Britain's negotiating position was very weak. The degree of their foreboding is obviously difficult to assess, but a detailed assessment is actually not necessary. In making the kind of diplomatic decisions being considered here, it was not essential for the British leaders to know with any precision the probability of American pressure on their lifelines. The mere possibility of Wilson's hostile action was a compelling reason for not answering his note with a rebuff. This was all the more true since the president's note had left them room within which to maneuver.

How far the British would feel forced to go in conciliating America was limited by the second major aspect of Britain's dependence upon America. An interruption in supplies was only something that might happen, and as long as this was the case, Britain's heavy dependence upon America for essential commodities was unlikely to cause the government to compromise their demands for victory. Much of this reluctance to compromise was due to their emotional commitment to win the war—an obsession which urged them to keep spending dollars at a terrific pace, despite their awareness of grave danger ahead.[61] Yet, in facing the threat of hostile action against supplies, there were perhaps also several rational considerations supporting this adamant attitude. Even if Wilson used his full powers, the Allies could keep going at full strength for several months. By moderating their efforts and conserving their resources, the Allies could reasonably expect to hold on longer. There would also be a fair chance of playing for time if Wilson interfered with supplies by attacking Allied credit. It was thought that such action would probably not cut off all American financing, because America now had an enormous financial interest in keeping the Allies afloat. It was also readily conceivable that expedients for gaining a little time would turn up. Proposals were later studied of changing debentures of the Canadian Pacific Railway from sterling securities into dollar securities, or the possibility of selling Britain's large holdings of South American securities to Americans. Thus, it was not unreasonable to expect that Britain would have something more than several months during which the political situation could change. Wilson might modify his policies after being conciliated by some relaxation of Allied restrictions on American trade and after feel-

[58] See CAB 1/21/6, 8, and 11.

[59] Roskill, 1970: 1: p. 347.

[60] Minutes of Anglo-French Conference, 26 Dec., 1916, CAB 28/2/13(a).

[61] See Bonar Law's statement on finance to the Imperial War Cabinet, 3 Apr., 1917, CAB 1/24/13(b).

ing the impact of his action on the American economy. Moreover, Germany might force dramatic changes in American policy by resorting to unrestricted submarine warfare. Even barring this eventuality, it seemed possible that something disastrous could happen to the enemy in the near future. But the real crux of the matter was that, if Wilson did decide to cripple the Allies' war effort, there would probably be enough time to come to the president's heel and negotiate a peace without victory *after* his attack on Allied supplies had become clearly imminent or even after it had become a fact. Supplies from America probably seemed necessary for victory, but it would not seem sensible in this situation to sacrifice the goal merely to insure the means, especially since the president's threats were vague.

Indeed, the threats to supplies were so indefinite that an almost sanguine view of the situation was possible. Though Spring Rice clearly pointed out the danger to Allied supplies and advised the wisdom of caution, he also conveyed various assurances that interference with supplies was unlikely.[62] The British ambassador's confidence may have been impressive in view of his reputation for excessive pessimism. There were even signs that the Foreign Office was beginning to feel reassured about the Federal Reserve Board's future course.[63] Yet, even without these encouraging signs, the British government would have remained firm.

Finding themselves in a vulnerable position but not yet faced with an imminent blow, the most reasonable course seemed obvious. The task was to develop a positive reply to Wilson which did not promote the president's aim of a peace without victory. This suggested the need for something more than a firm reply. It meant that they should formulate a persuasive defense of their determination to win the war and of the terms which made victory necessary. In short, it meant an exercise in wartime propaganda. This was in effect all that President Wilson's note demanded. Indeed, the note could be considered as an invitation to use a very prominent forum at a time when the British leaders had compelling reasons for finding an adventure in propaganda attractive. The fact that Britain was heavily dependent upon America for supplies made it seem very important that there should be widespread sympathy in the United States for their cause. The British government felt that they needed the sup-

port of an ever wider investing public in America in order to keep supplies moving, and public sympathy was obviously desirable in order to restrain both Wilson and Congress from possible hostile action. Discussion of ways to increase and improve Allied propaganda was very much in the air during this period. By apparently suggesting that the objects of the belligerents were similar, the president's note had actually helped to stimulate a desire for more propaganda. The fact that Wilson could get away with such a line in the United States seemed to emphasize America's colossal ignorance about the causes of the war and its meaning. Robert Cecil, like Spring Rice, was notably skeptical about the wisdom of many suggestions for mounting a big propaganda campaign in the United States, but he thought much could be accomplished in various ways. "Official propaganda known to be such is almost useless," he wrote on 29 December, "except, of course, in the form of State Papers."[64] He must have had the Allied reply to Wilson in mind. There seemed to be good grounds for believing the occasion propitious. Spring Rice had reported on 20 December that the prime minister's speech regarding the German peace overture had been favorably received in America.[65] The British leaders had, of course, always thought that they had a good case against Germany, and they knew that their terms could be justified by moral principles which had a wide appeal. For instance, during the enquiry into the peace question by Asquith's government, Balfour had pointed out how the "principle of nationality" alone could be used to obtain many objects desired by the Allies at the expense of Germany and the Austro-Hungarian Empire.[66] The British also generally felt that they had compelling moral justifications for the rest of what the Allies wanted. They could invoke such principles as the rights of small nations, security, reparation for victims of aggression, and the notion that the Turks were too barbarous to rule anyone but the Turks.

Robert Cecil's aforementioned memorandum on the American note illustrated this very clearly when he went on to consider an alternative to a negative response to the president. The positive reply which he proposed was along lines similar to the one that was to be used in the actual Allied note. Cecil suggested that the general objects of the war were well known, but that the Allies were willing to state them more fully. Occupied territory must be evacuated, and Belgium and Serbia restored. Beyond that, they wanted a territorial settlement with a chance of permanence, which must be based on principles "acceptable to human feeling, such as nationality and security." This would entitle France to a rearrangement of her eastern

---

[62] F.O. 371/2806/252387/260988; F.O. 371/2796/63430/262218; F.O. 371/2806/252387/262193.

[63] See the minute initialed by Rowland Sperling, chief clerk of the American Department of the Foreign Office, in F.O. 371/2796/63430/262218. Another consideration behind Britain's firm reply is worth noting. In an interesting twist to the problem of Britain's dependence upon America, Spring Rice warned that any appearance of weakening or anxiety for peace would damage Britain's credit. In other words, by compromising her demand for victory in order to maintain her supplies, Britain might incur the damage she sought to avoid. F.O. 371/2805/252387/259910; F.O. 371/2806/252387/262940.

[64] CAB 24/3/102.

[65] F.O. 371/2805/252387/258250.

[66] Balfour's memorandum was published in Lloyd George, 1933: 2: pp. 300–308.

frontier which would render her secure from "such an unprovoked attack as she had been the victim of in the present war." It would also regain for her those provinces which were ethnologically French. An autonomous Poland, including Poles ruled by Austria and Germany, would be created under the protection of the Russian czar. The same principles would apply to Italy, including her need for security in the Adriatic. In southeast Europe, a settlement "on sound national lines" was essential, which "would include the liberation of Slav peoples from German domination." Cecil recommended speaking very strongly about relegating the unspeakable Turk to Asia. He also advised explaining that on commercial and political grounds, Russia should control Constantinople, "with proper safeguards for free navigation of the Bosphorus and Dardanelles." In a revealing paragraph, Cecil added:

Without expressing any final opinion as to the desirability of either of the courses which I have sketched, I cannot help feeling that the second would give us an opportunity of explaining vigorously and effectively to the Americans and other neutral nations, as well as to our own people and the Germans, that our aims are really based on justice and liberty, and that when we use these phrases we have something definite in mind beyond mere verbiage.

The War Cabinet seemed to share something of Cecil's sense of opportunity. His memorandum together with a French draft of a reply to the American note were before the War Cabinet meeting on 23 December. The French draft and the first alternative in Cecil's memorandum were considered *evasive*. The War Cabinet was definitely "inclined" towards Cecil's second alternative, which the minutes referred to as a proposal that the Allies "should *explain* in general terms the objects for which we are fighting, including insistence on a final settlement of the Turkish question." [67] It was agreed that Cecil should prepare for the War Cabinet's consideration a draft reply on the lines of his positive response.

The emphasis upon Turkey here is also interesting. After the German overture had appeared but before they knew of the nature of Wilson's note, the War Cabinet had postponed publishing its agreement with France and Russia regarding the ultimate possession of Constantinople and the Straits.[68] Now they felt that they had an opportunity to present its terms in a favorable light. In his memorandum Robert Cecil said of the positive reply to Wilson: "It would . . . enable us to put on a proper footing the Constantinople question, which will assuredly be one of our great difficulties in the near future."

The British leaders further realized that Wilson's note presented them with an opportunity to score some propaganda points against the president himself. This inclination was clearly present in Cecil's memorandum.

---

[67] CAB 23/1/16/2. Italics added.
[68] War Cabinet minutes, 18 Dec., 1916, CAB 23/1/10/5.

He did not intimate that the Allies go out of their way to sound conciliatory. On the contrary, he suggested that the Allies might introduce their statement of terms by protesting "in the strongest way against the American assumption that both sides were fighting for the same objects," and by reiterating "with vigour and directness" the Allied view of the war's origin and purpose. More pointedly, he added: "There might then be a reference to the American claim to humanity, with an expression of regret that it had so far produced little active results, enumerating the various occasions in which they had failed to interfere to check or punish German outrages or atrocities." The president's position that a league of nations would guarantee future peace was another target. Cecil suggested that after expressing utmost sympathy with the proposal of a league, the Allies should ask whether the promised support of the United States meant that its government "had the will and the power to give armed support to the decisions of any such league?" He also advised referring to a recent speech by Senator Stone, chairman of the Senate Foreign Relations Committee, in which he had declared his opposition to membership in a league. "We should further enquire," Cecil added, "whether the province of the league was to extend to the American continent. . . ." The Allies could then profess readiness to enter more fully into the subject when they were satisfied on these points. Cecil was, to be sure, a sincere supporter of the league idea, but his immediate task was to expose the weaknesses in the president's position and to take a good defensive stance.

At the meeting on 23 December, the War Cabinet were also informed that Balfour was preparing a draft reply. The foreign secretary was now apparently feeling well enough to take a more active part in deliberations, though it may have been that he did not want to miss the opportunity Wilson had given him. Balfour had long known what line he wanted to take about the president's mediation. Grey had squashed an earlier attempt by Balfour to state his case in connection with the House-Grey mediation plan. Now he had another chance. Like Cecil, he wanted to assail Wilson's position, but he proposed doing it more thoroughly.

Balfour's draft begins by welcoming the president's declaration of America's ardent interest in securing the future peace of the world and relieving small and weak nations of the peril of wrong and violence. Balfour stated that America's influence and resources "may prove of incalculable value to the future of civilisation" and he expressed Britain's sympathy with the "big ideals of international morality which breathes through these declarations of policy."

Having thus politely declared Britain as moral as Wilson, Balfour then adopted a more critical tone. He expressed the "utmost difficulty" in accepting those passages in the note which "might be interpreted as meaning that, in the President's view, not only must the arrangement for permanently improving international relations be dealt with after peace has been arranged, but that their success would in no way be affected by the character of the peace itself." Balfour admitted that the belligerents probably must settle the terms of peace "before the civilised world attempted a solution of those wider problems in which the President is so deeply interested." (He after all did not want Wilson's mediation.) But Balfour declared that His Majesty's government could not separate the question of peace terms and the success of an international organization after peace was established. Neutrals as well as belligerents must consider what kind of peace ought to be desired.

The British foreign secretary continued in an almost sarcastic vein by stating that there seemed to be universal agreement on one all important point. He wrote:

The President states (on evidence not in possession of His Majesty's Government) that the Central Powers desire to make the rights and privileges of weak peoples and small States as secure against aggression or denial in the future as the rights and privileges of the great and powerful States now at war.

This, Balfour concluded, would make the full restoration of Belgium, Serbia, and Montenegro an easy matter.

Regarding other "more difficult problems," Balfour asked rhetorically whether any scheme for securing international peace would be served by reverting to the *status quo ante*. He answered, of course, that His Majesty's government believed it would not.

Nothing in their judgment would be of worse augury for the future than that Europe when the war is over, should find itself infinitely poorer in men and money, but no nearer to an arrangement of state boundaries in harmony with national ideals than it was when the war broke out.

Having invoked the nationality principle, Balfour then argued, in effect, that, unless almost all of the Allied demands that could be justified by that ideal were satisfied, the new era would have poor prospects. He also asserted that the British Empire had "no more direct and immediate interest" in these changes than the United States.

In this context, Balfour discreetly avoided mentioning some British aims outside Europe which might prove embarrassing. For example, he referred to freeing "Christian communities from Turkish tyranny," but he was careful not to mention the Ottoman Empire's Arab provinces. Balfour also avoided references to the German colonies. The British government had many reasons for this aversion. On the one hand, any suggestion that the captured colonies should be retained would invite accusations that Britain was prolonging the war for imperialistic gains. Sir Louis Mallet, the chairman of an interdepartmental committee on territorial changes, remarked that "it would be very awkward to tell dear Mr. Wilson of our intentions. I fear he would never understand our reasons."[69] On the other hand, any evasive, non-committal reference to the captured colonies would provoke powerful objections from imperialists in Britain and a storm in the Dominions. Moreover, the territorial changes committee had not completed its study of the question and there was not sufficient time to consult the Dominions (not to mention Japan) on so controversial an issue. There was also a feeling that Britain should not commit herself on the question. It was thought that the colonies might have to be used as bargaining counters in eventual negotiations.[70]

Balfour's draft was also evasive about Britain's treaty commitments to her allies in the handling of territorial changes. After acknowledging the existence of such agreements, he declared that, apart from "obligations of honour" every diminution of the territorial changes enumerated in his draft reply "would . . . imperil the prospects of those great ideas of international relationships to which the President had given such admirable expression." In this way Balfour cleverly avoided referring to Britain's treaty commitments which went beyond the principle of national self-determination.

The foreign secretary made two further points in his draft: (1) international law and enlightened principles must have an effective sanction, and (2) Germany's military terrorism and disregard for treaties, the laws of nations, and the laws of humanity must be proved unsuccessful. Otherwise the president's beneficent aims would be fore-ordained to failure. Balfour ended his draft reply with the following passage:

His Majesty's Government desire to express their appreciation of the services which the President has performed for the cause of humanity by publicly expressing to the world suffering, as never before, under the horrors of war, that the mere termination of hostilities would provide no sufficient cure for our ills; that what civilisation requires is some security that peace when it comes shall be honourable and lasting.[71]

In short, he was virtually thanking Wilson for creating a favorable opportunity to justify Britain's refusal to negotiate an end to the war.

Further signs of the British government's intention to exploit the opportunity created for them by Wilson can be found in Lord Cecil's account of the meeting he had with the American ambassador on the morning of

---

[69] Mallet to Drummond, 20 Dec., 1916, Balfour Papers, Add. MSS. 49748.

[70] As will be shown later, Lloyd George himself championed this view in the Imperial War Cabinet during Mar., 1917. CAB 23/43/First Meeting; CAB 23/40/13/5. As far as America was concerned the omission proved beneficial. Several months after the United States entered the war, Spring Rice recalled: "The absence of any mention of British claims in the Allied statement of last year created a good impression." F.O. 371/3121/157711/158304.

[71] CAB 37/162/31.

26 December. Page brought a circular telegram to the interview. It suggested that any reply which complied with the requests of the president's note should be made in strict confidence, though it would be understood that the United States government might convey the peace terms in confidence to the opposing side of belligerents. Wilson had probably realized that, if the belligerents publicized their terms, they would be publicly committed to a fairly specific set of demands which would make compromise more difficult. The Allies obviously could use the occasion to declare terms which Germany would not accept unless completely defeated. Perhaps Wilson also realized that in justifying such terms the Allies might make a good case for themselves and against a peace without victory. At any rate, these were the British government's intentions and they clearly required publicity. Hence, Cecil told Page that it would be "quite impossible" for Britain permanently to keep her reply secret; "public opinion," he said, "would not permit it. . . ." He added, however, that perhaps they might wish that nothing be divulged until the German reply had been received.[72] Cecil was, no doubt, aware of the advantages of seeing an opponent's cards. There was also a good chance that Germany would not state her terms, which would be a big windfall for Allied propaganda.

Cecil reported to the War Cabinet later the same day that Page had urged the desirability of "complete frankness" in dealing with the United States Government.[73] The American ambassador had, Cecil said, informed him of America's very limited appreciation of the issues involved in the war and the spirit in which the war was carried on by the Allies. Not surprisingly, the War Cabinet concurred that "frankness" was desirable. They also debated whether the Allies should reply with separate or identical notes. The War Cabinet agreed provisionally that it was undesirable for each power to formulate its own peace terms, but they also recognized that, if separate replies were used, appeals for restitution and reparation by states such as Serbia and Belgium could be very convincing in neutral countries. The final decision was deferred pending an imminent conference with French ministers.

The British and French had planned a conference on war matters—particularly Greece and Italy—for some time. When the president's note arrived they were fortunate to have a meeting between themselves virtually ready-made which could be used to decide upon a reply. Although the War Cabinet was inclined to return a positive response, the nature of the Allies' reply did not appear as a foregone conclusion at the start of the conference. The War Cabinet had not yet reached any final decision and French comments about the peace question tended to be rather bellicose.

Moreover, it might prove difficult to agree upon a relatively specific declaration of peace terms in a short period of time. Cecil commented in a Foreign Office minute: "The probable result of the Allied discussions will be [a] formless note of no signification whatever." [74]

The first meeting of the Anglo-French conference was held on 26 December. It began with a discussion of the German and American peace notes. A French draft reply to the German note was produced and amended. The British were particularly concerned that demands for the restoration of invaded territories might damage their claims in Mesopotamia and the German colonies. This was easily avoided by not mentioning invaded territories and the amended draft was accepted by the conference. The reply used essentially the same tactic as that adopted by Lloyd George in his speech before the House of Commons. It stated that a suggestion for negotiation without any conditions was not a peace offer, and accused the German note of being a maneuver of war. No peace was possible, the note said, until the "reparation of violated rights and liberties, the acknowledgment of the principle of nationalities and of the free existence of small states" was assured, and until the security of the world was guaranteed by suppressing the causes which have "menaced nations" for so long. In effect, peace negotiations were out of the question unless Germany capitulated. This was later topped off with a passage on the suffering of Belgium, who would only consider a peace settlement which assured her of just reparation, guarantees, and security. The note was subsequently handed to the American ambassador in Paris on 30 December. An advance copy reached Wilson on the same day. It was published in Paris on the thirty-first.[75]

When the conference went on during its first meeting to discuss the reply to President Wilson, Lloyd George as chairman posed the following points.

1. Should we go into any sort of detail? Should we state our terms to America, to the world, and to our own people? The War Cabinet themselves were undecided.

2. Should the Allies send an identic Note or should each nation send its own reply? The advantages of the latter course lay in this: that France, and also Belgium and Serbia, could say things to the Americans that this country could not.

A possible suggestion was that there should be an identic

---

[72] Cecil to Spring Rice, 26 Dec., 1916, F.O. 371/2806/252387/263429.

[73] CAB 23/1/17/2.

[74] F.O. 371/2806/252387/262697. Cecil's comment was elicited by an interesting minute, dated 26 Dec., by Sir Eyre Crowe, then an assistant under-secretary of state. Crowe feared mediation by the president and advised declaring that no mediation would be acceptable until the enemy was mastered. He argued that Wilson would support some unacceptable German demands, namely (1) independence of Ireland, (2) "freedom of the seas," and (3) disarmament and general arbitration. Cecil was not convinced.

[75] *Foreign Relations, 1916, Supplement:* pp. 123–125.

note with France, Belgium and Serbia adding certain individual observations.[76]

M. Ribot, French minister of Finance, argued that separate notes ran the risk of division among the Allies. He thought Belgium's tendency to consider herself a special case was dangerous. M. Berthelot, of the French Ministry for Foreign Affairs, supported this view. He also repeated Briand's opinion that the Allies must maintain their position as defendants, with Germany in the position of asking for peace. According to the minutes of the conference Berthelot argued: "If anything in the way of terms had to be announced, it was preferable to do so in answer to Germany, rather than in answer to the United States." As mentioned above, he said that Mr. Lansing had given them to understand that the American government knew the Allies' aims and only wanted to know the German aims. "That situation," he asserted, "should be maintained." In response to this, Lord Robert Cecil observed that "the American demand required very careful handling or the Americans might say that the Allies did not dare avow what they really wanted, namely, the destruction of Germany." He went on, "The effect of that would be bad in the United States and worse in Germany." After reiterating arguments which had been presented to the War Cabinet, Cecil expressed his fear that Briand's proposed reply to the American note "might be read as missing a great opportunity." He thought that his own draft made out a "very strong case."

M. Ribot said it came down to the following question: "Was our reply to be a diplomatic Note or an answer to the American people?" The conference agreed that their reply was essentially "an appeal to democracy." The minutes also record that "Mr. Balfour agreed with the Prime Minister that President Wilson's Note was addressed to the American people as much as to anyone else." The new British foreign secretary then presented the argument embodied in his draft reply to the effect that the United States must be made to realize that, unless the peace at the end of the war was what the Allies wanted, "the peace of the whole world" could not be established. "A reversion to the *status quo ante bellum* would not," he said "be in the interests of the world at large." Balfour added: "This point required serious attention because the United States had it in their power to compel peace." Cecil thought that Balfour's point should be made, but evidently wanted to go beyond debating the president's position. He expressed the notion that "in order to rouse American sympathies it was necessary to make a definite appeal to the United States."

Lord Curzon, who was a member of the War Cabinet, saw danger in making detailed statements for the benefit of public opinion in Britain and the United States. He said that "it meant in the first place, considerable negotiation among the Allies themselves." M. Ribot suggested that the two opposing views could be reconciled. Finally the conference agreed that on the following day they should consider the drafts by Balfour and Cecil and a fresh one to be prepared by M. Berthelot.

For the rest of that afternoon, and during the following morning the Conference was preoccupied with urgent questions about Greece and Salonika as well as the problem of extending the British line on the western front. The top ministers in Lloyd George's government endured a constant stream of demanding problems, and it should be remembered that the response to Wilson was devised in a context of various pressing matters. The conference did not mention the Allied reply to Wilson again until just before the members adjourned for lunch, and this was only to concert pressure upon Belgium not to make a separate reply.[77]

During the afternoon meeting of the twenty-seventh, the conference remained occupied with problems in Greece and did not consider the draft replies to Wilson as planned.[78] In addition to the pressure of other business, discussion may have been postponed because morning papers stated that the Germans had replied to the American note. Perhaps the Allied leaders merely wanted time to analyze the German reply, but they may have also realized that it had left the field entirely to them.

The Germans declined to state their terms. A "direct exchange of views" appeared to the Imperial government as the most suitable approach to lasting peace. One implication of this was that the president had been slighted. Not only was his request refused, but his mediation had been pronounced undesirable. A telegram from Spring Rice received by the Foreign Office about noon on the twenty-seventh stated:

President is disappointed at Germany's answer as he expected Germany to inform him of terms and thus put matter in his hands. It is thought Allies have a chance of gaining his sympathy by conciliatory (?statement) with sympathetic reference to league to enforce peace.[79]

The War Cabinet considered M. Berthelot's new draft on the morning of the twenty-eighth, and accepted it as a basis for a joint reply subject to certain amendments.[80] Later in the day, Lloyd George suggested to the Anglo-French conference that another draft be prepared by a joint committee which included Balfour and M. Cambon, the French ambassador.[81] A revised version of Berthelot's draft was approved in the early evening.

[76] CAB 28/2/13(a).

[77] CAB 28/2/13(b).
[78] CAB 28/2/13(c).
[79] F.O. 371/2806/252387/262556.
[80] CAB 23/1/21/3.
[81] CAB 28/2/13(d). The committee as constituted also included Lord Robert Cecil and M. Thomas, French minister of munitions.

Before the Allied reply was handed to the American ambassador in Paris on 10 January, 1917, there would be some complaints about the wording of various passages in the Anglo-French draft, some foot-dragging about certain terms, and some modifications made, but this draft formed the substance of the final note. The Belgian government eventually signed the Allied note, though it insisted on adding a separate reply as well.

The Anglo-French draft politely paid tribute to the lofty sentiments which inspired the American note and expressed support for the creation of a league of nations to insure peace and justice. The draft note added:

They [the Allied Governments] hope that they will be able to count on the assistance of the United States in providing the sanction necessary to the enforcement of such arrangements lest an illusory security should serve merely to facilitate fresh acts of aggression.[82]

The main general points were then stated: (1) a discussion of future arrangements to insure lasting peace presupposed a satisfactory settlement of the present conflict; (2) while having as profound a desire as the United States to terminate the war as soon as possible, the Allied governments did not believe it possible at the present moment to obtain a just and secure peace.

The draft note recognized the plight of neutrals for which the Allies were not to be blamed, having in no way provoked the war. It also contained a protest and an expression of regret that the American note was sent immediately after the German note, "thus giving the impression that one supported the other." This passage was eventually deleted at the prudent suggestion of Baron Sonnino, the Italian minister for foreign affairs.[83] The draft reply continued with an expression of satisfaction about the American declaration that the president's note was not associated with that of the Central Powers and professed their confidence in America's resolution not to support the "authors responsible for the war."

There followed the predictable protest about the "analogy drawn between the two groups of belligerents" in the American note. This referred primarily, of course, to Wilson's alleged implication that their aims were the same. The Allies expressed certainty that President Wilson did not associate himself with the misleading public declarations of the Central Powers, on which the analogy was based. The draft note then described the many sins of the Central Powers which, it stated, fully explained the Allied protest to the president.

The draft then turned to its statement of terms, declaring that the Allied governments experienced no difficulty in meeting the president's request. The demands which followed were substantially the same as Lord Robert Cecil had suggested in his memorandum of the previous week, though slightly more vague. The draft note insisted upon restoration and reparation for Belgium, Serbia, and Montenegro. France, Russia, and Romania were to be evacuated with reparations. Europe's reorganization was to be secured by a permanent settlement, based upon the following:

The principle of nationalities and the security of peoples small and great, safeguards for land and sea frontiers against unprovoked attacks, the restitution of provinces formerly torn from the Allies by force; the liberation of Italians, Slavs, and Roumanians from foreign domination [the final version also mentioned the Czecho-Slovaks]; the liberation of the peoples who now lie beneath the murderous tyranny of the Turks and the relegation into Asia of the Ottoman Empire. . . .

Poland was referred to by a line which suggested that the czar intended to create a "free" and united Poland.[84]

The list of terms ended with a declaration that the Allies did not seek "the extermination or political extinction of the German people." At the interesting suggestion of the Russian minister for foreign affairs, the word "people" was later made plural.[85] This was topped off with a reaffirmation of the Allies' determination to end the conflict with victory, upon which their safety and prosperity as well as the future of civilization depended.

The amendments to the Anglo-French draft which have not been indicated above were of minor significance as far as Anglo-American relations were concerned. The closest thing to an exception was the deletion of the expressed hope that the United States would help provide sanctions to secure the new international order. Baron Sonnino thought that the Allies might regret opening the door to United States interference in Europe, and recommended the complete omission of the passage.[86]

---

[82] F.O. 371/3075/2/1186.

[83] Telegram from Grahame (Rome), 1 Jan., 1917, and Foreign Office telegram to Grahame, 3 Jan., 1917, F.O. 371/3075/2/1186.

[84] The reference to Poland was actually quite peculiar. The line read as follows: "The intentions of His Majesty the Emperor of Russia regarding Poland have been clearly indicated in the proclamation which he has just addressed to his armies." This was intended to refer to the czar's order to the Russian Armies which was dated 25 Dec., 1916, and which appeared in the British morning press on 28 Dec. The czar stated that one of Russia's tasks was "the creation of a free Poland from all three of her now incomplete tribal districts." The Russian foreign minister later wanted to modify the Allies' note so that it would explicitly refer to the czar's intention to add German and Austrian Poland to Russian Poland, but would omit the reference to a "free Poland" contained in the czar's order to his army. The British Foreign Office, which was particularly concerned about the impact of this passage in America, feared that their enemies would exploit the omission. Telegram from Buchanan (Petrograd), 5 Jan., 1917, telegram to Bertie, Rodd and Buchanan, 6 Jan., 1917, and Foreign Office minutes, F.O. 371/3075/2/4588.

[85] Ibid. For a published version of the Entente Allies' reply, see Foreign Relations, 1917, Supplement 1: pp. 6–9.

[86] See telegram from Grahame, 1 Jan., 1917, F.O. 371/3075/2/1186.

The Foreign Office later advised Lloyd George, while he was attending an Allied conference in Rome, against this omission. On 3 January, 1917, a telegram, initialed by Robert Cecil, was sent to the prime minister containing the following argument:

We regard it as of very great importance that the Americans should realize that any scheme to enforce peace such as those of which they are now enamoured are the purest futility unless those who join in them are prepared to make sacrifices to enforce them.

There is a great danger that Americans carried away by the sounding phrases of amateur pacifists should think that by establishing a mere paper league to enforce peace they have prevented future wars and that therefore the only matter of real importance is to bring this war to an end anyhow.

To prevent this it is essential to bring them up against the realities of the situation and insist that unless they are prepared to fight for the decrees of their league of peace they will be treated by future militarists as so many scraps of paper.[87]

Cecil and Balfour did not have their way. On the suggestion of the Russian foreign minister, specific reference to America was omitted and a general line about the necessity of sanctions substituted.[88]

The Foreign Office more than made up for this change by sending a commentary by Balfour upon the Allied note, in which the foreign secretary elaborated his favorite points, lest they should be missed in their more cryptic form in the Allied reply. This supplementary note was more politely phrased and less barbed than his earlier draft reply, but it was equally emphatic about the fallacy of separating the terms of a peace settlement from future efforts to ensure peace, about the necessity of proving the unscrupulous methods of the Central Powers unsuccessful, and about the need for sanctions behind international law and behind treaties to prevent or limit war.[89]

The British government's addition of this commentary underlines its intention to use the replies to Wilson as an occasion to argue publicly against his apparent position on the peace question. The reply to the German note, which had been drafted with America very much in mind, was put to the same use. On 2 January, 1917, the day after the reply to Germany had been published in the British and American press, the War Cabinet decided "that action should be taken by the existing organisations for propaganda to ensure that the Replies of the Allies to the German and American Peace Notes should be published not only in the press of the principal cities of the United States but also in the provincial press."[90] On 13 January, the day after

the Allies' reply to Wilson was published, Lloyd George wrote to Balfour enthusiastically approving of the dispatch and publication of his supplementary note. The prime minister stated that it would "do no end of good both in America and at home."[91] The supplementary note was cabled to Washington, and Spring Rice privately delivered two copies of the document to Lansing on the fourteenth. Lansing and the British ambassador agreed that it would be wise to delay formal communication and publication of Balfour's commentary until the president had expressed his opinion on the effect of the note on public sentiment. Lansing said that the president should be given an opportunity of making verbal criticism from the point of view of publicity.[92] The Foreign Office was very impatient with this request. Immediately after receiving Spring Rice's report of it on the fifteenth, Balfour replied: "I think it is of great importance both from the view of public opinion in neutral countries and here that formal communication and publication should take place as soon as possible." Balfour could not see any advantage in waiting for Wilson's verbal criticism and he expressed his "fear that the President might take advantage of knowledge" of the contents of his commentary upon the Allied note to diminish the force of its special appeal to American public opinion. The foreign secretary requested "fuller explanation" of the ambassador's reasons for advocating delay.[93] Spring Rice pressed ahead with formal arrangements for publication, and after a short delay by the Foreign Office in case the president should raise a serious objection, the note was published on the morning of 18 January, 1917.[94] On the following day, C. H. Montgomery, an official in the News Department of the Foreign Office, sent a cable to the Washington Embassy stating that the Foreign Office was "anxious to know whether Mr. Balfour's dispatch has been widely published in the West and Middle West for instance in Sunday and small 'boilerplate' papers." He added: "If not we should be grateful for advice as to how such publications can be secured in this and future cases."[95]

The British government's emphatic desire to seek the widest possible publicity for its replies to the president's note is a fact which in itself indicates that the Foreign

---

[87] See telegram to Grahame, 3 Jan., 1917, F.O. 371/3075/2/ 1186.

[88] Telegram from Buchanan, 5 Jan., 1917, F.O. 371/3075/2/ 4588.

[89] Published in *Foreign Relations, 1917, Supplement 1:* pp. 17–21.

[90] CAB 23/1/25/8. When the reply to the German note was given to the American ambassador, he requested in the presi-

dent's name that the Allied reply to the American note should not be published until the president had had time to study it. The Allies allowed him forty-eight hours after the note was delivered on 10 Jan., 1917. With considerable justification a Foreign Office official commented: "The Americans expect to receive treatment far different from that which they accord to others." F.O. 371/3075/2/00006.

[91] F.O. 800/199.

[92] Telegram from Spring Rice, 14 Jan., 1917, F.O. 371/3075/ 2/11002.

[93] Telegram to Spring Rice, 15 July, 1917, F.O. 371/3075/2/ 11002.

[94] Telegram from Spring Rice, 15 Jan., 1917, and telegram to Spring Rice, 16 Jan., 1917, F.O. 371/3075/2/11946.

[95] F.O. 115/2263/Mediation/56.

Office felt that Wilson was threatening the Allies with peace. It also reveals a belief that the tables could be turned on Wilson and actually strengthen the British government's position. This reinforces the conclusion that Lansing had not spoiled Wilson's move. It never had a chance of success because of its inherent weaknesses. Indeed, Wilson's note perhaps facilitated Britain's rejection of peace negotiations. In effect, the world's leading candidate for the role of peacemaker had implied that the cause of peace would be served without actual peace negotiations, but merely by a declaration of terms and a kind of negotiation for the benefit of the galleries. There was admittedly an apparent risk that the Allies might become involved in disputes among themselves about the peace terms to be declared, but skill in the use of vague words and an acute awareness of this danger minimized this obstacle. The situation was, of course, not propitious for Wilson's peacemaking ambitions. The belligerents had uncompromising policies, amenable, if at all, only to the exertion of strong pressure by the United States. Yet, by December, 1916, it was probably too late to mount an effective threat in support of a negotiated settlement. Without a powerful military establishment, Wilson could not reasonably expect to have much leverage in Berlin. Furthermore, since there were no reliable signs that Germany would accept a return to the *status quo ante bellum* with perhaps minor, face-saving changes, there was no adequate justification for threatening the Allies with a disabling blow to their essential supplies if they refused to negotiate and continued to insist on winning the war. At a minimum such a blow would have to seem imminent, and it seems very likely that its first effects would have to be felt before the Allies would yield. In short, Wilson's peace move had little chance of promoting peace. Instead it promoted British propaganda in America for an Allied victory.

III. "PEACE WITHOUT VICTORY" AND THE APPROACH OF AMERICAN BELLIGERENCY

1. FIGHTING RHETORIC WITH RHETORIC

President Wilson delivered his famous "peace without victory" address to the Senate on 22 January, 1917. The text of the address was communicated to the British Foreign Office on the same day, and it was published in the morning press on the twenty-third.[1] The speech began with a reference to his recent request to the belligerent nations that they state their peace terms. He recalled that the Central Powers had not complied while the Allies had stated comparatively definite terms. Wilson then asserted that it is taken for granted that peace must be followed by some definite "concert of power" which will make another catastrophic war virtually impossible. Moreover, the United States must

[1] F.O. 371/3076/2/18095; London *Times*, 23 Jan., 1917.

"add their authority and power to the authority and force of other nations to guarantee peace and justice throughout the world." In his view, such a settlement could not be long postponed, and he declared that the United States government should formulate the conditions upon which it would feel justified in asking the American people to approve its "solemn adherence" to a league for peace.

As he had done in his note to the belligerents, the president indicated that the war must first be ended and that the United States would have no voice in determining the peace terms, but he virtually admitted his intention to influence the peace settlement. He stated that America would have a voice in determining whether the terms would be guaranteed by an universal covenant and that America's conditions should be announced before it was "too late"—presumably meaning too late to affect the peace terms.

Wilson believed that, if the peace "presently to be made" was to last, it must be "made secure by the organized major force of mankind." A new balance of power would be inadequate. "There must be," he said, "not a balance of power but a community of power; not organized rivalries, but an organized common peace."

Both sides in the war, he pointed out, had said that they did not intend to crush their opponents. These assurances implied first of all a peace without victory. Wilson phrased his case as follows:

Victory would mean peace forced upon the loser, a victor's terms imposed upon the vanquished. It would be accepted in humiliation, under duress, at an intolerable sacrifice, and would leave a sting, a resentment, a bitter memory upon which terms of peace would rest, not permanently, but only as upon quicksand. Only a peace between equals can last.

The president explained that the equality he had in mind was an "equality of rights" for small as well as big nations. Moreover, a lasting peace also required recognition of the principle that governments derive all their just powers from the consent of the governed. As an example, he suggested that statesmen everywhere are agreed that there should be a "united, independent, and autonomous Poland." More vaguely he added: ". . . henceforth inviolable security of life, of worship, and of industrial and social development should be guaranteed to all peoples who have lived hitherto under the power of governments devoted to a faith and purpose hostile to their own."

Other requirements were outlets to the sea for every great people, freedom of the seas for all in practically all circumstances, and limitation of armaments. The president believed that he had expressed the wishes of the American people and also that he was speaking for the liberals, the friends of humanity in every nation, as well as for "the silent mass of mankind" who had not been able to express their real sentiments about the death and ruin which had visited their homes and loved ones.

Just before noon on 23 January, the Foreign Office received a telegram from Spring Rice about the president's speech. His first point was that the Allies "should if possible retain the excellent position which we have gained by our sympathetic answers to his first proposals." Numerous other reports also suggested that their public statements on the recent German and American peace moves had made a generally favorable impression on the American public.[2] The problem was obviously how to maintain the favorable diplomatic position which Britain enjoyed in America. As far as the League of Peace was concerned, Spring Rice suggested that Britain could "safely return the most sympathetic answer in principle." He had long felt that the president's dream would be fruitless.[3] "Until Congress has taken action," he explained, "the proposal he [Wilson] makes has no practical value whatever as the Senate must empower him to enter into the proposed arrangements and has already declared itself against it in principle. We can therefore sympathetically await developments."

Spring Rice undoubtedly feared that the president's proposal of a peace without victory would be considered offensive in the Allied countries, and he was chiefly concerned that this would provoke a reply which would, in turn, offend Wilson. "The constant danger," he warned, "is that we should give way to some natural burst of indignation which would put the president on Germany's side which, if he is so at all at present, he is only through fear."[4]

For the British, freedom of the seas was potentially the most unpalatable condition in Wilson's speech. Their main concern was with the possible impact of Wilson's principle upon maritime rules applying to wartime. Spring Rice thought that there was ample room for evasive action on this question. He noted that at the Hague conference in 1907 the United States proposals advocating the exemption of private property from capture or seizure on the high seas made an exception of contraband of war. "This opens," the ambassador observed, "a wide field for discussion." Moreover, he added, "Damage to private property at sea can safely be put on the same basis as damage on land: i.e. be subject to compensation after the war." Since the United States government had already accepted this principle, the British government could feel not only reassured that the president's speech posed no immediate threat to their existing maritime measures against Germany but also knew that they would have some good arguments in the future peace settlement.

On 24 January, the Foreign Office received another telegram from Spring Rice about the president's speech. "There is a widespread belief," he wrote, "that President is thinking of third term in consequence of playing a great part in a world peace and that he is bent upon forcing acceptance of his mediation." Spring Rice warned: "There is therefore a danger lest he be encouraged to go too far and Germany is certainly egging him on." The ambassador concluded that, as the president's speech did not explicitly call for an answer, it seemed "safer to await developments in silence."[5]

Despite this advice, a member of the War Cabinet responded publicly to the president. Bonar Law, chancellor of the exchequer, made his reply during the course of a speech to a war-loan demonstration in Bristol on the evening of the twenty-fourth. He said that just as Wilson had spoken frankly, "it is right that any member of an Allied Government who refers to it should speak frankly too." The British government and the president could not possibly look at the question from the same point of view, Law reasoned, because the head of a neutral state must take a neutral attitude, and because America was "very far removed from the horrors of this war" while Britain was "in the midst of it." Britain believed that the essence of the conflict was the question of right and wrong. "We know," he said, "that this is a war of naked aggression." By far the worst crime of the horrible war was the initial one by which the German government started it.

He then elaborated on the theme that the British government, like President Wilson, also wanted peace and security. He observed that Wilson hoped to achieve it by means of a league of peace. As Spring Rice had advised, Bonar Law expressed some sympathy with the idea. He suggested that it was humane and in his opinion not altogether utopian. Yet he also retained a skeptical note. He stressed that Germany had already violated the international agreements which had been made to avoid and mitigate the horrors of war. No neutral had been able to stop the German atrocities, he observed, and no neutral country had made any effective protest. In his view, the question was one of life or death. "We must," he said, "have stronger guarantees for the future peace of the world."

Law's arguments were anything but novel. The only important difference between Bonar Law's task and the one which Balfour had faced earlier in connection with the president's note was that Wilson's speech suggested some general peace conditions. That is, Wilson was not quite so vulnerable to Balfour's contention that he fallaciously separated the problem of establishing a lasting peace from the terms upon which the peace would be based.[6] Otherwise, the chancellor

[2] Telegram from Spring Rice, 22 Jan., 1917, F.O. 371/3076/2/18011. For additional cables touching upon this point, see F.O. 371/3075/2/11062, 13532, 14763. For relevant letters from Spring Rice, see F.O. 371/3076/2/17114, 23669, 23675; F.O. 371/3080/8770/17118. See also, Hardinge to Sir Valentine Chirol, 4 Jan., 1917, Hardinge Papers 29.

[3] Gwynn, 1929: 2: pp. 215–216, 335.

[4] F.O. 371/3076/2/18011.

[5] F.O. 371/3076/2/19009.

[6] In view of the timing of Wilson's address, it might seem that he was responding to Balfour's commentary on the Allied note, but he had started discussing the project early in Jan.

of the exchequer could use familiar themes to attack Wilson's proposition that a lasting peace could be made without an Allied victory.

He repeated the idea that Britain had rejected peace negotiations not from lust for conquest and victory, nor from any feeling of vindictiveness, but because peace now would be based on a German victory. It would mean, he said, that an unbroken military machine would be in the hands of an aggressive nation, who would prepare for another war and at a time of their own choosing plunge Britain again into her present miseries. His argument was indeed a familiar one, but he added to it a memorable slogan: "What President Wilson is longing for we are fighting for." This scored a clever debating point against the president. The London *Times* reported that a great demonstration followed the remark, that the audience stood and cheered for a long time, and that there were cries of "Bravo Bonar Law." It was also a shrewd, evasive slogan. It avoided any definite reference to Wilson's various peace conditions such as freedom of the seas, while it simultaneously declared that Britain shared the president's aims.[7]

Bonar Law's colleagues may have been consulted about the tenor of his speech before it was delivered. If so, securing approval would undoubtedly have been a simple matter since no change in government policy was involved. On the other hand, this same fact makes it seem possible that the chancellor of the exchequer had felt no need to have his speech approved before its delivery.[8] In any case, it is not surprising that the War Cabinet minutes record no mention of Bonar Law's reply to the president. Indeed, the minutes do not even mention the president's speech.

As far as a formal reply from the Foreign Office was concerned, none was felt to be required.[9] Balfour did not record his reasons for this attitude. Perhaps he simply felt that the president's speech called for nothing more than another speech—that a formal diplomatic reply to his address would be inappropriate. Another

possibility is that he wanted to avoid more negotiations among the Allies about a reply to Wilson. There were grounds for believing that it would not be worth the trouble. The publication of his celebrated commentary on the Allied reply to the president was still very recent, and it defended a peace with victory very skillfully. Since Bonar Law had publicly referred to the president's address, Wilson should not feel that he had been ignored if the Foreign Office did not respond. Moreover, the British government expected the German government to launch an unrestricted submarine campaign very soon which, without Britain's help, would probably ruin the president's current efforts to mediate and would markedly change the diplomatic situation in the Allies' favor. The president was committed to break diplomatic relations with Germany if she attacked merchant and passenger ships without warning or without providing for the safety of passengers and crew. That commitment would have to be faced once Germany's all-out campaign started. He would almost certainly have to break diplomatic relations and, of course, it was likely that America would enter the war against Germany unless Berlin backed down.

Apart from the question of an official reply to the president, there was some brief consideration given by the Foreign Office officials to the task of discrediting in America the president's apparent suggestion that the "silent mass," as opposed to the British government, were for peace. But this seems to have been handled by Cecil's and Balfour's private secretaries and the News Department of the Foreign Office. It was not a serious problem.[10]

The general impression which emerges from a study of the British government's response to Wilson's famous address of 22 January is that it demanded little official attention. Indeed, this reaction was well suited to the political situation. Wilson's only chance of mediation between Germany and the Allies depended upon whether Germany could be drawn into accepting it. As was explained in the previous chapter, the president could put tremendous pressure on the Allies to make peace by interfering with their supplies, but he could exert no effective pressure against Germany short of war. In view of this fact, it is not surprising that the president's address appears to have been carefully designed to evoke Germany's assent to mediation by the president.[11] No doubt he also wanted to elicit pacific noises from the Allies as well, but Germany's agreement was the first essential requirement. Britain, meanwhile, could reasonably do little more than wait for Germany's next move, which they, of course, ex-

---

and had drafted most of his note by 11 Jan. Link, 1965: pp. 250, 252-253. An interesting footnote to this fact is that Wilson later asked Frederick Dixon to convey to the British government an explanation which made out that his speech was in response to Balfour's note. Dixon reported as follows: "The President suggested that having taken the lead in attempting to bring about peace negotiations, and having received your note indicating the advisability of a league to enforce peace after the war, he felt in honour bound to state the terms on which alone he could advise the entrance of the United States into such a league." Dixon to Balfour, received 23 Feb., 1917, F.O. 800/211. For Dixon's identity, see below, p. 37 and note 29.

[7] London *Times*, 25 Jan., 1917. Cf. Link, 1965: p. 274.

[8] It would have been very ironic if Lloyd George had complained about not being consulted. He had sprung the "knockout blow" interview on his colleagues when he was chancellor of the exchequer.

[9] See minutes by Hardinge and Balfour, 26 Jan., 1917, F.O. 371/3076/2/21908.

[10] Telegram from Mr. Leay (Boston) transmitting from Dixon for Locock, received 24 Jan., 1917, Cecil Papers, Add. MSS. 51092; minute by Drummond, 27 Jan., 1917, Cecil Papers, Add. MSS. 51093.

[11] May, 1959: pp. 369-370.

pected would be the commencement of unrestricted submarine warfare.[12]

2. THE GAMES WISEMAN PLAYED IN JANUARY, 1917

Another indication of the British government's response to the president's speech came from Sir William Wiseman, a young British intelligence officer who had been cultivating a close diplomatic relationship with Colonel House since December, 1916. On 20 January, House told Wiseman about the president's imminent speech to the Senate and urged that he advise his government to agree to an immediate peace conference. House was evidently acting on his own initiative, for Wilson wrote to him on the twenty-fourth that, though he would be "deeply interested in the opinions reported by Wiseman," he was "even more concerned to find out what Germany is thinking. . . ."[13] On 25 January, House, who resided in New York, wrote to Wilson that Wiseman had brought him a "depressing story from Washington" (presumably meaning from the British or Allied representatives there). Beneath the official cordiality with which the president's address to the Senate was accepted, there was deep resentment. "The underlying feeling," House reported, "was that you were making a proposal to enforce arbitration in the future while the Allies were giving up both blood and treasure now for the same purpose."[14]

Wiseman had warned that, by pressing the Allies too hard for peace at that time, the president would harm the cause of democracy. He had asserted that every belligerent government was in the hands of reactionaries and, if the United States were not careful, the reactionary forces would refuse to join a league for future peace and might turn upon America in order to save autocracy. It was a weak argument against Wilson's peace efforts, and House duly observed that the danger which Wiseman described seemed to be remote. On the other hand, what Wiseman had said about the Allies' reactions to the president's speech rings true.

This cannot be so easily said of Wiseman's remarks to House on 26 January. House's encouraging report to Wilson of this subsequent conversation contrasts markedly with his report of the previous day, and not surprisingly it has stimulated some speculation—particularly by Professor Link. "His [Wiseman's] whole tone had changed," House wrote. Wiseman told him

that the "atmosphere had cleared wonderfully since yesterday." House then informed his British colleague about the attempts that were being made to induce the German government to state moderate terms so that the president could bring about peace negotiations. "This pleased him," House wrote, "and we got down to a discussion of peace terms, and the conference which he seemed to now think could be brought about in the event that Germany returns a favorable reply." House also reported: "He [Wiseman] told me in *gravest confidence,* a thing I had already suspected, that he is in direct communication with the Foreign Office, and that the Ambassador and other members of the Embassy are not aware of it." House was "happy beyond measure" about this conversation, for he judged that Wiseman was reflecting the views of his government. "He [Wiseman] went so far as to discuss with me where the conference should be held," House enthused, "and whether or not there should first be a preliminary conference and afterwards a general one." House added, "I take it he has heard directly from his government since yesterday for he seemed to speak with authority."[15]

What is the significance of these comments? Professor Link has written:

This might have been the most important communication between London and Washington since the beginning of the war. It is, unhappily, impossible to know what it signifies because it stands starkly alone among the available evidence, and will stand alone until the documents of the British Foreign Office are open to scholarly view.

The Foreign Office documents are now open, but alas, they have not yet yielded any information which illuminates Wiseman's conversation with House. Until such documents are found, we are still left with speculation.

Link suggested two possibilities, among others. He observed firstly that Britain's knowledge of Germany's impending all-out submarine campaign led to the assumption that America and Germany would soon be at war, which would abruptly end Wilson's peace moves. Perhaps on this assumption Lloyd George and Balfour "instructed Wiseman to tell House that Britain would not refuse to go to a peace conference if the President obtained a favourable reply from Germany." Link added that it would be a cheap and safe way to earn badly needed credit with the Washington administration.

Secondly, Professor Link stated that it is also possible that Wiseman was in fact transmitting an authentic message from the British government. Link suggested that it is "not altogether inconceivable" that the British feared German victory due to the submarine campaign and the possible defection of Russia. The British must have known, he observed, that Germany could reverse their decision about all-out submarine warfare and accept Wilson's mediation instead.

---

[12] On 16 Jan., 1917, Lord Hardinge made the following comment in a letter to Sir R. Paget, British minister at Copenhagen: ". . . I am somewhat alarmed at what may happen when the Germans start again sinking everything at sight, which according to all indications, is to take place next month. Of course it may be only bluff, though I am inclined to think not. It will be interesting to see what President Wilson will do when the Germans sink the first American ship again." Hardinge Papers 29.

[13] Published in Link, 1965: p. 277.

[14] Published in Seymour, 1926: 2: pp. 420–421.

[15] Published in Link, 1965: 2: p. 280.

"Perhaps British leaders had concluded that the risks of Wilsonian mediation in a peace conference were less than those of a German victory through an undersea assault." Link went further. "Perhaps," he speculated, "they had even concluded that a peace settlement based upon the President's address to the Senate was good enough, especially if it brought American membership in a new world system."[16]

Link's first suggestion has considerable plausibility. The second has almost none. It seems very unlikely that the British would abandon their commitment to victory unless a catastrophic defeat seemed unavoidable without immediate peace negotiations. The Allies' great military strength continued while the Central Powers seemed to be in a strained condition.[17] Moreover, a reversal of policy appears all the more unlikely in view of the Foreign Office's skepticism about effective American membership in a new world system.[18] They much preferred relying on the strong possibility that America and Germany would soon be at war.

Actually, quite apart from the likelihood of American belligerency, Wiseman's comments were safe and noncommittal. According to House's report, Wiseman had merely "seemed to now think" that a peace conference could be brought about in the event that Germany returned a *favorable reply* to the president's request for moderate terms. Aside from a change in tone, this was not inconsistent with what the British government had been saying in recent months. Their avowed position was that they could not be expected to consider peace negotiations until Germany stated her terms. This clearly implied that moderate German terms would be considered. To disavow this implication would be to incur responsibility for slamming the door to negotiations. As we have seen, the British had announced terms which would mean victory if attained. For Germany to concede to these terms was undoubtedly what the British government would consider a favorable reply, if they were pressed on the question. In the meantime, Wiseman would be unlikely to dwell upon the obstacles to peace negotiations in his conversations with House. His role as a sympathetic

and discreet channel of communication between House and the British government required that he appear as congenial as possible.

There are also several possible interpretations which suggest that Wiseman's remarks, at least as reported to Wilson, were of little or no significance as far as London's attitude to peace negotiations is concerned. For instance, it is possible that House slanted his report to Wilson because he wanted to do something to reduce the danger to Anglo-American friendship posed by Wilson's peace moves. He may have feared that, if Wilson assumed that Britain would be resentful of such efforts and intractable about peace negotiations, the president would tend to cooperate with Germany without consulting the British. House had tried very hard in the past to assure that Wilson's mediation efforts did not alienate Britain, so it is not surprising to find a comment in his report to the president which clearly reveals this concern. "I know you will appreciate the difference," he wrote, "between any statement coming from the English as against one coming from the Germans."[19]

Another consideration is that House sometimes tended to hear only what he wanted to hear. It may have been, as it had been in the discussions which led to the House-Grey memorandum, that House leaped to the conclusions which he wanted to believe. Wiseman's efforts to be congenial would not have discouraged House's wishful thinking.

While there are grounds for doubting House's report to the president, it is also possible that Wiseman's comments were not based on instructions from London. Indeed, it is quite plausible that he made his remarks on his own initiative. The encouraging tone of his comments on 26 January may have been intended to compensate for his gloomy report on the twenty-fifth. What House told him about the new American effort to elicit a German statement of moderate peace terms may have promoted his change of tone. Wiseman may have felt it to be in Britain's interest for him to appear receptive and encouraging to this peace move. If the American initiative failed, Britain might well gain some ground diplomatically while Germany would surely lose. If it succeeded, Wiseman's remarks would not have cost Britain anything. As mentioned above, his comments could be interpreted as being within the limits of Britain's avowed position on peace negotiations. Moreover, the wording of House's report suggests that Wiseman had not said explicitly that his comments were based on instructions from London. He had, according to House, merely stated that he was in direct communication with their Foreign Office. Indeed, W. B. Fowler, an authority on Wiseman, has described

---

[16] *Ibid.*, p. 281.

[17] On 2 Jan., 1917, Lord Hardinge stated in a letter to Sir Arthur Hardinge, British ambassador at Madrid, that the Germans were "in a very bad way, for it is quite clear that they would never propose peace unless they were in desperate straits." Hardinge Papers 29. On 31 Jan., Hardinge commented in a letter to Mr. George Allen, one of his friends in India, that, although peace still looked far off, he believed it nearer than people imagined. "If we can only secure even a moderate success in the spring offensive," he wrote, "the German system will crack." Hardinge Papers 29.

[18] See Drummond to Spring Rice, 16 Jan., 1917, F.O. 800/242/fol. 285. Spring Rice frequently reiterated his doubts that the United States would join a league to enforce peace. For examples which were received by the F.O. during the week of Wiseman's conversations, see F.O. 371/3076/2/17114, 18011.

[19] House to Wilson, 26 Jan., 1917. Published in Link, 1965: p. 280.

it as a "prevarication, or half-truth." Fowler wrote:

He was not, at the moment, in direct touch with the Foreign Office proper. Rather, he was an agent for the Secret Service (M.I. 6), the espionage organization which, though financed by the Foreign Office, operated with nearly complete autonomy. His reports, like other intelligence reports, doubtless circulated anonymously in the Foreign Office, and his reports on conversations with House must have attracted special attention. But not until April did Wiseman become primarily an agent of the Foreign Office instead of a Secret Service officer who happened to send in useful political information.[20]

In Fowler's view, the prevarication to House was a means by which Wiseman propelled himself into a key position for the good of Anglo-American relations. He explained:

Wiseman recognized that House liked him and saw in their developing friendship the potential for drawing Britain and America closer. To heighten his importance in House's eyes he intimated that he was a special emissary for the Foreign Office. Impressed, House confided in him more and more. . . .[21]

Fowler did not mention Wiseman's comments about the British government's readiness to discuss peace, but the obvious implication of his interpretation is that Wiseman's remarks did not reflect the views of his government.[22]

Thus, there are a variety of reasons for doubting that Wiseman's remarks as reported by House represent an authentic reversal of British policy on the peace question. The statements which he made may have been a safe maneuver to gain credit with Wilson and House; the latter could have slanted or misinterpreted Wiseman's remarks; Wiseman might have distorted a genuine message from London; or perhaps he acted on his own initiative. All of these interpretations make some sense when placed in the context of the available evidence about the British government's attitudes. Link is, of course, quite right in stating that the lack of evidence to support the possibility that Britain had reversed its attitude towards peace does not necessarily mean such speculation is "necessarily incorrect." On the other hand, a lack of evidence plus plausible interpretations which fit with existing evidence makes such speculation seem very dubious.

3. LLOYD GEORGE'S CELEBRATION OF LINCOLN'S BIRTHDAY

Whichever interpretation of Wiseman's remarks may be correct, their potential impact (beyond attaining some credit in Washington) was cut short on 31 January, when the German government informed Washington about its unlimited submarine campaign and when it confidentially intimated to the president a set of peace terms which could only be attained by military victory.[23]

Wilson broke off diplomatic relations on 3 February, but postponed the crucial decisions about belligerency. He stated that he refused to believe that Germany actually intended to destroy American ships and take the lives of American citizens. "Only overt acts on their part," he declared, "can make me believe it even now." On the other hand, he added that, if his "inveterate confidence" should prove unfounded, if American ships and lives were sacrificed by German naval commanders, he would ask Congress for authority "to use any means that may be necessary for the protection of our seamen and our people in the prosecution of their peaceful and legitimate errands on the high seas." [24]

The British were undoubtedly disappointed by his decision not to bring America into the war immediately. In London on the following day, Lloyd George said of Wilson: "And so he is not going to fight after all! He is awaiting another insult before he actually draws the sword!" [25] It was in fact the beginning of two months of waiting for American belligerency. During this period, the threat of American attempts to mediate between the Allies and Germany had diminished. As far as Anglo-American relations were concerned, the British government's main tasks were firstly to promote America's entry into the war, and secondly, to prepare discreetly for as much cooperation as possible between the United States and the Allies as American belligerency became more certain.[26]

The main factors in the situation which would discourage a peace move by the president were all well known to the British government. The German submarine campaign and the breaking off of diplomatic relations between Germany and America were, of course, public knowledge, but, in addition, they also quickly learned that the United States government had the German peace terms and that Colonel House had said that they would not be acceptable to the Allies.[27] Nevertheless, some fear of American peace moves seemed to continue during February.

---

[20] Fowler, 1969: pp. 14–15.

[21] *Ibid.*, pp. 15–16.

[22] Fowler's omission of Wiseman's comments is somewhat odd in view of the attention which they have received from other historians. Link's speculations have been cited above. See also May, 1959: p. 383; Baker, 1937: **6**: pp. 441–442.

---

[23] The German peace terms were conveyed in the form of a letter from Ambassador von Bernstorff to Colonel House. *Foreign Relations, 1917, Supplement 1*: pp. 34–36.

[24] Baker and Dodd, 1926: **2**: pp. 422–426.

[25] Riddell, 1933: p. 238.

[26] There was, strangely enough, some skepticism about the advantages of having the United States in the war. In a letter to Sir Valentine Chirol, dated 15 Feb., 1917, Lord Hardinge expressed such doubts. But this was definitely not the dominant view in the British government. Hardinge added in his letter that the War Cabinet was anxious to have the U.S. enter the conflict. Hardinge Papers 29.

[27] Spring Rice reported this on 1 Feb., F.O. 371/3080/24839/25730. The information was subsequently included in a weekly report for the War Cabinet Secretariat. Western and General Report No. 2, F.O. 371/3080/27667/33230.

In view of Wilson's past efforts to avoid war by attempting to make peace, the British government could not rest assured that another sensational peace move would not come from the White House. In case the British should ever grow confident, their pessimistic ambassador in Washington could be counted on to remind them of the danger. On 5 February, the Foreign Office duly received a predictable warning. "It must . . . be remembered," Spring Rice cabled, "that war will not take place unless there is overt act on part of Germany and that President Wilson is bound to do all he can to promote peace should occasion be found." [28] On the following day another report arrived from an important Foreign Office informant named Frederick Dixon, who stated that tremendous efforts were being made to restore relations between Germany and America. William Jennings Bryan and Ambassador Bernstorff were, Dixon said, "both active." He also reported, after mentioning a long interview with the president, that the American government did not think war would follow.[29]

Though the British government was less anxious about possible peace moves by the president than they had been in previous months, they nevertheless continued to discourage American thoughts of a peace without victory. One forgotten but notable example of this effort was disguised in the form of a public tribute by the prime minister to Abraham Lincoln on the anniversary of his birth—12 February.[30] The tribute was initially suggested by Charles H. Grasty, one of the heads of the New York Times, who requested it on behalf of his own newspaper but also engaged to have it appear simultaneously in leading papers throughout America. The British government had long made use of quotations from Lincoln's speeches to parry peace moves and to justify Britain's desire for victory, so the situation in early February proved an excellent opportunity for the prime minister to imply—while ostensibly paying his respects to a great American statesman—that the United States should support Britain's war against Germany rather than try to bring about an immediate peace.

Though eager to have the United States join in the war, the British government was wary of overtly appearing to promote American belligerency. It was feared that British encouragement might retard rather than hasten America's entry into the war. On 2 February, in a letter to the prime minister which related a conversation with Ambassador Page, Balfour remarked: "It would, I take it, be bad policy to say anything which might be regarded in America as showing a desire on the part of the British Government to force the U. S. A. into war; but this is a point on which you are quite as good a judge as I." [31] There was, in fact, a consensus on this point in the Foreign Office.[32] Lloyd George was accordingly somewhat cautious about appealing in public for the United States to enter the war, but his tribute to Lincoln was nevertheless a veiled plea for American belligerency and against American peacemaking.

Lloyd George's tribute again drew parallels between Lincoln's position and that of the British government. He suggested that just as Lincoln fought against slavery to save the union, Britain was fighting against a militarist slavery to save the world. He also declared that, like Lincoln, they believed that they must fight on to a finish in order to avoid a more costly fight for freedom at some later day. The conclusion of his message is worth quoting in full.

It would, indeed, be impossible to state our faith more clearly than Lincoln stated it himself at the end of 1864. "On careful consideration," he said, "of all the evidence it seems to me that no attempt at any negotiation with the insurgent leader could result in any good. He would accept nothing short of severence of the the Union—precisely what we will and cannot give. His declarations to this effect are explicit and oft-repeated. He does not deceive us. He affords us no excuse to deceive ourselves. . . . Between him and us the issue is distinct, simple and inflexible. It is an issue which can only be tried by war and decided by victory." That was the judgement of the greatest statesman of the nineteenth century during the last great war for human liberty. It is the judgement of this nation and of its fellow nations overseas today. "Our armies," said Lincoln, "are ministers of good, not of evil." So do we believe. And through all the carnage and suffering and conflicting motives of the Civil War Lincoln held steadfastly to the belief that it was the freedom of the people to govern themselves which was the fundamental issue at stake.

So do we today. For when the people of Central Europe accept the peace which is offered them by the Allies, not only will the Allied peoples be free as they have never been free before, but the German people too will find that in losing their dream of an Empire over others, they have found self-government for themselves.[33]

Though Wilson would not endorse the Allies' recent announcement of peace terms, some of these sentiments would find expression seven weeks later when the president asked Congress to recognize that a state of war existed between America and the German government.

[28] F.O. 371/3108/27635/28452.

[29] Telegram from Mr. Leay (Boston), 5 Feb., 1917, F.O. 800/211. Dixon, a British subject, was editor of the prestigious Christian Science Monitor. He had access to the Foreign Office through the British Consul in Boston. Many of his reports were sent in cypher and received close attention.

[30] A copy of the Lincoln Day message as well as several letters about the project can be found in F.O. 395/65/329/15832. It was published first in the New York Times on 11 Feb., 1917, and in the London Times on 12 Feb.

[31] Lloyd George Papers, E/3/2/12. A copy of this letter with slightly different phrasing is in F.O. 800/199.

[32] See Mr. Montgomery's and Lord Hardinge's minutes in F.O. 395/65/329/29033; the minutes in F.O. 371/3112/28438/ 49496; Eric Drummond's minute on the back of a letter from H. Cust to Balfour, 1 Feb., 1917, F.O. 800/211.

[33] London Times, 12 Feb., 1917.

4. WILSON'S ATTEMPT TO MEDIATE BETWEEN AUSTRIA-HUNGARY AND BRITAIN

When President Wilson broke off diplomatic relations with Germany on 3 February, 1917, he avoided a break with Austria-Hungary so that he could use her in further peace moves.[34] The Austro-Hungarian government, for its part, was prompt to encourage the president. The foreign minister, Count Ottokar Czernin, not only reciprocated the desire that diplomatic relations be maintained but also urged the president to continue his peace efforts. He declared Austria-Hungary's readiness to negotiate on the basis of a peace without victory which Wilson himself had suggested, and he argued that it was now up to the Entente to accommodate themselves to that basis. Czernin asserted that as long as the Entente retained their published aim of the dismemberment of Austria-Hungary, it was impossible to talk peace or to give up any means of defense. But he predicted an end to the submarine war, peace for the world, and immortality for the president, if Wilson would force the Entente to accept the American point of view about ending the war.[35]

Wilson grasped at the straw and promptly instructed his ambassador in London to convey a confidential, informal appeal for a separate peace with Austria-Hungary. Ambassador Page was told to speak to the leading members of the British government rather than to the Foreign Office, because the president did not intend his message to be official. He wished Page to ascertain informally what he might expect if proposals he now foreshadowed should be made to the Foreign Office. The president stressed that Austria intensely desired peace and that the chief obstacle was her fear of virtual dismemberment. She needed only reassurance on that point, in Wilson's view, chiefly with regard to the older units of the empire. He thought that "the large measure of autonomy already secured to those older units is a sufficient guarantee of peace and stability in that part of Europe so far as national and racial influences are concerned" and that what opportunity and security Austria required to the south could be obtained by giving her rights of way to the sea guaranteed by a concert of nations. He did not doubt that Austria could be satisfied without depriving the Balkan states of their political autonomy and territorial integrity. Thus, if the Entente governments would make it possible for the president to assure Austria on this point, "he could in a very short time force the acceptance of peace upon terms which would follow the general lines of his recent address to the Senate regarding the sort of peace the United States would be willing to join in guaranteeing."[36]

On 10 February, Page obtained an interview with the prime minister and told him the "general substance" of the president's proposals. It is possible that British Intelligence had provided Lloyd George with the text of the president's instructions to Page even before the ambassador arrived at 10 Downing Street. According to Page's report of the meeting, the prime minister welcomed the overture and immediately answered all of the questions which Page had prepared before the ambassador could mention the details of the message.

Lloyd George said that he knew that Austria wanted to quit. Not only was she suffering badly, but if the Teutonic powers won the war, she would be a vassal of Germany. That would be worse for her than an Entente victory. Germany already managed the country and commanded Austrian armies.

Page reported that the prime minister continued by saying: "Of course, the Austrian emperor wishes as far as possible to save his empire." He then added a very interesting remark in view of the Entente Allies' recent statement of peace terms. As was mentioned above, the Allies called for the liberation of Italians, "Slavs," Rumanians, and Czecho-Slovaks from foreign domination.[37] This declaration was open to widely different interpretations. The Allied note did not specify whether the liberated peoples were to be granted sovereignty, autonomy, states' rights in a federal system, or some other halfway house. In contrast to the Austro-Hungarian foreign minister's interpretation of the Allies' statement, Lloyd George said:

We have no objection to his [the Austrian Emperor] retaining Hungary and Bohemia. We have no policy of sheer dismemberment but we must stand by the nationals of our allies, such as the Roumanians, the Slavs, the Serbians, and the Italians. Their just demands must be met by the principle of nationality.

Like Wilson, Lloyd George was obviously very selective and flexible when he applied his principles. His remarks to Page amounted to an assertion that the principle of nationality applied primarily to allies. As far as other people under foreign domination were concerned, some measure of autonomy rather than sovereignty was usually what the British government had in mind at this stage of the war.

After professing to Page his willingness to be lenient toward Austria-Hungary, Lloyd George then began piling on arguments to justify rejecting Wilson's proffered mediation. He declared that neither the British government nor its allies could afford to lose the support of Italy. He suggested that the blockade of Germany might be broken on the Austrian side. More-

---

[34] Link, 1965: p. 314.
[35] Ambassador Penfield to Lansing, 5 Feb., 1917, *Foreign Relations, 1917, Supplement 1:* pp. 38–39.
[36] Lansing to Page, 8 Feb., 1917, *ibid.,* pp. 40–41. Wilson

himself drafted the telegram. For a more detailed account of the document, including some critical comments about the president's views, see Mamatey, 1957: pp. 54–59.
[37] For Foreign Office discussion of terms featuring autonomy, see CAB 24/6/43. See also Balfour's statement to the second meeting of the Imperial War Cabinet, CAB 23/43.

over, the German troops and officers holding the Austrian armies together would be released to strengthen the German line in more important places, and Austrians released from the army would go to Germany and add to her productive power. Austria, he argued, was an increasing military and economic burden to Germany, and Germany would probably give in sooner with Austria on her back than if Austria were out of the war.

The prime minister repeated that Britain held no animosity for Austria and, in fact, wanted to safeguard her future freedom. The present question, he maintained, was purely one of military expediency. Ambassador Page recorded the main point as follows: "For these and other reasons," the prime minister said, "we cannot now even receive formally any peace offer from Austria nor authorize any discussion of peace with her on our behalf." Lloyd George did not, however, want to close the door completely. He added that, if the president, acting only for the United States, chose to receive specific Austrian proposals and to transmit them to him "in private confidence," he would be informed as soon as they could be formally received and considered. "I shall be willing," he declared, "and in fact very glad to have such proposals proceed on the principle laid down in the President's recent speech to the Senate." [38]

This congenial remark did not, of course, commit the prime minister to much, since he had refused to let the president go ahead with mediation. But this fact does not imply that the prime minister did not mean what he said. In negotiations of a separate peace with Austria, the president's "Peace Without Victory" address would not seriously conflict with Britain's interests. It is highly possible that Lloyd George was looking ahead to the day when he might want to use the president as a mediator. In any case, there can be little doubt that the British government was very interested in a separate peace with the Hapsburg Empire, despite the prime minister's comments to the contrary. In fact, it seems almost certain that Lloyd George's justification for his rejection of the president's mediation was insincere.

Some secret minutes of the War Cabinet contain proof of this. At a meeting on 18 January, they discussed certain approaches recently made to the British minister in Christiania (now Oslo) by persons professing to be accredited Austrian agents, with a view to a separate peace between Austria-Hungary and the Allies. The chief of the Imperial General Staff gave his opinion that a separate peace with Austria would be a decided military advantage, and he estimated that it would eliminate 47 Austro-Hungarian divisions now on the eastern front and thus set free 149 divisions to deal with 78 German divisions then on the eastern

front.[39] Moreover, the submarine menace in the Adriatic would be removed. He added that these advantages would more than counterbalance the possibility of Italy withdrawing from active participation in the war. This is such a persuasive observation by Robertson that it seems very unlikely that Lloyd George could have believed in his argument to Page that Britain could not afford to lose Italy as an ally. It would be more characteristic of Lloyd George to attempt to arrange a separate peace with Austria-Hungary and still maintain Italy's participation in the war.

Lord Robert Cecil also expressed an opinion which contrasts sharply with Lloyd George's remarks to Page. Cecil suggested that even though a separate peace would make the blockade situation more difficult, the shortage of shipping would enable the Allies to prevent any substantial supplies from reaching Germany through Austria.

The War Cabinet then agreed upon two steps. Firstly, Balfour should informally indicate to the allied ambassadors in London that, in the event of tentative approaches being made to the British government, they proposed to ascertain whether a real offer was intended, unless their allies objected. Balfour was to make it clear that no actual negotiations would be entered upon without consulting Britain's allies. If no objection were raised, the next step would be to inform the persons who had approached the British minister in Norway that the British government wanted a much more precise proposal of conditions for negotiations and more proof that the offer was from a responsible quarter.[40]

Sir Francis Hopwood[41] was subsequently sent to Scandanavia at the beginning of February to ascertain whether or not the Austrians had made a genuine peace move and to report any further proposals.[42] The results of his mission were still unknown when Lloyd George met with Page on 10 February. Thus it seems that the prime minister refused to allow Wilson to proceed with mediation, not because the British government was uninterested in a separate peace with Austria, but because the British were already testing some direct Austrian overtures and would prefer negotiations without the president's mediation, if possible. Lloyd George's preference for keeping negotiations entirely in the British government's hands was—like the attitude of an anxious motorist who is reluctant to let anyone else drive—not necessarily rational. On the other hand, several specific considerations may have promoted the prime minister's initial refusal to permit the president to mediate. Lloyd George undoubtedly

[38] Page to Lansing, 11 Feb., 1917, *Foreign Relations, 1917, Supplement 1:* pp. 41–43.

[39] Presumably the figure 149 was the sum of divisions already facing the Germans, plus those who would be freed from facing the Austrians.
[40] CAB 23/13/37(a).
[41] Later Lord Southborough.
[42] For Hopwood's report on his mission, see F.O. 371/3079/7661/66517.

knew that negotiations with Austria-Hungary would be delicate. If Germany learned of the peace moves, she would stop them. There was also a risk of serious dissension among the Allies, if they (particularly the Italians) learned of the talks before Britain could tactfully inform them. Perhaps Lloyd George felt that as long as he had the choice, it would be prudent not to involve the United States in the peace moves because the State Department might not be able to keep the matter secret.[43] It is also possible that, having a choice, Lloyd George wanted to keep the negotiations entirely in British hands because he feared that Wilson might want to attempt a general peace settlement rather than limit negotiations to a separate peace. As will be shown later, Lloyd George was wary of any hint of mediation which might entangle him in negotiations with Berlin. We do not know precisely what Page meant when he said that he conveyed the "general substance" of the president's dispatch to the prime minister. In the past he had read somewhat similar messages. If he did so on this occasion, Lloyd George may have heard the following lines:

The President knows that peace is intensely desired by the Teutonic powers, and much more by Austria than by any of her allies. . . . He is trying to avoid breaking with Austria in order to keep the channels of official intercourse with her open so that he may use her for peace. . . .
The effort of this Government will be constantly for peace even should it become itself involved.

In view of Wilson's recent efforts to promote a general peace settlement, his dispatch could plausibly be interpreted as meaning that he wanted negotiations with Austria to lead quickly to negotiations with Germany. The British government was well aware of the fact that from the president's point of view, a quick end to the war would be the best solution of the crisis precipitated by Germany's unrestricted submarine campaign. Consequently, *direct* negotiations with Austria-Hungary might have seemed distinctly preferable to Wilson's mediation. On the other hand, it is doubtful whether any considerations of this kind would be strong enough to rule out mediation by the president, if there were no clear alternative. It will be remembered that Lloyd George took care to leave the door open to Wilson's mediation between Austria and the Allies at some future time. Perhaps he foresaw that the approaches by Austria then being examined in Scandinavia would prove fruitless and that later he might want to use the president. In any case, this is what happened.

On 15 February, Sir Francis Hopwood reported that he had received a German overture proposing informal conversations between himself and a German agent.[44] The overture had been promoted and conveyed by a Dane who had just returned from a meeting with the German chancellor. It was suggested that the King of Denmark should secretly initiate the talks with confidential invitations to the British and German governments. The plan depended upon British consent.

Lloyd George and Balfour were perturbed by the news. On the seventeenth, the prime minister wrote the following comments to the Foreign Secretary:

Has any answer been sent to Hopwood's last telegram? Do we want even informal conversations with Germany at this stage? Austria is quite a different matter. To open up negotiations with Germany through the Danish King might destroy any chance there is of detaching Austria. What is your view?[45]

Balfour sent a telegram on the same day telling Sir Francis Hopwood not to meet with the Germans. "We have no desire," he stated, "to negotiate with Germany. . . ." Hopwood was further warned "that nothing should be said directly or indirectly to the Germans: and suggestions to the contrary effect . . . should receive no favour at your hands." Balfour also pointed out that Hopwood's mission would now have little chance of success. ". . . We cannot believe," he wrote, "that Germany will allow separate negotiation with Austria to go on under her nose without interference." Balfour mentioned several facts which must have made the "whole position plain" to the Germans, and he concluded that it was "doubtful" whether Hopwood's mission could now "do all the good" which they had hoped for from it.[46] Balfour was obviously very pessimistic, though momentarily he may not have given up entirely. He asked for Hopwood's advice on whether or not the latter should await an approach by a very credible Austria agent, whom the British had been led to expect.[47] But whatever glimmers of hope which still remained in London must have been virtually snuffed out by a message from Hopwood in Copenhagen on the eighteenth, which reported evidence that the Austrian minister had announced at a dinner table that he expected peace and had suggested that something was already going on in Copenhagen. "It is inconceivable," Hopwood concluded, "that Germans have not also heard it."[48] Very soon thereafter the British government attempted to open up a different channel for peace negotiations with Austria-Hungary.

[43] For a warning at that time about the lack of secrecy in Washington, see Spring Rice to Balfour, 19 Jan., 1917, Gwynn, 1929: 2: p. 373.

[44] F.O. 371/3080/33142/36932. This overture was also reported by Sir Ralph Paget, the British minister at Copenhagen. F.O. 371/3080/33142/36539.
[45] Lloyd George to Balfour, 17 Feb., 1917, F.O. 800/199 or Lloyd George Papers, F/3/2/13.
[46] F.O. 371/3080/33142/36932.
[47] The British expected Count Mensdorff, who had been the Austro-Hungarian ambassador in London when the war broke out.
[48] See enclosure no. 14 in Hopwood's report on his mission, F.O. 371/3079/7661/66517.

On 20 February, Page reported that the prime minister had changed his "first views." The ambassador stated:

He has just told me and authorized me to telegraph you that if you formally submit a peace commission proposal on behalf of Austria-Hungary his government will be glad to receive it formally and to consider it on its merits, on condition that every precaution be taken to insure the utmost secrecy, as if the Germans realize it they will stop. I reminded him of what he had said about his willingness not to disrupt the Austro-Hungarian Empire by the loss of its older units Hungary and Bohemia. He repeated what I reported in my above-mentioned telegram on that subject.[49]

The condition of secrecy was clearly a means of limiting the negotiations to a separate peace. This particular aspect of the prime minister's move has been questioned in Professor Link's major biography of Wilson. Link stated that it was not known whether this proposal was simply an additional British move to detach Austria-Hungary from her major ally or part of a large scheme aimed at peace negotiations with Germany. He mentioned some evidence that the possibility of a settlement with Germany was considered by Bonar Law and Lord Milner, and he also speculated that the prime minister may have actually been heading in this direction. Link wrote: "Lloyd George certainly knew, as Wilson did, that the shortest route to peace talks with Germany now ran through Vienna. Perhaps he was contemplating negotiations that would begin with the Hapsburg authorities and then involve the German government." He added, however, that the truth of this matter would remain hidden until "the essential British documents are opened to investigation."[50]

These documents are now available and they make it clear that both Lloyd George and Balfour wanted to avoid negotiations with Germany at this stage. Lloyd George's aforementioned letter of 17 February together with Balfour's telegram to Hopwood on the same day definitely prove this. Lloyd George was presumably turning to Wilson because any approach which the president made would probably go to an Austrian with authority. This would overcome the major frustration of the Hopwood mission. Another reason is that the British attitude toward the terms of settlement with Austria harmonized quite well with Wilson's attitude. Both Britain and America essentially wanted

Austria-Hungary to stop fighting, and they were quite willing to leave her most of her territory in order to persuade her. The British government had agreements with allies which made this very difficult, but they were nevertheless willing to try to get around them.[51] Indeed, Britain's secret treaties may have been one of the reasons for using President Wilson. Lloyd George may have thought that in negotiations with Austria-Hungary he could use pressure from the president as a good excuse for reducing British commitments.

The prime minister's remarks to Page quickly produced an American move. The United States government promptly approached the Austro-Hungarian minister of foreign affairs with a discreet offer to mediate between Austria-Hungary and the Allies, on the condition that it be kept secret from all other governments.[52] But Czernin refused to consider a separate peace, and, after a fruitless attempt to persuade him to think again, the discussions with Austria-Hungary were not pursued further at this stage.[53] When the president would make his next peace move, he would be at war.

5. PLAYING UPON WILSON'S AMBITION TO BE A PEACEMAKER

In the course of Lloyd George's maneuvers concerning negotiations with Austria-Hungary, he made a very interesting appeal to the president for America to join the war against Germany. The appeal was made during the prime minister's conversation with Ambassador Page on 10 February, just after he had rejected the president's offer to mediate between Austria and the Allies. The ambassador quoted Lloyd George as follows:

We want him to come into the war not so much for help with the war as for help with peace. My reason is not mainly the military nor naval nor economic nor financial pressure that the American Government and people might exert in their own way against Germany; grateful as this would be [sic] I have a far loftier reason. American participation is necessary for the complete expression of the moral judgment of the world on the most important subject ever presented to the civilized nations. For America's sake, for our own sake, for the sake of free government, and for the sake of democracy, military despotism must now be ended forever. The President's presence at the peace conference is necessary for the proper organization of the world which must follow peace. I mean that

[49] Telegram from Page to Lansing, 20 Feb., 1917, *Foreign Relations, 1917, Supplement 1:* pp. 55–56. The ambassador's reports to Washington contain speculation about what caused the prime minister's change of mind. Telegram from Page to Lansing, 21 Feb., 1917, *ibid.,* p. 56; letter from Page to Wilson, 22 Feb., 1917, Wilson Papers, Series 2. Yet, he may have eventually realized that he had been manipulated. Page remarked in his diary that "the British trick about the Austrian peace project shows how the British use us!" Page Diary, 24 Feb., 1917.

[50] Link, 1965: p. 385.

[51] See Lord Hardinge's minute, *ca.* 18 Jan., 1917, F.O. 371/3079/7661/13580. See also Eric Drummond's memorandum on a separate peace with Austria, dated 12 Feb., 1917, as well as another minute responding to it by Lord Hardinge, dated 17 Feb., 1917, CAB 24/6/43.

[52] Lansing to Ambassador Penfield, 22 Feb., 1917, *Foreign Relations, 1917, Supplement 1:* pp. 57–58.

[53] Ambassador Penfield to Lansing, 27 Feb., 1917, *ibid.,* pp. 62–63; Lansing to Ambassador Penfield, 3 Mar., 1917, *ibid.,* pp. 63–64; Ambassador Penfield to Lansing, 13 Mar., 1917, *ibid.,* pp. 65–66. The author's conclusions about this episode were reached independently of an outstanding unpublished dissertation about British relations with Austria-Hungary. See Fest, 1970.

he himself must be there in person. If he sits in the conference that makes peace he will exert the greatest influence that any man has ever exerted in expressing the moral value of free government. Most of the present belligerents will have suffered so heavily that their judgment also may have suffered and most of those that win will want some concrete gain, old wrongs righted, or boundaries changed. Even Great Britain, who wants nothing for herself, will be prevented from returning the German colonies. South Africa and Australia will not permit the giving back of lands that would make them neighbors to German subjects and give Germany secret submarine bases throughout the whole world. The United States wants nothing but justice and an ordered freedom and guaranties of these for the future. Nobody therefore can have so commanding a voice as the President. Convey to him this deep conviction of mine. He must help make peace if the peace made at the conference is to be worth keeping. American participation in the war would enable him to be there and the mere moral effect of this participation would shorten the war, might even end it very quickly.[54]

After raising the question of whether Lloyd George believed what he said, Professor Link suggested in passing: "Perhaps he did, for he was capable of lofty sentiments, even though they were usually fleeting."[55] One could probably come closer to what was going on in Lloyd George's mind by beginning with the assumption that he generally only expressed "lofty sentiments" when it suited his interests. This leads in turn to the question: what down-to-earth considerations were behind the prime minister's lofty remarks? Several answers are plausible.

This approach does not necessarily imply that Lloyd George was being completely insincere. He may have actually believed that Wilson might be politically useful at a peace conference. Though the British government was still unwilling to negotiate with Germany until Britain's military position had markedly improved, they could neither count upon Germany's collapse nor Britain's immunity from war-weariness. Consequently, they could by no means rule out negotiating with Germany when she was still very powerful and when the Central Powers still occupied Allied territory. It is clear that the prime minister envisioned the possibility of using the captured German colonies as bargaining counters, despite Australian and South African opposition.[56] In such a situation, Wilson's support would be welcomed. Moreover, Lloyd George's references to returning the German colonies in his appeal to the president suggests that he, in fact, had this possibility in mind.[57]

He may have also foreseen that, once Britain's main aims of liberating Belgium and perhaps most of occupied France had been assured, it might prove politically impossible, if not merely absurd, for Britain to carry on the war in order to gain new territory for Italy, Rumania, Serbia or even France. This would be even more evident if the German submarine campaign and further military offensives markedly increased Britain's miseries. Thus, here was another possible situation in which the president might be useful in helping Britain back out of her commitments. At the same time, of course, Wilson might put pressure on Germany to make concessions. In this sense, Lloyd George could exploit the basic fact that neither Britain nor the United States wanted any territory on the Continent for themselves.

The timing of his appeal—his meeting with Page on 10 February—obviously suggests another motive. In an earlier conversation with Page on 5 February, Lloyd George had expressed a similar line of persuasion, but only briefly.[58] His interview five days later provided a much more opportune moment. He was then trying tactfully to put off Wilson's mediation. Flattery was probably intended to compensate the president for a negative response to his peace move.

The main purpose of Lloyd George's remarks, however, was undoubtedly to promote America's entry into the war by playing upon the president's peacemaking ambitions. The prime minister eagerly wanted America to enter the war, and, as Professor Link commented, "he surely knew the force of such an appeal to Woodrow Wilson."[59] The president's ambitions to be a peacemaker were virtually axiomatic in Whitehall.

IV. FROM "PEACE WITHOUT VICTORY" TO "PEACE THROUGH VICTORY"

President Wilson's transition from neutrality to belligerency seemed frustratingly slow to the British government. He wanted to avoid both war on the one hand and submission to Germany's unrestricted submarine campaign on the other. At the same time he

[54] Page to Lansing, 11 Feb., 1917, ibid., pp. 41–44.
[55] Link, 1965: p. 318.
[56] Lloyd George strongly advocated this view in the Imperial War Cabinet during the spring. CAB 23/43/First Meeting; CAB 23/40/13/5. See also Hankey, 1961: 2: p. 599.
[57] The lack of reference to the German colonies in the Allies' reply to the president's peace note had caused some alarm in the southern Dominions. See Louis, 1967: p. 78. Walter Long, secretary of state for the colonies, catered to the Dominions by declaring on 31 Jan., that no man should think the German colonies would return to German rule. London Times, 1 Feb., 1917. This was an untimely remark as far as America was concerned, and several days later the prime minister took a more circumspect position. In a speech at Canarvon he stressed that the issue must be considered as a part of the whole peace settlement. London Times, 5 Feb., 1917. It is just possible that Lloyd George's remarks to Page were also intended to nullify the bad impression which Long may have given Wilson. Long subsequently retreated from his statements of 31 Jan. Parliamentary Debates, Commons 90: cols. 1242–1243 (20 Feb., 1917).
[58] See Page to Lansing, 6 Feb., 1917, Foreign Relations, 1917, Supplement 1: pp. 119–120.
[59] Link, 1965: p. 318. According to Jane Addams, the president pointed out to members of the American Peace Federation on 28 Feb., that American participation in the war would gain for him a seat at the peace table. See Link's discussion of Wilson's decision for war, ibid., p. 414.

was under tremendous pressure to take some kind of action, because American commerce was being seriously disrupted by the refusal of many American and other neutral ships to venture into the war zones declared by Germany. Wilson first tried resorting to a policy of armed neutrality. This move suffered a temporary but irritating setback when a small group of senators staged a filibuster and blocked a bill to arm merchant ships, but the president pressed ahead with the policy on his own authority. Meanwhile, the tide of American feeling against Germany was distinctly rising, and despite occasional lulls, would continue to rise. It was doubtless helped along by the publication of the Zimmermann telegram, but even without such sensational disclosures, war would have seemed to be drawing near. The president was committed to resist unrestricted submarine warfare. The *Sussex* pledge, which he had exacted from Germany the previous spring, had limited his room to maneuver. At most, he could allow the pledge to be modified. To abandon it entirely would have been very embarrassing. The Germans, however, would not accept restrictions—not even on neutral shipping. Berlin had closed all of the options which might have enabled Wilson to maintain both peace with Germany and America's trade with Europe. The "overt acts" were bound to occur and increase in number. The Cunard liner *Laconia* was sunk without warning late in February, and two Americans were among the large number of people killed. The first sinking of an American ship without warning occurred on 12 March. On 18 March, three more American ships were sunk, two without warning. Yet, the president still had not gone to war. In the summary of events for the week ending on 21 March, L. S. Amery impatiently commented: "Meanwhile, President Wilson seems to be becoming increasingly fastidious in his selection of a really suitable 'overt act' for precipitating hostilities. . . ." [1] However, on the twenty-first, Wilson requested Congress to meet on 2 April "to receive a communication concerning grave matters of national policy." By then, the reports from Washington reflected confidence that the president would ask Congress to declare that the United States was at war with Germany.[2]

1. THE LAUNCHING OF AN AMERICAN CRUSADE

The first part of Wilson's address to Congress reviewed Germany's submarine policies and concluded that Germany's submarine campaign against commerce was "warfare against mankind." He explained that armed neutrality now appeared impracticable.[3] Amer-

ica could not, he declared, choose the path of submission. Stressing his awareness of the solemn and tragical character of the step he was taking, the president advised that Congress accept the status of belligerent which the Imperial German government had "thrust upon it." In outlining some of the necessary war measures, Wilson commented that waging the war would involve the "utmost practicable cooperation in counsel and action with the governments now at war with Germany." Yet, he obviously wanted to avoid any suggestion that, in taking the momentous step from neutrality to war, he was abandoning his past objectives and adopting the aims of the Entente. Indeed, he maintained that his motives and objects were the same as when he delivered his "Peace without Victory" speech on 22 January. The constant objective was "to vindicate the principles of peace and justice . . . as against selfish and autocratic power and to set up amongst the really free and self-governed peoples of the world such a concert of purpose and of action as will henceforth insure the observance of those principles."

Wilson emphasized that the quarrel was with the Imperial German government and not with the German people. He absolved the latter of any responsibility for the war. The conflict, he said, had been determined upon as in the "old unhappy days" when wars were waged in the interests of dynasties or of little groups of ambitious men who used their fellow men as pawns. The president also stressed that a concert for peace could only be maintained "by a partnership of democratic nations." Autocratic governments could not, in his view, be trusted to observe its covenants.

Having established this assumption, he then proceeded to grant Russia the necessary credentials. In this respect, the March revolution had been very timely. Wilson declared that the wonderful recent events in Russia had added assurance to the hope for future peace. Russia, he explained, was always democratic at heart. The autocracy there was not, in fact, Russian in origin, character, or purpose, and now that it was gone, the Russian people added their "naïve majesty and might" to the forces fighting for freedom, justice, and peace. "Here," he said, "is a fit partner for a League of Honor."

The president then elaborated on the unfitness of the Prussian autocracy for friendship with America. He spoke of spies, criminal intrigues, and the designs of a government that did what it pleased and told its people nothing. He asserted that Americans were accepting the "challenge of hostile purpose" because they knew that such a government could not be a friend and because there was no assured security for democratic governments where its power was present.

Having decided for war, the president was clearly determined upon victory over the German government.

---

[1] F.O. 371/3080/27667/63514.

[2] Telegram from Barclay, 21 Mar., 1917, F.O. 371/3109/27635/60363.

[3] To be effective, armed ships would have to attack submarines on sight, which according to international law was not the privilege of neutrals, and armed conflict at sea with Germany would very probably lead to war anyway.

America was, he said, about to accept the gage of battle with a "natural foe of liberty and shall, if necessary, spend the whole force of the Nation to check and nullify its pretentions and its power." The president described the meaning of this effort in the loftiest of terms.

We are glad, now that we see the facts with no veil of false pretense about them, to fight thus for the ultimate peace of the world and for the liberation of its peoples, the German peoples included: for the rights of nations great and small and the privilege of men everywhere to choose their way of life and democracy. Its peace must be planted upon the tested foundations of political liberty. We have no selfish ends to serve. We desire no conquest, no dominion. We seek no indemnities for ourselves, no material compensation for the sacrifices we shall freely make. We are but one of the champions of the rights of mankind. We shall be satisfied when those rights have been made as secure as the faith and the freedom of nations can make them.

His peroration portrayed the war as virtually a religious crusade, emphasizing, of course, that it was for American ideals.

To such a task we can dedicate our lives and our fortunes, everything that we are and everything that we have, with the pride of those who know that the day has come when America is privileged to spend her blood and her might for the principles that gave her birth and happiness and the peace which she has treasured. God helping her, she can do no other.[4]

The president's address was received with a tremendous roar of approval, and though Congress debated the question for several days, their decision was never in doubt. The United States was formally declared to be at war on 6 April.

2. COURTING A WARY ALLY

The president's speech and America's entrance into the war were, of course, warmly welcomed by the British. As Robert Cecil commented to Balfour, they were "all gushing over the U. S.—a little overdoing it."[5] Public statements by Lloyd George and Bonar Law were full of extravagant praise. They said that the "glowing phrases of the President's noble deliverance illumine the horizon," that it was "a speech worthy of Abraham Lincoln," that America's entry was "the greatest event" of the war and the "turning point" in the struggle. There was also the inevitable echo of Canning, namely that "the New World has been brought in, or has stepped in, to redress the balance of the Old."[6]

The British government was delighted, of course, primarily because America's great potential strength could now be exerted against Germany. The Imperial War Cabinet's first reaction to the president's speech was to initiate arrangements for sending a special mission to Washington to explain the needs of the Allies.[7] This action quickly ripened into a high-powered mission under the leadership of the British foreign secretary himself.

Lloyd George's and Bonar Law's public statements duly acknowledged the importance of American resources but they placed an equal or greater emphasis upon less mundane and more rhetorical considerations. They welcomed America's entry into the war for the moral justification it gave to Britain's cause. It once and for all stamped the conflict "as a struggle against military autocracy," and was a "fitting pendant to the revolution which . . . brought the Russian people . . . into the circle of free nations. . . ."

Lloyd George said that an even more important consideration than America's war effort was that she would "ensure a beneficent peace." Echoing his confidential appeal of February to the president, he said that, glad as he was for American help during the war, he rejoiced "even more in the knowledge that America is going to win her right to be at the conference table when the terms of peace are being discussed. That conference," he said, "will settle the destiny of nations . . . for God knows how many ages. It would have been a tragedy for mankind," he continued, "if America had not been there, and there with all the influence and the power, and the right, which she has now won by flinging herself into this great struggle."[8]

The official public statements also stressed the common ground between America and Britain. It was claimed that, like America, the British Empire had been forced into the war and that neither country was animated by lust for conquest or any other selfish ends. Above all, it was stressed that Britain shared the aims and ideals expressed in the president's speech. In the House of Commons, Bonar Law said: "The aims and the ideals to which President Wilson has given . . . such noble expression are our ideals too; and, as we found earlier, so the American people have found now, that there is no method by which these aims can be secured except by fighting for them."[9]

Balfour's mission, which arrived in Washington on 22 April, released a further flood of rhetoric. Predictably, the foreign secretary stressed the common danger which Britain and America faced and the common ideals for which they were fighting. He freely invoked the War-for-Democracy-against-Autocracy theme, and played up the historical significance of

[4] Baker and Dodd, 1927: 1: pp. 6–16.

[5] Cecil to Balfour, 22 Apr., 1917, Balfour Papers, Add. MSS. 49738.

[6] London *Times*, 7 Apr., 1917 and 13 Apr., 1917; *Parliamentary Debates*, Commons 92: cols. 1669–1670; statement for American press, Bonar Law Papers, 81/5/1.

[7] CAB 23/40/7/1. The Imperial War Cabinet was one of the *ad hoc* institutions which brought representatives of the Dominions and India together with the British War Cabinet. It met during the spring of 1917 and the summer of 1918.

[8] London *Times*, 13 Apr., 1917.

[9] *Parliamentary Debates*, Commons 92: cols. 1669–1670.

America's wholehearted commitment to the struggle. The drawing together of the English-speaking, "freedom-loving peoples" seemed momentous.[10]

Behind the scenes, Spring Rice predictably expressed misgivings about the future of Anglo-American cooperation and the president's position. His view of the situation was clearly stated in dispatches dated 13 April, which were circulated to the War Cabinet. He wrote:

> The President in entering into the war has probably taken the action . . . at the earliest possible moment. If it had been taken before it is extremely doubtful whether the country would have followed him. His political method is to ascertain from various sources of information what is the predominant sense of the country. He has never taken any action in which he was not moderately sure of at least the acquiescence of the majority. His tendency has been to follow very exactly the dictates of popular opinion.[11]

The British ambassador had accepted only the somber elements of a generally sanguine outlook which Colonel House had promoted during the last phase of American neutrality. House had probably been trying to allay British frustrations over the president's reluctance to go to war. During February and March he had granted several reassuring interviews to J. Allen Baker, a member of Parliament. On 23 February, House had said, according to Baker, that Wilson's personal "desires for action were much in advance of anything to which he could give public expression." The president "must seem to be pushed into action" in order "to carry a united people with him," especially the West and Middle West which were "difficult to get into line." The president must have "the whole nation at his back." House clearly wanted this version of events to be conveyed to British leaders, and Spring Rice, Balfour, and Lloyd George were all eventually informed of this interview.[12]

House's interpretation probably only reinforced the ambassador's convictions about America's aversion to hostilities with Germany. Spring Rice explained on 13 April that it was plain to everybody that the president had wanted to avoid war, yet had been forced into it as the only alternative to abject surrender. The ambassador asserted that the country still maintained its reluctance to fight. Spring Rice also remained apprehensive about American sensitivity to British influence. "Above all," he added, "there is a strong dislike to take part in the war as allies and especially as

allies of England."[13] Elsewhere he warned:

> . . . The greatest care must be taken by the Allied Governments in dealing with this Government. It must not be supposed that the entry of the United States into the war means an alliance for definite and tangible objects with the other Powers, but rather a common action forced upon them. . . ."[14]

The president had, in fact, been reluctant initially to receive the Balfour mission, because he feared that it might appear as if Britain were assuming a great influence upon American policy.[15]

The two most salient aspects of Wilson's attitude were impressed upon Balfour by the president himself in their first meeting on 23 April. Several days later the foreign secretary cabled a report of the conversation to the prime minister as follows:

> Most important pronouncement made by President was a two-sided declaration that he did not think it would be expedient to bind himself by any Treaty obligations such as those to which other allies had already entered into with each other but that nevertheless having joined us in conflict he meant to throw himself wholeheartedly into it and to see it through to a finish.[16]

In short, Wilson was going to reserve his independent diplomatic position but his military goal was victory.

Balfour appreciated the president's desire for independence from the Entente. "Were I in his place," he wrote, "I should have decided as he has done." He also tried to explain the two reasons which lay behind it. Firstly, the president thought that treaties with European powers would be unpopular in America, merely because they were treaties. Balfour did not gather that the president shared this prejudice himself, but it could not be neglected as a political factor. The second reason was of greater importance from Britain's point of view. The foreign secretary observed:

> He [the president] is of course aware of the general tenour of mutual engagements by which European Allies have bound themselves and he contemplates possibility that a time might come when though all essential objects of war had been attained one or other of allies relying on strict letter of treaties would show themselves uncompromising and unpractical over some questions of detail.
> He evidently thought in that event United States being themselves unfettered might exercise powerful and valuable influence.

There would, of course, have been some obvious advantages in having the United States formally committed to fight for some of the Allies' terms. Britain was not merely committed by treaty to support the ambitions of her Allies. She would also be reluctant to release her hold on the German colonies or the conquered Turkish territories. Certainly the Dominions of South Africa, New Zealand, and Australia would

---

[10] New York *Times*, 22 and 26 Apr., 1917.

[11] CAB 24/12/622.

[12] J. Allen Baker to Balfour, 2 Apr., 1917, F.O. 800/211. Drummond forwarded a copy to Lloyd George's secretary, J. T. Davies, on 4 Apr. with the comment that "events are justifying Colonel House's predictions." Lloyd George Papers, F/3/2/16. As will be shown below, Balfour was relatively receptive to House's view, but Lloyd George remained skeptical.

[13] CAB 24/12/623.

[14] Spring Rice to Balfour, 13 Apr., 1917, F.O. 899/12/155.

[15] Fowler, 1969: pp. 25–26.

[16] Telegram dated 26 Apr., 1917, F.O. 371/3119/86512/86512.

be adamantly against restoring the German colonies which they had captured. If Wilson were bound to these terms as well, it would have reduced the danger of his making embarrassing demands to the Allies to renounce some of their ambitions or of trying to force a "premature" end to the war.

On the other hand, the British did not necessarily feel that the president's keeping a free hand was devoid of possible advantages. It was pointed out in the previous chapter that Lloyd George may have thought that this aspect of Wilson's independent position might prove useful at a peace conference in case a complete victory proved unattainable. Certainly the British government thought that some of the Allies' war aims might have to be reduced, and that some of the captured Turkish territories and German colonies might have to be returned.[17] If compromise did become necessary or desirable, Wilson could conceivably make it easier for Britain to back out of her solemn commitments by exerting pressure on all of the interested Allies. In any case, when Balfour conversed with House on 28 April, he was more than willing to welcome the idea of America going to the peace conference with a free hand. House wrote in his diary:

> I asked if he did not consider it wise for us to keep clear of any promises so that at the Peace Conference we could exert an influence against greed and an improper distribution of territory. I said to him, what I once said to Grey, that if we are to justify our being in the war, we should free ourselves entirely from petty, selfish thoughts, and look at the thing broadly and from a world standpoint. Balfour agreed to this with enthusiasm.[18]

Perhaps the enthusiasm was primarily intended to please House, but it is also quite likely that he, in fact, considered Wilson's independent position to have great potential benefits for Britain.

As for the president's commitment to wage a vigorous and determined fight for victory, Balfour confidently believed him. The Cabinet, however, were apparently not so sanguine. Certainly they were disappointed at the slowness of America's war preparations. On 25 April, the Foreign Office sent Balfour a very confidential cable stating that the "War Cabinet are somewhat disturbed at the apparent attitude of the American people towards the war. Put quite shortly, they do not think that the American people are taking the war quite seriously enough. . . ."[19] Balfour tried to reassure London in a cable on 30 April. "You need not fear," he wrote, "either that (?people) here underrate gravity of situation or that they mean to spare themselves in the efforts to improve it." The delays,

he explained, had other causes.[20] But there was still apprehension in the War Cabinet. Indeed, there was some fear that Wilson might be more interested in peace projects than in waging the war vigorously. This fact emerged clearly in a dispute over who would represent Britain in America after Balfour's return.

On 6 May, Balfour cabled the suggestion that Lord Grey should come to America as a special envoy.[21] The War Cabinet "after some hesitation agreed," and the prime minister wrote to Grey urging him to accept the position.[22] Grey traveled from his home in Northumberland to London and discussed the matter with Lloyd George and various other colleagues. The prime minister reported his meeting with Grey to the War Cabinet on 16 May. According to the minutes, he said that Grey "had replied that he felt he was not the right man at the moment, but if after Mr. Balfour's return he found President Wilson, Colonel House and Mr. Page all desire that he should go to Washington, he might be willing to reconsider the position."[23] Lloyd George, meanwhile, had changed his mind. He told the War Cabinet that after his conversation with Grey, he concluded that the ex-foreign secretary was not the right man for Washington at that juncture. Hankey paraphrased the prime minister's comments as follows, "His [Grey's] mind was too much fixed on peace and too little on the active prosecution of the War. His [Lloyd George's] fear was that if Lord Grey were sent he and President Wilson would be talking of peace when they ought to be preparing for war."[24] The prime minister went on to describe the type of man required as one who could put pressure on the heads of America's great supply departments to assist the Allies actively in the war instead of talking about it. He, in fact, wanted Lord Northcliffe, the newspaper magnate, and though there were vigorous objections, Lloyd George pressed the appointment through by the end of May, before Balfour returned from America.[25]

Undoubtedly Lloyd George decided against persuading Grey to accept the appointment for a variety of reasons.[26] Not least, he wanted to get Northcliffe out

---

[17] See Balfour's statement to the Imperial War Cabinet on 22 Mar., 1917, CAB 23/43/Second meeting. See also the Imperial War Cabinet discussion of 1 May, 1917, CAB 23/40/13/5.

[18] House Diary, 28 Apr., 1917. Published in Seymour, 1928: 3: pp. 44–45.

[19] F.O. 371/3113/28438/85223.

[20] F.O. 371/3113/28428/88809.

[21] F.O. 800/383/U.S./17/5.

[22] Telegram to Drummond, 11 May, 1917, Balfour Papers, Add. MSS. 49738; Lloyd George to Grey, 11 May, 1917, F.O. 800/383/U.S./17/7.

[23] CAB 23/13/140a.

[24] Ibid. Apparently Grey had actually given Lloyd George good grounds for fearing that his mind would be on peace. In a memorandum on his own attitude, Grey wrote that while he was reluctant to accept the post, "the prospect of continuing with House in the United States the same intimate exchange of ideas as we had together in London is attractive. . . ." The prime minister knew all too well that when House had last been in London he had been trying to arrange American mediation to stop the war. F.O. 800/383/U.S./17/9.

[25] CAB 23/2/147/10; CAB 23/2/151/7.

[26] Cecil remarked in a cable to Balfour that he thought it

of England. But his fear that it would be harmful to provide encouragement to the president's interest in peacemaking was probably more than a mere rationalization. The president's peace moves were still a fresh memory.[27]

Balfour, nevertheless, had good reasons for taking a more confident view of America's intention to fight. There was the evidence of the warm and enthusiastic American audiences, but more importantly, he realized that Wilson had committed himself to mount an effective war effort. In Balfour's report on his mission, dated 23 June, 1917, the foreign secretary wrote:

He has, I think, taken a considerable risk in entering the war. In his own opinion he did so at the very first moment at which public sentiment was sufficiently favourable to his policy. . . . However this may be, war was declared, and we may be confident that the Democratic party, which declared it, will use every endeavour to prosecute it successfully. Apart from all higher motives, their political future probably depends on its results. It is, therefore, to them and especially to the President, who is their leader not merely in name but in fact, that we must chiefly look to rouse the apathetic, and organise effectively the vast resources of the country.[28]

Balfour must have also been encouraged by the president's lack of protest about the secret treaties. Perhaps he was a little relieved, as well. On his first day in Washington, the foreign secretary agreed with Colonel House that it would be best to avoid discussing peace terms, and, according to House, Balfour said that "he would not talk to the President about peace terms unless the President himself initiated it." This was a prudent policy for several reasons: (1) as we have seen, Balfour assumed the president was already aware of the tenor of the secret treaties; (2) America's belligerent status gave her a strong claim to be informed; and (3) he was likely to ask for information. In fact, the president subsequently directed House to discuss the question of war aims and the secret treaties with Balfour and to arrange a later conversation on the question at the White House. House duly raised the matter on 28 April. Balfour's response was tempered with discretion. He discussed the European arrangements freely and he readily agreed to carry out House's request that the president be given copies of the secret treaties, but he did not raise some sensitive

topics. House recorded emphatically: "We did not touch upon the German Colonies, neither did we touch upon Japan, China, or the Eastern question generally." Balfour was probably relieved that House did not press him on these matters.

Two days later, on 30 April, Balfour and the president had an informal conference about war aims. Things went equally well for the foreign secretary. House, who was also present, recorded that the ground covered was "exactly the same" as he and Balfour had covered in their meeting. House noted that he asked Balfour again about the desirability of giving copies of the secret treaties to the president. The foreign secretary again agreed to do so.[29]

Balfour had to cable to London for copies of the treaties. He eventually sent the documents to the president on 18 May. Ray Stannard Baker, Wilson's official biographer, long ago listed the contents of Balfour's dispatch and carefully noted the omissions. Balfour sent only Britain's agreements which related to Europe and the Middle East. He did not send any documents referring to the provisional division between Britain and France of Germany's West African possessions, Togoland and the Cameroons; more importantly, he did not send a copy of the agreement with Japan about the German islands and German rights in Shantung.[30]

These omissions have preserved interest in the controversy which erupted after the peace conference about the extent to which the British government informed the American administration of the secret treaties during the war. The suspicious aspect of the omissions in Balfour's conversation and correspondence with the administration is that they were questions which would be most likely to embarrass the British. This was particularly true of the agreement with Japan, and the British government was well aware of it. America's policy of the "open door" in China, her sensitivity about questions involving China's "political or territorial integrity," and her general apprehension about Japan's increasing power were all well known in the Foreign Office. Moreover, the relevance of these points had been clearly acknowledged when the assurance regarding Shantung and the Pacific islands had been considered in January and February, 1917. Indeed, when the War Cabinet had discussed the proposed agreement on 13 February, they had before them

---

would have been possible to persuade Grey. Telegram to Drummond for Balfour, 17 May, 1917, 5:30 P.M. Balfour Papers, Add. MSS. 49738.

[27] In his memoirs Lloyd George wrote: "I cannot help thinking that in his heart he [Wilson] hoped that the mere act of ranging the States with their infinite resources on the side of the Allies would lead to Peace before any American blood was shed." Lloyd George would not go so far as to say that the president "deliberately dawdled his preparations" in order to give the Central Powers time to reconsider their attitude in view of the power which America could add to the Allies, but he thought it "must have been an element" in the slow American mobilization. Lloyd George, 1934: 3: p. 563.

[28] F.O. 371/3073/158680/158680.

[29] House Diary, 22, 26, 28, and 30 Apr., 1917. Extracts published in Seymour, 1928: 3: pp. 38-49.

[30] Baker, 1939: 7: pp. 74-75. Baker noted that two further agreements were not mentioned: (1) the Franco-Russian understanding of February–March 1917, regarding Germany's western and eastern frontiers, and (2) the recent negotiations at St. Jean de Maurienne (19 Apr., 1917) which supplemented the treaty with Italy. But he conceded that these omissions might be understandable. Britain may not have been completely informed of the first agreement and the latter might be regarded as not yet completed.

a Foreign Office memorandum which contained a section entitled "The Attitude of America." The memorandum quoted the identical note sent by the United States in May, 1915, to China and Japan declaring that no agreements or undertakings which impaired American treaty rights in China, the political or territorial integrity of China, or the open door policy could be recognized. The memorandum also recalled various warnings which had been conveyed to London about Washington's attitude. For example, it was pointed out that on 16 January, 1917, Lansing had told Spring Rice that "he was anxious about the attitude assumed by Japan, who seemed to be asserting rights in China and in particular in Shantung which could not be admitted by the United States." The Foreign Office memorandum went on to observe:

For many months the American press has been very apprehensive as to Japan's inheriting the German rights in Shantung, and acquiring the German Islands north of the Equator, and there will evidently be considerable excitement when it is known that we have formally agreed to support Japan in her claims.

Finally, the memorandum stated that the Foreign Office had heard "privately that Mr. Wilson intends, at the end of the war, to call a Conference of the Powers interested in China, and to endeavour to come to an agreement for the maintenance of Chinese integrity, and the policy of the open door." [81]

Even before seeing this Foreign Office memorandum, the War Cabinet manifested apprehension about America's attitude. The War Cabinet minutes of 5 February, 1917, read as follows:

The War Cabinet decided that: the possible entry into the War of the United States of America increased the necessity for an early decision in regard to Japan and Shantung and the occupied German islands north of the Equator, in order to avoid negotiations on the subject with another Power. The War Cabinet therefore desired the Foreign Office and the Admiralty to expedite their reports on this subject as much as possible. . . . [32]

In short, the British government wanted to reach a decision on the agreement with Japan before America became a belligerent, because they feared consulting the United States.

Hence, Balfour must have feared that disclosing the agreement with Japan was likely to cause difficulties in Anglo-American relations at a time when Britain urgently needed America's wholehearted cooperation. In particular, they urgently needed shipping and financing, without which it seemed highly possible that the war would be lost. The spring of 1917 was obviously no time for raising sensitive issues which might disturb the efforts of the new belligerent.

It is true that Balfour was often careless about details, but it would be stretching the point to suggest

that he simply overlooked the question. [33] Had he been asked about it, he probably would have responded frankly, but the Americans apparently made discretion easy for him by not asking, and he probably felt that the most prudent way to inform Wilson would be to send a copy of the agreement along with the copies of the rest of the secret treaties.

A new piece of evidence on this question supports the view that he did intend for this collection of secret treaties to be complete. His cable requesting that they be sent to Washington simply asked for "copies of various political agreements we have concluded with Allies." [34] This evidence is not absolutely conclusive. It is just possible that before he departed for America, Balfour and his Foreign Office colleagues decided that the United States would not be informed about the agreement at that stage of the war. In this case, when the Foreign Office received Balfour's request that copies of Britain's various political agreements with the Allies be sent to Washington for the president, they would have assumed that the Anglo-Japanese agreement was to be omitted. But this possibility seems most improbable.

Why then was a copy of the agreement with Japan not sent to Washington? There are two plausible explanations. The first is that the Foreign Office simply made a clerical mistake. When the controversy broke out in 1919, Sir Eric Drummond admitted this possibility in a Foreign Office minute. He recalled that during the war the treaties were collected by the War Department of the Foreign Office, while Shantung was handled by the "China Department." [35] This explanation at least fits with the existing evidence. The Foreign Office's record of the documents which were sent to Washington was written by C. Howard Smith, a junior clerk in the War Department. It was initialed by Lancelot Oliphant, Sir Ronald Graham, and Lord Hardinge, none of whom were members of the Far Eastern Department. [36] On the other hand, it would not be unreasonable to suspect that one of them noticed the omission. The second possible interpretation is that the Foreign Office deliberately withheld the document without Balfour's knowledge. Perhaps on the advice of the Far Eastern Department and the

---

[81] CAB 24/3/118b.
[32] CAB 23/1/54/6. For the Admiralty report, see CAB 1/23/5.

[33] In some minutes referring to a letter from Spring Rice dated 12 Oct., 1917, Balfour wrote: "When I was in the States I took pains to qualify American views of Japan." Balfour Papers, Add. MSS. 49740. In a letter to Milner dated 19 Jan., 1918, Balfour commented: "When I was in America, I found that the State Department took a profoundly gloomy view of Japanese policy. I did what I could to combat suspicions which seemed to me, on the evidence, somewhat excessive. . . ." F.O. 800/203/Japan.
[34] Telegram from Balfour transmitted by Spring Rice, 2 May, 1917, F.O. 371/3081/89749/89749.
[35] See Drummond's minute dated 16 Oct., 1919, F.O. 371/3695/16000/140033.
[36] Smith's minute dated 3 May, 1917, F.O. 371/3081/89749/89749.

American Department of the Foreign Office, it might have been decided to make a deliberate clerical mistake, or perhaps a clerical mistake was allowed to go uncorrected by officials who feared a controversy with the United States. Sir Walter Langley, who was superintending undersecretary of the Foreign Office's American Department as well as of the Far Eastern Department, was undoubtedly aware of the dangers of informing the United States about the Shantung agreement. Aside from troubling Anglo-American relations at a crucial time, there was an obvious risk that, if America objected to the agreement, she might precipitate a general discussion about Japan's position in China. The Foreign Office had been trying to avoid such a discussion since the beginning of the war, because Japan would have a great advantage while Britain was preoccupied in the West.[37]

Had the Foreign Office been specifically asked to inform the United States of any arrangements with Japan, they no doubt would have done so. Indeed, when Lansing enquired in August, 1917, about any understandings which Britain had with Japan as to the ultimate settlement in the Pacific, the Foreign Office complied with the request, though their answer was reluctant and a little misleading.[38] They were careful to reveal nothing more than was absolutely necessary. Only that part of the Anglo-Japanese agreement which related to the German islands was disclosed. The Foreign Office did not mention the promise to support Japan's inheritance of German rights in Shantung, apparently on the grounds that Shantung is not actually in the Pacific.

Nevertheless, the point remains that, if Wilson's administration had conscientiously sought information about any agreements with Japan, it could have obtained full information from either Mr. Balfour or the Foreign Office. In fact, the Americans too were reluctant to raise sensitive questions which might impair cooperation with the Allies and thus hamper the war effort against Germany. Wilson was not as wary as House. He wanted to take the opportunity to discuss the question of war aims with Balfour, but, as Charles Seymour pointed out, House's diary indicates that the president evidently did not think it worth while to make an issue of the secret treaties.[39] Elsewhere, Seymour succinctly described the president's position as follows: "The United States had its own quarrel with Germany, wished to make war as efficiently as possible, and found the most efficient method in close military cooperation with the Allies."[40] Wilson could not have stood by, while Germany sank American ships, waiting for the Allies to revise the secret treaties. The best he could do was to keep a free hand until the war was won. Nevertheless, he felt (rather overconfidently) that he would still be able to have his own way at the end of the war. In July, he wrote the following well-known remarks to House:

England and France have not the same views with regard to peace that we have by any means. When the war is over we can force them to our way of thinking, because by that time they will among other things be financially in our hands; but we cannot force them now. . . .[41]

In effect, Wilson gave the goal of victory priority over his war aims, a fact which the British foreign secretary no doubt perceived with satisfaction.

At the same time, Balfour had no illusions that Wilson's discretion about the Allies' territorial war aims meant tacit approval. We know that areas of disagreement were made clear to him by House. During their conversation of 28 April, House indicated that he thought Italy should not gain Trieste. He said that Austria should not be shut off from the sea. Balfour, on the other hand, cited Italy's argument that she needed the Dalmatian Coast for the protection of her own east coast because there was "no seaport from Venice to Brindisi [suitable for a naval base]. . . ."[42]

House showed more emphatic disapproval of the arrangements for disposing of the Turkish Empire, except for the plans concerning Constantinople, which House may have misunderstood.[43] On hearing Balfour's description of the Allies' agreements for dividing up the region, House told him that it was all bad and that the Allies were making a breeding place for future war.

Balfour and House also disagreed about Poland. Assuming Germany would be the chief menace in the future, Balfour did not want Poland to be independent

---

[37] See the minute by T. H. Lyons of the Far Eastern Department dated 29 June, 1917, F.O. 371/2954/118705/128955.

[38] Telegram from Spring Rice, 2 Aug., 1917, and telegram to Spring Rice, 11 Aug., 1917, F.O. 371/2954/153795/153795. The Foreign Office gave an inaccurate historical account of the negotiations which led to the agreement. The most suspicious error was the statement that the only understanding on the subject was come to in the autumn of 1916. If this was simply a mistake, it was a convenient one. The Foreign Office suggested that one reason His Majesty's government went ahead with the agreement was that America was "not in the war." Of course, America was not in the war in mid-February, 1917, either, but she had by that time broken relations with Germany. By then war was an obvious possibility, and as we have seen, the War Cabinet hastened their decision for precisely that reason.

[39] House Diary, 30 Apr., 1917; Seymour, 1928: 3: p. 49.

[40] Seymour, 1942: p. 269.

[41] Wilson to House, 21 July, 1917, quoted in *ibid.*, p. 270.

[42] House Diary, 28 Apr., 1917.

[43] House noted his agreement with Balfour that Constantinople should be internationalized. In fact, it had been promised to Russia, though it was to be a free port. Seymour suggested that House may have interpreted "free port" to mean "free city." Seymour, 1928: 3: p. 45n. There are other plausible explanations including the possibility that Balfour was referring to what he thought should be done with Constantinople rather than what had been promised to Russia. They may have also realized that Russia might renounce her claims to Constantinople.

of Russia for fear that it would prevent Russia from coming to France's aid in the event of a German attack. House, for his part, assumed that Russia would be the chief menace and that a strong independent Poland would act as a buffer state. Perhaps Balfour assumed this to be the president's view. He may well have recalled that the president had come out in favor of a united, independent, and autonomous Poland in his "Peace without Victory" address of 22 January.[44]

Another difference of opinion between House and Balfour concerned the question of an outlet to the sea. Balfour suggested that Danzig might be made a free port, but House thought that this would only cause antagonism and future trouble. House's view at this moment did not bear much resemblance to the position which the Americans later adopted at the Paris Peace Conference, but every expression of difference was a warning of potential trouble.[45]

There were, of course, signs of agreement on various points as well. They took it for granted that "Alsace and Lorraine would [?should] go to France, and that France, Belgium, and Serbia would be restored."[46] Moreover, they agreed "that Austria must return [?give up] Bosnia and Herzegovina but that Serbia . . . should give to Bulgaria . . . part of Macedonia. . . ." Balfour and House thought that Rumania should receive a "small part of Russia which her people inhabited and also a part of Hungary for the same reason." Neither wanted to dismember the Austro-Hungarian Empire. House wrote: "We thought Austria should be composed of three states, such as Bohemia, Hungary and Austria proper." Even on the disposition of the Turkish Empire, Wilson's adviser managed to find some areas of agreement with the British visitors. House indicated to Sir Eric Drummond that while he looked unfavorably on the division of Asia Minor between the "Western Powers," he agreed that Britain must fulfill her undertakings to the Arabs.[47] This, in effect, meant forcing the Turks out of the Arab regions.

Discussions about a separate peace with Germany's Allies were also harmonious, despite the fact that House's comments were somewhat contradictory. During his first meeting with Balfour, he was asked what he thought about negotiations for a separate peace with

those powers. House replied that he "thought well of Austria and Bulgaria but believed that we should put Turkey into the scrap heap along with German militarism." Balfour "assented to this."[48] In another conversation with the British foreign secretary on 13 May, House spoke of making concessions to Turkey as well as Austria if those states were willing to break away from Germany. Balfour also "agreed to this."[49] Moreover, a week later House gave Balfour's private secretary the impression that he strongly favored a separate peace with Turkey. In the meantime, he had grown pessimistic about detaching Austria.[50] The British foreign secretary probably shared this view.[51]

House usually only raised points on which the British could easily agree. Furthermore, on potentially troublesome subjects which seemed necessary to raise, he was tactful and undemanding. For example, on 20 May, House asked Drummond whether he should travel to Holland if he received a direct official request from the German government that he should go there to discuss peace. This question could have raised the specter of separate American talks with Germany, but House added some reassuring comments. He said that he would not go to Holland without first consulting the British and French governments. He intimated that he had received various indirect proposals that he should talk with unofficial German representatives in Holland, but he had not even replied to them. According to Drummond, House also expressed the following attitude:

If the German Government asked for a peace discussion, he would make it clear that a first preliminary to any talk must be the evacuation of Belgium and France and that the Allies would not treat except with real representatives of the German people as opposed to the military clique.[52]

In effect, these conditions demanded a tremendous military improvement in the Allied and American military position and more moderate leadership in Germany even before a discussion of peace could begin.

House made another interesting suggestion to Drummond. He thought "that a statement should be made by the Allies or by the President speaking for the

---

[44] It should be noted that there was a difference of opinion in the Foreign Office on the Polish question. An important F.O. memorandum written by Ralph Paget and Sir William Tyrrell in Aug., 1916, advocated a solution similar to House's. CAB 29/1/5. The Russian Revolutions soon made this disagreement academic.

[45] See Tillman, 1961: pp. 203–209.

[46] House Diary, 28 Apr., 1917. This particular passage was not quoted accurately in Seymour, 1928: 3: p. 43. Seymour and House sometimes changed the diary when the *Intimate Papers* volumes were prepared. Most of these changes are insignificant, but occasionally the meaning has been altered.

[47] Memorandum by Drummond, 21 May, 1917, Balfour Papers, Add. MSS. 49687.

[48] House Diary, 22 Apr., 1917. Austria and Turkey had severed diplomatic relations with the United States during April, but there was no declaration of war against these powers. Moreover, diplomatic relations were even maintained with Bulgaria.

[49] House Diary, 13 May, 1917.

[50] Memorandum by Drummond, 21 May, 1917, Balfour Papers, Add. MSS. 49687.

[51] On 23 Apr., 1917, Balfour told Lansing that the British government had had indications of Austria's anxiety for a separate peace though the difficulty of separating herself from Germany seemed for the present overwhelming. Cable from Balfour for prime minister, transmitted by Spring Rice, 26 Apr., 1917, F.O. 371/3119/86512/86512.

[52] Memorandum by Drummond, 21 May, 1917, F.O. 371/3082/118656/118656. According to the House Diary this conversation occurred on 20 May.

Allies, to convince the German people that while the reactionary group ruled [in Germany] any peace negotiations were impossible." [53] Drummond drafted the following declaration embodying House's idea:

The United States and the Allies are determined to carry on the struggle till the aims set out by the President have been secured. To effect this purpose the people of America will spare neither treasure nor life, no matter how long the war continues. In 1918 there will be one and a half million American soldiers on the Western front.

The Allies can never abandon the cause of democracy and civilization. But they have already declared that they have no quarrel with the German people; they have no desire to dismember Germany. The war against democracy was inspired and caused by a small military autocracy in Prussia which imposed its wishes even on the German Emperor. With this autocracy the representatives of the democratic countries can never deal. People must treat with people, otherwise there can be no peace. Germany now can never hope for a favourable decision by force of arms. [54]

Charles Seymour pointed out that the points in this document "formed the basis for the public statements of President Wilson during the remainder of the war: Peace to the German people, endless war on German militarism." [55]

As far as the question of peace was concerned, it was possible to see an implicit danger in this formula. If Germany changed its constitution in a democratic direction or, perhaps, even if it merely seemed to, the president might want to stop the war before Britain had achieved all of the aims which seemed attainable. This danger would, in fact, cause some apprehension in London later on in the war, but the British government was not very concerned about this aspect of the president's position in the spring of 1917. Indeed, the Imperial War Cabinet seemed quite willing to endorse the formula when America entered the war. On 5 April, they authorized Lloyd George to send a message to President Wilson on their behalf "cordially welcoming the co-operation of the United States, and laying special stress on the fact that we too regarded the war as one not against the German people, but against the system of Prussian autocracy." [56] It must be noted that Lloyd George's subsequent statement did not go very far in this direction. When he delivered the message to leading American journalists, he placed all of the emphasis on the war being against the Prussian autocracy and left the peaceful intentions towards the German people to be implied. [57] British public statements at this time were generally wary of the president's formula to this extent. [58] Yet, according to

House, Balfour approved of the statement which Drummond had drafted. [59] One is left with the general impression that the British at this stage did not fear that the policy would prove incompatible with a victory over Germany.

Actually, the logic of the president's formula implied that his commitment to victory was at least as strong as the existing system of government in Germany, and, in fact, the system did not break down until Germany was decisively defeated. Perhaps Balfour foresaw this, or perhaps he merely felt that he must go along with the president and House. In either case, however, it does not seem likely that he felt he was approving a policy of peace without victory.

The draft statement was soon rendered "somewhat obsolete." Near the end of his visit to Washington, Balfour and Wilson discussed a public message for Russia, which the president intended to issue in the near future. [60] This proclamation is worth examining, for it clearly reveals the transformation of Wilson's position which had taken place since his peace moves of the previous winter.

The message set out to correct any confusion about war aims, and suggested that, since the war had now begun to go against Germany, she was trying to escape ultimate defeat by misleading propaganda. The president reiterated that America did not seek material profit or aggrandizement, but was fighting for the liberation of people everywhere from the aggressions of autocratic force. He developed the theme that the ruling classes in Germany were lately professing a similar liberality, but only to preserve the power they had set up in Germany and the selfish advantages which they had wrongly gained all the way from Berlin to Baghdad and beyond. The president asserted:

Of course, the Imperial German Government and those whom it is using for their own undoing are seeking to obtain pledges that the war will end in the restoration of the *status quo ante*. It was the *status quo ante* out of which this iniquitous war issued forth, the power of the Imperial German Government and its widespread domination and influence outside of that Empire. That status must be altered in such fashion as to prevent any such hideous thing from ever happening again.

He went on to warn against considering remedies "merely because they have a pleasing and sonorous sound," and argued that "effective readjustments"

---

[53] Memorandum by Drummond, [?21–23] May, 1917, Balfour Papers, Add. MSS. 49687.

[54] Drummond's draft statement, *ibid.* Copy also in House Papers.

[55] Seymour, 1928: **3**: p. 59.

[56] CAB 23/40/8/3.

[57] London *Times,* 7 Apr., 1917.

[58] In reference to a question to be asked in Parliament about

the President's formula, a fear was expressed in the Foreign Office that British endorsement of it would offend the French public. F.O. 371/3081/94228/94228.

[59] House's minute, dated 23 May, 1917, concerning Drummond's draft statement, House Papers.

[60] See the note added to Drummond's memorandum about his draft statement of [?21–23] May, 1917, Balfour Papers, Add. MSS. 49687. Balfour stated later that this interview took place on 23 May, when the president called on him. F.O. 371/3073/158680/158680. There must be some doubt about this date. The meeting may have occurred in the late afternoon of 21 May. See Baker, 1939: **7**: p. 80.

would have to be made. These would be guided by the following principles:

No people must be forced under sovereignty under which it does not wish to live. No territory must change hands except for the purpose of securing those who inhabit it a fair chance of life and liberty. No indemnities must be insisted on except those that constitute payment for manifest wrongs done. No readjustments of power must be made except such as will tend to secure the future peace of the world and the future welfare and happiness of its peoples.

The president concluded with an appeal for practical cooperation and sacrifices. ". . . If we stand together," he declared, "victory is certain and the liberty which victory will secure." The president added: "We can afford then to be generous, but we cannot afford then or now to be weak or omit any single guarantee of justice and security." [61]

Not surprisingly, Balfour told Wilson that the proclamation was admirable. He had doubts only about the line: "No people must be forced under a sovereignty under which it does not wish to live," and on that point, the president provided some personal reassurance. A month later, Balfour recalled Wilson's explanation, in essence, as follows:

He was pleading the cause of nationalities, such, for instance, as Poland; and nationality involved, in his view, the idea of a political organisation and a national self-consciousness which had manifested themselves historically. . . . We agreed that no single phrase could be found which was beyond cavil; cases of doubt and difficulty abounded; all that could be accomplished in such a manifesto as he had drafted was to indicate the general trend of the policy which he desired to pursue.[62]

This was particularly reassuring in relation to the captured Turkish provinces and German colonies.

The proclamation as a whole clearly supported Balfour's view that the president was now intent on a peace *with* victory. The president had, in fact, somersaulted into essentially the same position which the British had occupied when they defended themselves against Wilson's own efforts to end the war. Balfour himself had taken a very similar line against Wilson in the past. Indeed, his favorable reaction to the president's message must have been spiced with some sense of irony.

3. USING THE NEW ADVOCATE OF VICTORY

The recent champion of a negotiated peace had become its most effective opponent, and in subsequent public statements he elaborated his newly adopted themes. On 14 July, Flag Day in the United States, the president spoke at considerable length about the

dangers of negotiating peace with the German government while it held its present advantages. He warned of a plan to "throw a broad belt of German military and political power across the center of Europe and beyond the Mediterranean into the heart of Asia." The greater part of the plan, he observed, had already been executed. The net had been spread from Hamburg to the Persian Gulf, and the enemy had other valuable pawns as well. Its armies pressed close upon Russia, had overrun Poland, occupied valuable territory in France, and held almost all of Belgium. It was from this position that the German government, without disclosing its terms, promoted talk of peace. Berlin wanted to negotiate a settlement before it had to retreat. The president went on to suggest that, if Germany's military masters were forced back, their power at home and abroad would fall to pieces. A government accountable to the people would be set up in Germany, and the world could unite for peace. On the other hand, if they secured peace while they still held their immense advantages, they would have gained by force what they had promised to obtain. "Their prestige will be secure," he explained, "and with their prestige their political power." They would be safe, the world would be undone, and "America would fall within the menace." The United States and the rest of the world would have to remain armed, ready for the German government's next aggressive step.

Wilson then tried to discredit the liberals, the socialists, the leaders of labor, and the thinkers who were promoting an early peace. Indeed, he portrayed the talk of peace as a sinister intrigue which was being carried out by agents, dupes, and friends of the Imperial German government. America, he declared, had chosen to help set the world free, and woe be to those who stood in the way.[63]

The tenor of this address contrasted sharply with the "Peace without Victory" speech. Not surprisingly, it caused the small group of British radicals, who advocated a negotiated settlement, "no little anxiety." [64] However, to the British government the president's transformation from peace without victory to advocating peace through victory was not only welcome but also very timely.

During the summer of 1917, the British government faced a mounting problem of war weariness. In Russia, the problem had grown to alarming proportions. In Western Europe, though it was not nearly as bad, the problem caused serious apprehension. Following the Nivelle offensive, part of the French army had mutinied and there were gloomy reports about the French home front. There were also some doubts about Italy's capacity to stay in the war.[65] Britain was the least war weary of the Allies, but the government was grow-

---

[61] Baker and Dodd, 1927: **1**: pp. 49–51. The message was delivered to the Russian provisional government about the time of an American Mission's arrival there on 26 May, but it was not made public in Washington until 9 June, 1917.

[62] Balfour's report on his mission to the United States, 23 June, 1917, F.O. 371/3073/158860/158860.

[63] Baker and Dodd, 1927: **1**: pp. 60–67.

[64] Martin, 1958: pp. 136–137.

[65] Minute by Lord Robert Cecil, 10 July, 1917, F.O. 800/214.

ing increasingly concerned about the morale at home and the dangers of pacifist propaganda.[66] The German submarine campaign continued at a frightening pace, and, since it directly affected vital commodities like coal for France and Italy and food for Britain, it promised to have an adverse effect on the war spirit. More generally, the war had been going on for almost three years and now that Russia was crumbling, the Allies faced a bitter prospect of prolonged sacrifice.

The war weariness found expression in the movement for a revision of the Allies' war aims. The chief source of this pressure was, of course, Russia. The revolution's leaders adopted the formula of peace "without annexations or indemnities on the basis of the self-determination of peoples." They also supported the project of holding an international socialist conference at Stockholm, and pressed the Allies to revise their war aims at an official conference.

The British agreed in principle to an Allied conference to reconsider war aims.[67] They could not risk giving Russian "pacifists" the pretext for arguing that the Allies were prolonging the war for imperialistic aims.[68] Revising the war aims also had the attraction of improving the chances of a separate peace with Germany's Allies. Moreover, the war was not going well and it appeared increasingly unlikely that the Allies would be able to attain the full terms of their note of January to President Wilson.[69]

Yet, the British government wanted to postpone an Allied discussion of war aims as long as possible. Revising war aims in an alliance was a very hazardous undertaking. It was likely to damage the unity of the alliance and weaken the war effort.[70] Moderating war aims might improve the moral case for the war, but it removed some of the material motives. After giving up important war aims, an ally might be less willing to fight, or even want to make a separate peace. Moreover, haggling over revising war aims might produce nothing more than bad feeling in the Entente. Each government was likely to insist that its allies make most of the concessions. Another danger, which was likely to worry the more imperial minded members of the British government in particular, was that Britain would be pressed to give up her conquests of the German colonies so that the Allies could secure their main interests.[71]

The British government remained opposed to peace with Germany at that stage of the war, though the prospects of victory looked increasingly bad. Not surprisingly there were some grave doubts about this attitude. Lord Robert Cecil, in particular, was very worried and wanted to aim at peace in the autumn. He was tempted to consider putting up with the *status quo ante* in Europe and essentially the war map outside the continent. At the same time, however, he felt that Britain was "bound" to her Allies, and his list of their minimum demands was, in fact, not consistent with the *status quo ante bellum* in Europe. Cecil also recognized that the Entente would at least have to win a considerable military or diplomatic success before Germany could possibly be induced to accept peace on anything resembling the lines he described.[72] The crux of the matter was that the closer the Allies seemed to defeat, the less likely the German government was to compromise with the British. Even if Cecil could have secured the War Cabinet's acceptance of his minimum position, the Germans would have considered it far too much to sacrifice. In a letter to the British ambassador in Stockholm, Hardinge commented: "According to our information Germany is not prepared to discuss any terms of peace except on the basis of the present military map and repudiates any mediation that would not allow her the fruits of victory."[73] In any case, the British government would not consent to peace negotiations until the Germans stated their terms, particularly with reference to restoring Belgium and the occupied territory in France.

Cecil's great fear was that Russia, France, and Italy could not be relied upon to continue the war beyond 1917. His main point was that, if the peace was to be unsatisfactory, Britain had better try to negotiate at the least unfavorable moment. His anxious suggestions precipitated enquiries by the Foreign Office at the end of July about war weariness in France and Italy, but, as Hardinge observed, the idea of early negotiations did not find "any general favour. . . ."[74]

One dilemma posed by Cecil's suggestion was that any sign of weakening by Britain would only incline

---

German Colonies & sometimes talks lightheartedly as tho [*sic*] they could be thrown back to the German wolves."

[72] Minute by Lord Robert Cecil, 10 July, 1917, F.O. 800/214. The document was circulated by Balfour on 17 July.

[73] Hardinge to Sir Esmé Howard, written in late June or early July, 1917, Hardinge Papers 33, fol. 215. See also "Memorandum on German War Aims," 15 July, 1917, produced by the Intelligence Bureau in the Department of Information. CAB 24/23/1792. It pointed out that the only result of the war which could be satisfactory to Britain involved a net loss to the Central Powers and this was universally treated in Germany as unthinkable. The memorandum had a postscript dated 25 July which dealt with the Reichstag resolution of 19 July. It pointed out that the resolution was being interpreted in an elastic fashion.

[74] Hardinge to Sir Rennell Rodd and Hardinge to Lord Bertie, 31 July, 1917, Hardinge Papers 33.

---

[66] War Cabinet minutes, 5 June, 1917, CAB 23/3/154/22; War Cabinet minutes, 20 Aug., 1917, CAB 23/3/220/2.

[67] War Cabinet minutes, 26 June, 1917, CAB 23/3/169/13.

[68] See Sir George Buchanan to Hardinge, 2 July, 1917, Hardinge Papers 33.

[69] War Cabinet minutes, 31 July, 1917, CAB 23/13/200A.

[70] Balfour to Lord Bertie, 21 June, 1917, F.O. 371/3082/115538/125021; War Cabinet minutes, 16 July, 1917, CAB 23/3/187/19.

[71] Curzon to Balfour, 29 June, 1917, F.O. 800/199. When Lord Curzon expressed this fear to Balfour, he also complained: "The P.M. is rather indifferent to the fate of the

the Allies to make the separate peace which the British feared. Moreover, even if Britain's Allies agreed to make a general rather than a separate peace, it would be likely to be negotiated on the basis of the *status quo ante* which was not acceptable to the British government, despite Cecil's panic and Russia's frightening deterioration. On 31 July, Hankey wrote in his diary:

Lunched with Lloyd George, Carson and Milner. All rather upset by the bad Russian news . . . I tried to test whether there was any inclination towards peace, by inquiring whether in the last resort they would be willing to hand back the German colonies in exchange for a German evacuation of Belgium. Not much response. In fact the talk was still of a war *à outrance,* and getting President Wilson to come over and swear to support us. . . .[75]

In a War Cabinet meeting on 2 August, Balfour warned against disclosing British views of the difficulties ahead to the Allies lest they conclude that the *status quo ante* was the best they could attain and press Britain to make peace on that basis.[76]

As far as the question of peace was concerned, the British government faced a complicated task. They had to oppose the idea of peace negotiations with Germany without appearing to prolong the war for imperialistic reasons. It was difficult to avoid making references to war aims, but they had to be wary of stating war aims which provoked dissent in Russia. At the same time, they had to avoid showing weakness or lack of support for their western Allies or for the Dominions. Moreover, if any peace move was made from an influential quarter, there would be pressure to reply and the Allies would want to be consulted. This might bring about the discussions of war aims which the British government wanted to prevent.

In this situation the president proved useful. One simple and obvious tactic was to identify British aims with Wilson's. For instance, in Lloyd George's well-known speech at Glasgow on 29 June, the prime minister began his remarks about war aims with the following passage:

In my judgment this war will come to an end when the Allied Powers have reached the aims which they set out to attain when they accepted the challenge thrown down by Germany to civilization. These aims were set out recently by President Wilson with his unrivaled gift of succinct and trenchant speech. As soon as these objectives are reached and guaranteed this war ought to come to an end, but if it comes to an end a single hour before, it will be the greatest disaster that has ever befallen mankind.[77]

The president could readily be used in this way because the British statements on peace and war aims were, in fact, substantially in harmony with Wilson's recent pronouncements. Indeed, Lloyd George's Glasgow speech as a whole was remarkably consistent with the president's speeches. When he referred to particular war aims, the prime minister went as far as he could towards a non-annexationist position without actually renouncing the imperial *desiderata*. Mesopotamia would be left to the peace conference, but it would never be restored to Turkish tyranny. The question of the German colonies would also be settled at the peace conference, and the choice of the "future trustees" would take into account the sentiments and interests of the people themselves. Lloyd George even came close to Wilson's theme of war against the German government and peace to the German people. He suggested that the British would be less suspicious about entering negotiations with a free government in Germany than about dealing with a government which was dominated by Prussian militarism.

By far the most interesting use of Wilson to oppose peace negotiations followed the pope's peace move in August, 1917. Benedictus XV urged the belligerent governments to agree on the following points: (1) the simultaneous and reciprocal decrease of armaments; (2) the institution of international arbitration; (3) the true freedom and community of the seas; (4) reciprocal condonation of damages, allowing for certain exceptions in special cases; (5) the evacuation of Belgium and France and the restitution of the German colonies; (6) the examination of territorial questions between Italy and Austria, Germany and France in a conciliatory spirit, taking account of the population as far as is just and possible; (7) a similar examination of the questions of Armenia, the Balkans, and Poland. In presenting these bases for peace negotiations, the pope's note expressed the hope that they would be accepted and that there would thus be "an early termination of the terrible struggle which has more and more the appearance of a useless massacre."[78]

The note was dated 1 August, 1917, but the British War Cabinet did not learn of it until 10 August. The matter was discussed on the tenth and the fifteenth, but no decisions were reached on a reply pending further investigation and consultation with the Allies.[79]

The first reports from America were encouraging. In a telegram received on 16 August, Spring Rice reported: "I gather President is considerably put out by proposals coming at time when United States Government are doing their utmost to kindle a warlike spirit throughout States and to combat pacifists." The ambassador also commented that with the exception of the Hearst newspapers, the general tone of the press was hostile to the pope's proposals. "Special stress," he observed, "is laid on fact that American aims have been repeatedly and clearly defined by President and that there can be no peace that will leave Germany

[75] Roskill, 1968: 1: p. 418. See also CAB 23/13/200A.
[76] CAB 23/13/203A.
[77] Published in Scott, 1921: pp. 107–114.

[78] *Ibid.,* pp. 129–131.
[79] F.O. 371/3083/156310/156416; CAB 23/3/210/10; CAB 23/3/215/4.

free to begin again." [80] But he added that a carefully considered and courteous reply was advocated.

The Foreign Office had also received an indication of President Wilson's attitude. At Balfour's request, Sir William Wiseman, who was in London at the time, had cabled House that the pope's note would raise many difficult questions and asked for the president's views about what reply, if any, should be made. [81] Wilson's response was transmitted by House in a telegram which Balfour promptly conveyed to the War Cabinet on 20 August. The minutes recorded Balfour's report of this cable as follows:

Information has been received from a private but reliable source to the effect that President Wilson is doubtful if he will reply at all, but that if he does, his answer will probably take the form of an appreciation of the humanitarian consideration which had animated the Pope's reply, but will point out the following objections:—
(1.) That there is no ground for the belief that the Pope's proposals would meet the views of any belligerent, and for this reason they did not form a good basis for negotiation.
(2.) That they practically advocate the *status quo* before the war.
(3.) That the entire disregard of International Law by the enemy makes it impossible to rely on any undertakings that he might give, and that Germany is morally bankrupt. President Wilson, however, was understood to hold the view that the door to negotiation should not be entirely closed. [82]

The last sentence quoted is misleading. House's telegram shows that it was merely his personal opinion that the door should not be shut abruptly. In fact, the president took a much harder line than his adviser. [83]

Balfour pointed out to the War Cabinet that on 16 August the Foreign Office had politely acknowledged receipt of the pope's note. The discussion which followed focused mainly upon "the question of whether the Allies ought to reply to the Pope's proposals by a re-statement of their war aims." The War Cabinet agreed that "this was not desirable." It was believed that "the reply of the Allies [in January] to President Wilson's Peace Note . . . had produced good results in inclining the President of the United States to make common cause with the Allies." On the other hand, it was felt that "its effect in other neutral countries had not been favourable." Moreover, "in the enemy countries its effect had been to enable the Governments to stimulate their peoples to still greater efforts by the implication that unless they continued the war to a successful conclusion they would suffer irretrievable loss." The War Cabinet recognized that it would be very difficult for a conference of the Allies to state their "war

aims in a less drastic manner." They also agreed generally that "it was undesirable to revive the idea of a Conference for the revision of treaties, for which the Russian Government had been pressing a month ago, but which had now fallen somewhat in the background." [84]

The point was also made that the Allies' reply to President Wilson had been used as anti-war propaganda in Britain and elsewhere to prove that their war aims were "imperialistic and grasping." Without repudiating them, it seemed wise to allow their "*desiderata* as expressed in January . . . to fall into the background." Ironically, it was thought that Wilson, who had provoked the January statement, might now be used to hide it from view. The minutes continue:

It was suggested that this might be achieved by encouraging President Wilson, who stands somewhat aloof from the general cause of the Allies, to send a reply stating the ideal and moral objects for which the Allies are fighting. It would then be in our power, if convenient, to express our concurrence in this reply.

This proposal was, however, supplanted by another consideration. It did not seem necessary for the Allies to answer the pope promptly. The Allies had already stated their war aims, but the Central Powers had merely expressed a willingness to present their terms at a peace conference. In this situation, the Allies could merely indicate that they would await the reply of the Central Powers. The War Cabinet preferred this option, so the possibility of using Wilson was held in reserve. [85]

A telegram to the Vatican was duly drafted and sent to Rome on 21 August. The British representative at the Vatican was instructed to convey the opinion that no progress was likely until the Central Powers "have officially announced the objects for which they are carrying on the war, the measure of restoration and reparation which they are prepared to concede, and the methods by which the world may be effectively guaranteed against any repetition of the horrors from which it is now suffering." The cable continued: "Even as regards Belgium, where they have owned themselves in the wrong, we have no clear intimation of their intention either to restore its complete independence or to repair the injuries which they have inflicted upon it." The telegram also pointed out that Austria and Germany had not issued any statements corresponding to the Allies' reply to Wilson's peace note and added that it seemed useless to attempt to bring the belligerents into agreement until they knew clearly the points of difference. [86]

[80] F.O. 371/3083/156310/160966.

[81] Telegram from Wiseman to House, 10 Aug., 1917, Wiseman Papers.

[82] CAB 23/3/220/1.

[83] Telegram from House to Drummond for Balfour, received 20 Aug., 1917, Balfour Papers, Add. MSS. 49687. See also House Diary, 18 Aug., 1917.

[84] It had originally been agreed to hold the conference in Aug., but this had been put off until Sept. CAB 23/3/187/19. The conference, in fact, never took place.

[85] War Cabinet minutes, 20 Aug., 1917, CAB 23/3/220/1. See also War Cabinet minutes, 21 Aug., 1917, CAB 23/3/221/8.

[86] F.O. 371/3083/156310/164623.

The War Cabinet's motives behind this telegram were mixed. It was observed that, if the Central Powers formulated terms which included "the evacuation of Belgium, it would show a marked advance on the part of the Central Powers toward a settlement." Undoubtedly, a clarification of the German position was being sought, but this did not mean that the British would be willing to negotiate on the basis of the evacuation of Belgium alone. Some ministers felt that in view of the dangerous condition of their allies, it might be prudent to try to commit Germany at least to the evacuation of Belgium.[87] On the other hand, the British government was also resorting to a tactic which was calculated to discredit the German government. The War Cabinet minutes state that, if the Central Powers showed no intention of leaving Belgium, "it would prove that no basis whatsoever for discussion existed." Moreover, if the Central Powers again refused to state their terms except at a conference, the Allies "should reply that we could not enter a Conference unless there was a reasonable basis for negotiation." [88] All of these tactics were designed to sidestep the pope's move. The British felt that the terms in the papal note favored the interests of the Central Powers, and they wanted to avoid getting involved in any correspondence or discussions on the unfavorable basis proposed by the Vatican.

A copy of the British government's telegram to the Vatican was sent to Ambassador Page for transmission to Washington. Balfour also cabled House about it. He stated that he was "in fullest sympathy with the President's line of thought" as expressed in House's recent telegram and he hoped that his message to the Vatican would receive the president's approval. Balfour added that he greatly dreaded the idea of any joint endeavor of composing an elaborate document. "Drafting difficulties alone," he observed, "seem to render the task impossible." [89]

A difficulty of another kind soon arose in connection with the British telegram to the Vatican, whose secretary of state seized on the particular reference to Belgium and asked Germany for an official declaration on the question. He also asked the British representative at the Vatican, Count de Salis, for his opinion of this move. The latter "felt anxious" to avoid appearing to encourage discussion with Germany, but he replied that a German declaration seemed desirable, as the point was especially important for Britain, though it was only one of many issues. When the Foreign Office learned of this development on 25 August, they were apprehensive. They feared that Count de Salis was running the risk of committing Britain to a "piecemeal method of negotiation." As Harold Nicolson explained, a German assurance about Belgium would give the Germans a right to demand a similar assurance about the Colonies, and from there the exchange might lead to a "dislocation of 'la victoire intégrale.'" [90] Count de Salis was accordingly warned that it was undesirable to intervene in negotiations between the Vatican and Germany and that he should decline to give his opinion on them.[91]

Meanwhile, a telegram from Colonel House arrived late on the twenty-fifth with news of another development. Without being urged by the British government, the president was going ahead with his own reply. Colonel House's telegram to Balfour read as follows:

The President has composed an answer to the Pope's peace overture, and will probably send it within a few days.

It will serve, I think, to unite Russia and add to the confusion in Germany.

If the Allied Governments could accept it as their answer to the Pope, it would, in my opinion, strengthen their cause throughout the world. If the United States are to put forth their maximum effort, there must be a united people, and the President has struck the note necessary to make this possible.[92]

Balfour had gone on holiday and Lord Robert Cecil acted for him. In a minute on House's cable, Cecil commented: "It is very desirable we should see proposed answer before it is sent if possible. We cannot buy even the President's pig in a poke."

Since the president had entered the war, he had gone to great lengths to maintain a free hand in his relations with the Entente. He insisted that the United States was an "associate," not an ally, and he was demonstrably reluctant to send any American representatives to Allied conferences and councils—even when the Allied council had been proposed by the United States. The British were well aware that the president's independent stance was particularly intended to preserve a free hand as far as peace terms were concerned. As was mentioned above, Wilson had made his attitude very clear to Balfour personally. Moreover, Spring Rice and Wiseman reiterated the

---

[87] Lord Milner clearly expressed his fear of "accidents" which might befall the Allies despite their "preponderance of power." See Milner to Sir John Willison, 17 Aug., 1917, Milner Papers 144.

[88] CAB 23/3/220/1.

[89] Telegram to Colonel House, 21 Aug., 1917, Balfour Papers, Add. MSS. 49687. Published in Seymour, 1928: 3: pp. 155-156. The published version is dated the twenty-second and there are some other minor differences between the two texts.

[90] See the minutes and telegrams in F.O. 371/3083/156310/166198. For a summary of the episode, see also F.O. 3084/156310/239583. Harold Nicolson was quite junior in the F.O., but he achieved a prominent voice on the subject of the pope's peace move. He was technically a third secretary in the Diplomatic Corps, who had been "temporarily employed" in the F.O. since Oct., 1914.

[91] Telegram to Count de Salis, 26 Aug., 1917, F.O. 371/3083/156310/166198.

[92] Telegram from Col. House, received 25 Aug., 1917, Balfour Papers, Add. MSS. 49687. Published in Seymour, 1928: 3: pp. 166-167.

point.[93] The British realized that the president's aloof position could be a distinct asset to the Allies when it came to defending themselves against peace negotiations, but this could only be true as long as the president spoke only in generalities and avoided stating controversial peace terms. A departure from this policy could make the president's independent stance very embarrassing. Wilson had generally avoided trouble in the past few months, but Cecil could not be sure that his discretion would continue. The president might blunder. As a neutral, he had made what seemed to the British very much like gaffes. Some of his remarks had become notorious in London. After the sinking of the *Lusitania,* Wilson had said: "There is such a thing as a man being too proud to fight." In his major speech before the League to Enforce Peace, the president had declared: "With its [the war's] causes and its objects we are not concerned." From the text of his peace note of December, 1916, the British remembered the words: "The objects . . . on both sides . . . are virtually the same. . . ." Since entering the war, the president had made at least one slip in the direction of excessive altruism. On 12 May, he had said: "We have gone in with no special grievance of our own." Critics had argued that, if there was no grievance, there was no need for entering the war.[94]

A more dangerous possibility was that Wilson might change course. The president's commitment to victory and his opposition to peace negotiations at that time were well established, but it was also realized that he disapproved of some of the Allies' war aims. At some stage he was likely to press moderation upon them. Indeed, there was a widespread feeling that America as well as Russia was a force for revision of the Allies' terms. During July and August the Foreign Office had received several dispatches from Spring Rice which warned of this danger.[95] Moreover, on 21 August, Lord Robert Cecil had circulated a memorandum on Anglo-American relations by Sir William Wiseman in which the latter predicted: "Public opinion will soon force the President to make some more definite statements regarding the concrete aims of the war, and the Allied Governments must be prepared for this."[96]

There were several territorial questions on which the president might be embarrassing: Dalmatia, the division of the Turkish Empire, or perhaps the German colonies.

Some non-territorial questions could also be referred to in an unfavorable way. Freedom of the seas was always a sensitive topic. Another controversial issue was postwar economic policy. The latter, in particular, was receiving an increasing amount of attention by the British government during the spring and summer of 1917. As Britain's military prospects looked increasingly bleak, the idea of discriminating against Germany's postwar trade, or at least threatening to discriminate, became increasingly attractive. If Germany could not be defeated and the danger of German expansion were to continue, it was felt that protectionist economic measures would be necessary in order to frustrate the enemy's economic recovery and to develop the Allies' relative strength. Another consideration was that "most-favored-nation" treatment might be bargained for territory which was held by the enemy. This could be an attractive alternative to restoring the German colonies. The British detected alarm in Germany at the idea of a *post bellum* trade war.[97] Moreover, America's entry into the war added tremendous potential for making effective economic threats. A major obstacle, however, would be to gain American consent. This was clearly acknowledged in a memorandum on trade war dated 27 June, which was discussed in the War Cabinet on 20 July. It stated:

If we are to possess, from the real possibility of a subsequent trade war, the maximum of bargaining power, it is of the greatest importance to secure the consent of the United States to such a possibility. We have every reason to be aware of the alarm and distaste at present felt in the United States and we can only hope to secure United States co-operation in this connection if it is made clear that such a trade war is only contemplated, as a necessary evil, in the event of inadequate peace terms which would leave Germany certain to remain aggressive, and which would therefore leave it all important to check her economic recovery; and, further, that it would be freely bargained away to secure terms which were calculated to discredit the present military party or to limit at least, and more directly, the opportunities at their disposal.[98]

A variant of the theme of *post bellum* trade war was discussed in the War Cabinet on 20 August, shortly after the problem of replying to the pope's peace note was considered in detail. The French minister of commerce, M. Clémentel, who was visiting Britain at the time, had outlined certain proposals to Lord Robert Cecil. His essential idea was to use the Allies' preponderant control of essential raw materials as a weapon in peace negotiations. He wanted to organize the Allies' and America's control of raw materials and then give the enemy an ultimatum: if they did not make peace with the Allies within a certain time, the raw

[93] Spring Rice to Balfour, 20 July, 1917, Balfour Papers, Add. MSS. 49740; telegram from Spring Rice, 21 July, 1917, F.O. 371/3115/29503/144189; Wiseman to Drummond, 7 Aug., 1917, Lloyd George Papers, F/60/2/29.

[94] For the British Embassy's reports on this "misunderstood" comment and its subsequent clarification, see F.O. 371/3120/116932/116932; F.O. 371/3120/116932/128149.

[95] Telegram dated 14 July, 1917, F.O. 371/3120/139607/139607; telegram received 31 July, 1917, F.O. 371/3111/27635/150233; Spring Rice to Balfour, dated 25 July, 1917, and received 13 Aug., 1917, F.O. 371/3121/157711/158304.

[96] F.O. 371/3112/27635/168236.

[97] Memorandum by Ernest M. Pollock, 27 June, 1917, CAB 24/20/1447.

[98] *Ibid.;* War Cabinet minutes, 20 July, 1917, CAB 23/3/191/8.

materials would be permanently withheld.[99] Other schemes were also discussed. There were various doubts about the plan, but it was agreed that "the economic factor provided assets of great value to the Allies, and that peace would very likely in the end be a balance of and compromise between the territorial victories of the enemy and the economic advantages of the Allies, and that from this point of view it was desirable to investigate the matter fully."[100]

Aside from these proposals of a *post bellum* trade war, Britain had other discriminatory policies in mind. At the Paris Conference back in June, 1916, the British government had agreed to the resolution in which the Allies expressed their determination not to grant most-favored-nation treatment to Germany for an unspecified number of years after the war. They had also agreed to work out special arrangements among themselves to reduce their dependence on enemy countries for essential supplies and to strengthen their economic position in relation to enemy countries.

At the Imperial War Cabinet in the spring of 1917, the committee established to study the economic and non-territorial *desiderata* had reported that the Paris resolutions did not offer satisfactory guidance on peace terms. The attitude of some of the Allies and the entry of the United States into the war had introduced "doubtful and new elements" into the situation. But the committee had emphatically endorsed one principle underlying the Paris resolutions, namely, that the Allies should withhold most-favored-nation treatment from the enemy powers.[101]

This committee had also recommended that the terms of peace should not contain any condition which would prevent the British Empire from controlling its natural resources. Indeed, the Imperial War Cabinet had agreed to "the principle that each part of the Empire, having due regard to the interests of our Allies, will give specially favourable treatment and facilities to the produce and manufactures of other parts of the Empire."[102] In August, 1917, an Imperial Trade Policy Committee was set up to study the methods and machinery by which to give effect to this resolution.[103]

This general movement in the direction of discriminatory policies, aimed particularly at the enemy countries, was accompanied by many misgivings. Serious domestic as well as international opposition could be expected, and the government handled the question warily. Yet, at the very least, they did not want to commit themselves to any peace terms which seemed to renounce economic discrimination. As far as the president's imminent reply to the pope was concerned, Cecil may have realized that it might be awkward if Wilson referred to economic questions. In any case, it would be prudent to examine what he was asked to approve. On 26 August, Drummond sent House the following message from Cecil:

I am grateful for information contained in your telegram of 25 August. My view is that it would be very desirable for British and other allied governments to accept the President's reply as their answer to the Pope. The question is however one of such importance that I shall have to consult the Cabinet and also our Allies. I assume the President's reply follows the lines already sketched out but I should be very grateful if it were possible to send me a summary of it if the President sees no objection.[104]

This telegram was based on a draft by Drummond which Cecil modified. In a minute referring to his draft, Drummond commented:

I suppose the matter will have to be brought up at the War Cabinet, but I feel sure that if the President has made up his mind to send in a reply within the next few days, nothing will stop him and it would be a mistake to try to dissuade him from doing so. He is however likely to be amenable as regards changes, if we wish for any.[105]

Wilson, in fact, gave the Allies no time to make suggestions. On 28 August, the Foreign Office received a telegram from Spring Rice notifying them that the president's reply to the pope was already on its way to London for transmission through the Foreign Office to the Vatican.[106] Ambassador Page delivered the document on 29 August.[107]

The president's reply began with polite praise of the pope's motives and then proceeded to argue that the pope's proposals would not lead to a stable peace. He stated that in substance the pope had advocated a re-

---

[99] Cecil mentioned that M. Clémentel further proposed that the economic weapon might be used as a means of keeping the peace after the war and "he rather relied on this aspect of the question to secure the adhesion of President Wilson to the scheme."

[100] CAB 23/3/220/3.

[101] "Report of Committee on Terms of Peace," 24 Apr., 1917, CAB 29/1/15. Various government committees had considered steps which might be necessary to safeguard British industries after the war. The War Cabinet considered publishing some of these reports in June, 1917, but decided not to do so, partly because they feared American reactions. See CAB 23/3/165/11.

[102] Imperial War Cabinet minutes, 24 Apr., 1917, CAB 23/40/11/10; Imperial War Cabinet minutes, 26 Apr., 1917, CAB 23/40/12/16.

[103] Memorandum by Sir Edward Carson, 20 Sept., 1917, CAB 24/4/156.

[104] Telegram from Drummond to House, 26 Aug., 1917, Balfour Papers, Add. MSS. 49687.

[105] See the minutes on the telegram from House to Drummond, received 25 Aug., 1917, Balfour Papers, Add. MSS. 49687.

[106] F.O. 371/3083/156310/167853. Sending the note through Britain was necessary because the United States had no diplomatic representative at the Vatican.

[107] Telegram to Spring Rice, 29 Aug., 1917, F.O. 371/3083/156310/170416. Cecil soon received something approaching an apology from House. His cable stated: "I am sorry your message came too late to comply with your request [to see the president's reply] since note was already in process of transmission. I hope it meets with the approval of the Allied Governments. Our people have received it with great satisfaction and approval." Telegram from House for Wiseman for transmission to Lord Robert Cecil, received 30 Aug., 1917, Balfour Papers, Add. MSS. 49687.

turn to the *status quo ante bellum*. In addition, the pope had called for such terms as disarmament, a concert of nations based on the principle of arbitration, and freedom of the seas. Wilson argued that the *status quo ante* would not be a satisfactory basis for this part of the Vatican's program. The object of the war was to remove the menace and power of a vast military establishment controlled by an irresponsible government. Peace on the basis of the pope's plan would enable that government to recuperate and renew its policy. This would make it necessary to create a permanent combination of nations against the German people, who are that government's instruments, and would mean abandoning the new Russia to intrigue and counterrevolution.

Wilson also declared that responsible statesmen must now see "that no peace can rest securely upon political or economic restrictions meant to benefit some nations and cripple or embarrass others, upon vindictive action . . . or any kind of revenge." He stressed that America wanted no reprisal upon the German people, who had suffered all things in this war which they did not choose. Americans, in his view, believed that peace should rest on the rights of peoples, great or small, "to freedom and security and self-government and to a participation upon fair terms in the economic opportunities of the world, the German people of course included if they will accept equality and not seek domination."

The president went on to renounce selfish or vindictive war aims. He reiterated once again that America sought no material gain, and he added: "Punitive damages, the dismemberment of empires, the establishment of selfish and exclusive economic leagues, we deem inexpedient and in the end worse than futile. . . ." In conclusion, Wilson declared that the United States could not take the word of the present rulers of Germany as a guarantee of anything that was to endure unless clearly supported by the will of the German people. America must await new evidence of the purposes of the great peoples of the Central Powers.[108]

Cecil gave the president's message a very polite reception. In a telegram to Spring Rice on the twenty-ninth, he recorded his remarks to Ambassador Page upon receiving the note:

I read it and, speaking for myself, expressed the warmest approbation of it. I said that I thought that the unfavourable reference to economic leagues might cause a certain amount of comment in this country, but as far as I am concerned I had no objection to it. I hoped that the delivery of the note [to the Vatican] might be of service to the Allied cause.[109]

On the following day, the War Cabinet discussed the president's note. They agreed that it "contained passages to which they could not give unqualified assent, and for this reason it was impossible to express official agreement on it." Cecil was authorized to inform the Allies that in view of the president's reply and the British government's earlier message to the Vatican, "no further reply should be sent until the answer of the Central Powers was received. . . ."[110] A telegram was promptly sent to Paris, Rome, Petrograd, Havre, and Tokyo, and its text was repeated to Washington for the information of the United States government.[111] Spring Rice reported, in a cable received on 1 September, that Lansing "showed [the] greatest satisfaction at His Majesty's Government's suggestion to the Allies and said he felt sure that [the] President would be much gratified."[112]

This was followed by a message from House (conveyed by Spring Rice) which suggested that the president was, in fact, anxious for the Allies to avoid further replies of their own. It expressed the hope that the Allies would use Wilson's reply to the pope "at least as a means of showing a united front." The message was also reassuring about Wilson's references to peace terms. "Do not attach too much importance," it stated, "to expressions relating to terms of peace which are subject to modification from day to day and will be determined by the march of events." The message continued: "The real importance of these expressions is their immediate effect on public opinion. This has been most satisfactory and President is meeting with almost universal support."[113] Eric Drummond commented in a minute that the message "obviously comes direct from the President himself," and that it required a reply.

Meanwhile the French came forward with a proposal for a communiqué in response to the pope's peace move. The British Foreign Office disapproved of the suggestion. In addition to criticizing some inaccuracies in the French draft, the British gave the following reasons:

It is of very great importance that all the Allies should unite in endorsing President Wilson's attitude as far as we can. Not only should such an attitude be exceedingly pleasing to the Americans but it avoids probable divergencies of opinion among the other Allies. The Russians for instance want to underline the omission from the Pope's Note of all reference to the Russian occupied territories. The Italians will insist on some reference to their national claims and aspirations. If we once start on that road we shall emphasize one or more aspects of those war aims

<hr />

[108] Baker and Dodd, 1927: 1: pp. 93–96.
[109] F.O. 371/3083/156310/170416. In Cecil's minute of 10 July, 1917, in which he advocated aiming at peace in the autumn, he made the following comment on economic policy: "Trade after the war is by far the most difficult question. The best thing would be to keep it out of the peace negotiations

altogether, and I think the furthest we could go would be to undertake not to make any specific treaties or conventions directed against Germany." F.O. 800/214.
[110] CAB 23/3/226/12.
[111] F.O. 371/3083/156310/170419.
[112] F.O. 371/3083/156310/170706.
[113] This telegram was sent through H. M. Consul General in Boston, received 1 Sept., 1917, Balfour Papers, Add. MSS. 49740.

unduly or each Ally will issue its own reply which will give an impression of disunion. On the whole therefore it seems better either to issue no communique or else a bare statement that in view of President Wilson's note the Allied Governments do not think it necessary to make any further reply to the Papal message. There are phrases in the President's note about economic policy and the impossibility of treating with the present German Government etc. which makes it difficult to go further than this.[114]

This telegram to Paris was repeated to Washington for the ambassador's "personal information only." Spring Rice replied that it seemed "absolutely in accordance" with the views which House had expressed to him. Drummond and Cecil were encouraged by this remark and promptly instructed Spring Rice to inform House of the substance of the telegram to Paris. Prudently, however, the ambassador was also told to omit the reference to phrases in the president's note which referred to economic policy and the impossibility of treating with the German government.[115]

There were undoubtedly various opinions as to why the president's comments on the German government were objectionable. As we have seen, Cecil feared that peace negotiations must come soon. Evidently he was anxious to avoid ruling out peace talks with the German government. Lord Milner shared this view. It must be noted that his willingness to consider enemy peace terms had important qualifications. Britain's Allies would have to be consulted. Moreover, in the autumn of 1917, he was very wary of conceding territory to Germany at Russia's expense.[116] Nevertheless, he clearly wanted enemy overtures to be investigated. This desire was expressed in an extraordinary message to Colonel House during November. His highly confidential remarks were conveyed by William H. Buckler, who worked at the United States Embassy in London. Milner complained of the British fear of a "peace trap" and urged the American government not to imitate Britain's "timidity" in handling enemy peace feelers. According to Buckler, Milner asked: "How are we to know what our enemies will offer, unless we keep our ears open?"[117]

In addition, Milner had other grounds for objecting to Wilson's attitude toward the German government. Buckler reported that Milner wished "the President had not insisted so strongly upon what amounted to a revolution in Germany. . . ." The tactful reason given was that a revolution was "almost impossible to bring about during war."[118] Milner probably dis-

approved of the president's attempt to encourage revolution in Germany because he feared that such efforts might destroy Europe's social and political structure.[119] Perhaps he also disliked the president's attacks on the German government because he thought that they would only promote Germany's internal unity against foreign interference.[120]

Balfour, too, was wary of appearing to impose a form of government on Germany. On the other hand, the foreign secretary had said in July that it was hard to see how a stable peace could be negotiated with an unreformed Germany.[121] Lloyd George's view was subject to rapid change and can only be inferred. In sharp contrast to Cecil's attitude, he had said on 21 July: "It is with a Germany dominated by an autocracy that we can not make any terms of peace."[122] This was a harder, more Wilsonian line on the issue than was usual among British leaders. It expressed a passing mood which may have softened by the end of August, as the Russian situation deteriorated. Furthermore, intransigent public references to the impossibility of peace negotiations were growing impolitic in the face of increasing war weariness.

The president's comments on the German government were not nearly as important as his references to economic policy. Wilson's condemnation of discriminatory economic restrictions and "exclusive economic leagues" was undoubtedly the main stumbling block to an explicit British endorsement of the president's reply to the pope. His remarks had also raised the danger of public controversy on the subject. Lord Robert Cecil tried hard to avoid trouble by publicly denying that there was any difficulty. In a statement issued to the press on 31 August, he declared that there did not appear to him to be "anything inconsistent as between the President's note and the economic policy of the Allies declared at the Paris Conference." He argued that the Paris Conference resolutions were purely defensive measures, aimed at restoring the Allies' economies after the war and protecting themselves "against any aggressive and militarist commercial policy which might be pursued by our enemies after the war."[123]

[114] Telegram to Lord Bertie, 1 Sept., 1917, F.O. 371/3083/156310/170713.

[115] Telegram from Spring Rice, received 2 Sept., 1917, Balfour Papers, Add. MSS. 49740; telegram to Spring Rice, 3 Sept., 1917, Balfour Papers, Add. MSS. 49740.

[116] War Cabinet minutes, 24 Sept., 1917, CAB 23/16/238(a); War Cabinet minutes, 27 Sept., 1917, CAB 23/16/239(a).

[117] Buckler's notes of his conversation with Milner, dated 3 Nov., 1917, enclosed in House's letter to Wilson, 9 Nov., 1917, Wilson Papers, Series 2.

[118] Ibid.

[119] Milner had been growing increasingly worried about the future since the March Revolution in Russia. In Apr., 1917, one of the reasons he was glad that the United States had entered the war was that he thought "they may exercise a steadying influence to prevent the dissolution of all human society." See Milner to Glazebrook, 21 Apr., 1917, Milner Papers 144.

[120] Lord Milner manifested this view at a Supreme War Council meeting in Feb., 1918. See CAB 28/3/44.

[121] Scott, 1921: p. 127.

[122] Ibid., pp. 118–119.

[123] Cecil also pointed out that restrictive economic policies could be valuable in a peace-keeping role. He suggested that "a league of nations, properly furnished with machinery to enforce the financial, commercial and economic isolation of any nation determined to force its will on the world by mere violence would be a real safeguard for the peace of the world."

Actually there was a grain of truth in Cecil's contention that the president's note was not inconsistent with the Paris Conference—or at any rate, with the idea of an economic alliance which excluded Germany. In the United States, the press learned "in an authoritative quarter," that the president's note had been misconstrued on this point. It was suggested that Wilson's remark about "exclusive economic leagues" should be read in connection with the statement which preceded it, namely, that to make peace upon the terms proposed by the pope would necessitate the creation of a permanent combination against the German people. The president meant, it was explained, that the Allies would be forced to combine commercially to prevent the resumption of German ascendency for military purposes. In short, Wilson had implied that unless the Allies achieved a victory, the United States would approve of postwar economic discrimination against Germany.[124]

This clarification of the president's position evaded the fact that the Paris Economic Conference resolutions were not conditional upon whether Germany was defeated or reformed. The press was told by State Department officials that the president did not have the Paris Economic Conference in mind when he wrote his note to the pope, but they "declined to discuss or speculate regarding the attitude of this country toward the Paris Conference."[125] Clearly, the administration wanted to keep their suspicions of the Allies' intentions concealed for the time being. Apart from the need for unity in wartime, the Americans wanted to minimize any obstacles to an Allied endorsement of the president's note.

American cooperation undoubtedly helped the British to *imply* that the president had replied for the Allies. The weak point in this tactic was, of course, that the British could not explicitly endorse Wilson's note, because it would associate them too closely with his objectionable phrases. The best that the British could do in this position was to say as little as possible, but the vague and evasive quality of the government's line on the pope's peace move did not pass unnoticed. In the months which followed, two pacifist M.P.'s, Mr. Joseph King and Mr. C. P. Trevelyan, asked questions in Parliament as to whether the president's reply was to be taken as expressing the Allies' answer, and whether the British government intended to reply. Balfour answered very briefly on 22 October that there seemed "to be no reason at present, for adding anything to the acknowledgment which has been already sent by His Majesty's Government."[126] Early in De-

cember, Mr. King asked why the pope's peace note received no reasoned reply from the British, French, and Italian governments. Cecil answered with the bare statement that those governments "considered that no reply to the Papal Note was necessary beyond that returned by President Wilson."[127]

This reserve was undoubtedly a little embarrassing. Wilson's reply to the pope had not been ideal from the British point of view. On balance, however, it had been very useful. Despite his transition to a peace-through-victory position, the president still had the image of a statesman who was relatively disinterested, idealistic, and even relatively pacifist. The fact that he had disapproved of the pope's peace proposals made it easier for the British to evade them without appearing guilty of prolonging the war for imperialist and aggressive reasons. As we have seen, the British were anxious to avoid the formulation of an Allied reply because of the danger of dissension in the alliance. The president's reply undoubtedly made this policy more feasible than it otherwise would have been. Indeed, they used the president's reply as a major reason for maintaining this policy. Thus, Wilson's note helped preserve the alliance from quarrels, the British from the accusation of being warlike, and the war against Germany from a negotiated peace.

V. THE SEASON OF PEACE TALK, 1917–1918

The belligerent powers, like farmers, were strongly influenced by the change of seasons. There was a time for offensives, and a time, after the grisly harvest had been reaped, for peace moves and statements of terms. Whitehall could easily anticipate that in the months following the pope's note and President Wilson's reply to it, talk of peace would increase. This chapter is about British-American relations concerning various questions of peace during the war-weary season of 1917–18.

1. THE DREAM OF A PAX ANGLO-AMERICANA

On 18 September, 1917, Lord Robert Cecil circulated a paper to the War Cabinet which reveals something of the Foreign Office's desire for close cooperation with the Americans. The document was actually a note which Cecil had sent to Balfour at the end of August regarding the problem of British representation at Washington. Once again, Cecil advocated replacing Spring Rice by Lord Grey. Cecil's efforts to make Grey the ambassador to Washington were fruitless as long as the war lasted,[1] but his note is worth

---

Perhaps this was calculated to appeal to Wilson. (See footnote 99 above.) *New York Times,* 1 Sept., 1917.

[124] *New York Times,* 31 Aug., 1917. Several months later, Wilson would make this threat much more explicit.

[125] *New York Times,* 1 Sept., 1917.

[126] *Parliamentary Debates,* Commons **98**: cols. 468–469.

[127] *Parliamentary Debates,* Commons **100**: cols. 573–574 (6 Dec., 1917).

[1] Grey was H. M. ambassador extraordinary and plenipotentiary on special mission to the United States from Aug., 1919 to Mar., 1920. The purpose of his mission, which began in Sept., 1919, was to deal with questions arising out of the peace settlement. His main task was to urge Wilson to compromise

quoting at considerable length for its comments on British-American cooperation.

Cecil considered Britain's diplomatic representation to be weak in Washington, and he argued that this was not only regrettable because of the mass of "business negotiations" connected with waging the war, but also because of the imminence of peace moves. He explained:

If serious peace propositions were made, the attitude of America would be all-important and in this connection the attitude of America really means the attitude of President Wilson. It cannot be too often insisted that, in Foreign Affairs, President Wilson is an autocrat; and, if we are to secure the complete cooperation of America during the war, and her friendship afterwards, we ought to have at Washington an Ambassador who will be in sympathy with his personality.

President Wilson might perhaps be described as in political opinion, a Gladstonian liberal. We ought therefore to have as Ambassador a man who will understand that type of mind, and for that purpose Lord Grey would seem suitable.

Cecil went on to relate that he had been told very recently that "the qualities the Americans really admire are what they describe as the typical English qualities, that is to say: straightforwardness, disinterestedness, idealism, or, if you like, the religious temperament." Cecil considered Grey to be pre-eminently strong in these things. He also pointed out that Grey enjoyed a close relationship with Colonel House.

Cecil shared a prevalent dream of British-American cooperation in international affairs, and he suggested that Grey as ambassador would help bring it to fruition. Cecil's glittering vision of the British wisely and benevolently guiding the young world power seems destined to be cited frequently by historians.

Sir William Wiseman told me the other day that he understood from Colonel House that the President desired to work closely with us when it came to a discussion of terms of peace. Indeed, he contemplated a state of things in which we should consult privately as to what terms of peace we propose to insist upon, and then go into the Council and back one another up. I do not know how far this may be true, but it is certainly a possibility when one remembers that, though the American people are very largely foreign, both in origin and in modes of thought, their rulers are almost exclusively Anglo-Saxon, and share our political ideals. But there seems to me to be more at stake even than cooperation in the terms of peace.

The United States are entering upon an entirely fresh chapter of their history. For the first time they are taking a part in international European affairs; they will soon begin to realize what vast power they have; and, unless they are very different from any other nation that has ever existed they will wish to make use of that power. If they make use of it rightly, it may be of incalculable benefit to the human race: and by rightly I mean in accordance with our ideas of right and justice. There is undoubtedly a difference between the British and the Continental point of view in international matters. I will not attempt to describe the difference, but I know that you will

agree in thinking that, where it exists, we are right and the Continental nations are, speaking generally, wrong. If America accepts our point of view in these matters, it will mean the dominance of that point of view in all international affairs. I am convinced that there is no one who is a better exponent of what I call the British point of view, both by nature and by training, than Lord Grey, and . . . there is no one more capable of upholding that point of view in the mind of President Wilson.[2]

Cecil's particular expression of the dream of a *Pax Anglo-Americana* was perhaps unusually moralistic in its terminology, but behind the desire for close cooperation there were undoubtedly very practical, political considerations. Part of the simple logic involved was as follows: the old balance of power had broken down; Britain's existing alliances were not capable of ensuring peace or even Britain's security; another great factor must be added to the European situation on Britain's side; the United States was the obvious candidate. Below this rudimentary formula, of course, lurked the stark realization that an extraordinarily great power was rapidly maturing across the water and that it was imperative that harmonious relations should be cultivated. The president obviously intended to make his influence felt on questions of peace, and there could be no doubt that he would have tremendous leverage in his hands whenever these questions arose.

2. HANDLING KUHLMANN'S PEACE INITIATIVE

Cecil was right about the imminence of enemy peace moves. On 18 September, the British ambassador in Madrid was told by the Spanish foreign minister that a "very exalted personage" in Germany wanted to know whether Britain would receive a communication in regard to a peace settlement. Very soon thereafter the British Foreign Office was also informed by Ambassador Cambon of a German approach to the French. Balfour reported to the War Cabinet on 24 September that a German diplomat named von Lancken had approached ex-Premier Briand through a lady who was personally acquainted with the French statesman. Von Lancken was acting under orders from Richard von Kuhlmann, the German foreign secretary. The following terms were suggested to the French: cession of Alsace-Lorraine by Germany; restoration of Serbia; territorial concessions to Italy; colonial concessions to Great Britain; restoration of Belgium. These proposals were, in view of the Allies' military position, suspiciously favorable to Britain and France. It was readily observed, too, that neither Russia nor Rumania was mentioned.[3] Furthermore, this approach was "of an entirely informal character."

In contrast to the overture to the French, the Germans approached the British through an official channel. Balfour considered it absolutely necessary to reply and he strongly advocated (1) agreeing to listen to the

---

in order to secure the Senate's ratification of the League. The president refused to see him.

[2] CAB 24/26/2074.
[3] CAB 23/16/238(a).

German proposals and (2) stating that the British government could only consider the proposals in consultation with their five largest allies. (In this instance, the United States was referred to as an ally rather than "associate.") Balfour also wanted to summon the ambassadors of these five governments to inform them of the reply he intended to make. He feared the dangerous consequences of the British acting without such a preliminary. The Germans themselves, he thought, might betray Britain's failure to consult her allies.[4]

The War Cabinet did not readily accept the foreign secretary's advice. The prime minister wanted to ascertain whether Russia's collapse would make victory impossible and to examine the possibility of making peace at Russia's expense. He advocated learning what Germany had to propose before communicating with any of the Allies. On second thought, however, Lloyd George decided that M. Painlevé, the French premier, must be told in view of his frankness with the British government.

Balfour, of course, agreed that the French must be consulted, but he wanted to inform the American government as well. "President Wilson," he pointed out, "was particularly interested in all matters connected with terms of peace." Undoubtedly Balfour had other reasons for consulting the United States. A difficult situation could easily develop if Wilson should learn that the British were keeping things back, particularly matters connected with questions of peace.[5] British candor might have also been seen as a means of preventing the president from engaging in peace moves behind the backs of his "associates." That is, Wilson might feel obliged to reciprocate Balfour's frankness. This could be important. The war spirit in America was obviously rising and the president was deeply committed to achieving some kind of victory, but there was always the possibility that he might react to a German peace move in a way which would embarrass the Entente. He might also seek a separate peace with Germany's allies in such a way that would alienate Italy. This could force Britain into an embarrassing position because of her commitments under the Treaty of London. Anglo-American consultation would at least give the Foreign Office a chance to mitigate a dangerous move by the president. More generally Balfour wanted, as part of his basic policy, to cultivate a close relationship with Washington through wide-ranging consultation whenever practicable.

The prime minister, however, did not consider it necessary to inform the Americans of the German overture. He said that at present the British government

wanted the United States to fight and "there was no need to discuss questions of peace with them." The War Cabinet followed suit. The minutes record the following conclusion:

The Prime Minister was authorized to inform M. Painlevé of the German proposal, and to tell him that the War Cabinet were disposed to receive a communication if sent. It was generally agreed that we could not refuse to hear what the German proposals were, but all action in regard to the reply to be made, and as to any communication with our allies, other than France, was postponed until after the Prime Minister's conversation with M. Painlevé.[6]

After this meeting, Balfour wrote to the prime minister stressing the dangers of holding "any communications of an important kind with the Germans without previously communicating the fact to the Russians." He wanted Lloyd George to have the risks fully in mind when he met M. Painlevé.[7]

On 27 September, after a brief trip to France, the prime minister reported to the War Cabinet that both Painlevé and M. Ribot did not want to enter into the negotiations which had been offered to them. They seemed to doubt whether the French would continue fighting if it were known that the Germans had offered nine-tenths of Alsace-Lorraine and all of Belgium. As for the German approach through Madrid, M. Painlevé was "willing that Great Britain should act as a post office. . . ."[8]

Balfour resumed his efforts to convince his colleagues about the necessity of informing Britain's allies about peace moves. He emphasized "that the danger of Russia going out [of the war] would be enormously increased if it got about that we are prepared to make peace at her expense." Abruptly changing his position, Lloyd George now "agreed" with Balfour, though he still thought that the War Cabinet could consider the question among themselves.[9] Quite clearly he was reluctant to abandon the idea of peace at Russia's expense. The prime minister argued "that the American people would not continue fighting merely to prevent Germany from obtaining peace at the expense of Russia, when she [Russia] declined to fight herself for her own possessions." He added that this was also "probably true of the British public."

George N. Barnes, a new member of the War Cabinet, had suggested earlier that "no great importance" needed to be attached to America's attitude since the United States was not yet contributing much to the war

---

[4] *Ibid.* See also memorandum by Balfour, 20 Sept., 1917, CAB 29/1/22.

[5] Balfour deleted the following lines from the explanation recorded in the minutes: "Otherwise there might be a difficult position. There was a feeling in the United States that we were keeping things back. . . ."

[6] CAB 23/16/238(a).

[7] Balfour to the prime minister, 24 Sept., 1917, Lloyd George Papers, F/3/2/30.

[8] CAB 23/16/239(a).

[9] *Ibid.* Lloyd George had not been unmindful of the dangers of proceeding without consulting Britain's allies. In fact, early in the War Cabinet meeting on the twenty-fourth, he was inclined to pursue the informal negotiations offered to the French, because he thought they could be repudiated, if necessary. CAB 23/16/238(a).

effort outside of financial assistance.[10] Balfour, of course, argued against this notion, and at the end of the meeting, he reiterated his view that the allies should be informed of the German peace offer which had been conveyed through Madrid.[11] The War Cabinet discussion was apparently inconclusive on this point, but Balfour kept up his campaign. He secured a telegram from the British ambassador in Russia saying that there was no choice but to tell Russia.[12] Lord Hardinge subsequently implied in a private letter that this telegram was decisive.[13] In any case, Balfour had his way soon after Ambassador Buchanan's cable arrived on 4 October.

On the same day, he sent a cable to Colonel House concerning the German overture. The message indicated the line which Balfour proposed to take in reply to the peace move, namely that the British would listen to terms, but would not discuss them without consulting Britain's co-belligerents. The foreign secretary added that no decision had been reached as to whether to inform the other principal allies before sending a reply. He also mentioned that he had informed only the French ambassador in London about the overture.[14]

This message was sent through Sir William Wiseman, who discussed the matter with House on 5 October. They drafted a reply which Wilson promptly approved. Their advice did not correspond exactly to Balfour's position. They suggested that he should refuse even to consult his co-belligerents "until a more definite proposal" was made.[15] Balfour, as we have seen, was particularly anxious to consult the Russians before making any reply. In this he had his way before the House-Wiseman draft arrived in London.[16]

On 6 October, the ambassadors of France, America, and Japan, along with the chargé d'affaires of Italy and Russia, met at the Foreign Office and were informed of the German overture. Balfour also revealed the following reply which he proposed to send to Madrid: "His Majesty's Government would be prepared to receive any communication that the German Government may

desire to make to them relating to peace, and to discuss it with their Allies." [17]

This brief and cautious message was duly sent to Madrid, and, as Balfour hoped, the Germans did not respond. The Foreign Office was pleased at having had its way. On 11 October, Hardinge wrote to Sir Walter Townley, British minister at the Hague, that they had to be "very wary to defeat Mr. Khulmann," for he was the cleverest of the German officials then in power. But Hardinge was convinced that the Foreign Office would hear no more from Spain, "especially," he added, "as we have indisputable proof that the whole aim of his [Kuhlmann's] advance was to sow distrust between America and ourselves." [18]

3. CONSULTATION ON WAR AIMS AND POSTWAR POLICIES

During the autumn months, British and American leaders conferred on a wide range of diplomatic questions. A national home for the Jews was one fateful topic. America's large and powerful Jewish minority gave her a special interest in Zionism. On 3 September, the War Cabinet decided that the opinion of President Wilson should be obtained before any declaration was made on the subject. The acting secretary of state for foreign affairs was requested to probe the United States government's views as to the advisability of a declaration of sympathy with the Zionist movement.[19] Cecil promptly asked Colonel House to ascertain Wilson's attitude.[20] On 12 September, he received a reply. House stated that the president thought that the time was "not opportune for any definite statement further perhaps than one of sympathy provided it can be made without conveying any real commitment." He explained that things were in "such a state of flux" at the moment that Wilson "did not consider it advisable to go further." [21] This reply may have puzzled the British slightly in view of the fact that they were only considering an expression of sympathy.

The subject came before the War Cabinet again on 4 October. The foreign secretary warned that the Germans were actively wooing the Zionists. Arguing for a positive British declaration, he asserted that the movement had behind it the support of a majority of Jews in Russia and America. Balfour also said that he knew President Wilson was extremely favorable to the movement. In opposition, Edwin Montagu, the secretary of state for India and an anti-Zionist Jew, argued that Colonel House had revealed the president's current opposition to a declaration. The War Cabinet

---

[10] George N. Barnes had been given Arthur Henderson's place in the War Cabinet after the latter had to resign in Aug., 1917, during the controversy over the Stockholm Conference.

[11] CAB 23/16/239(a).

[12] Lloyd George Papers, F/3/2/32.

[13] Lord Hardinge to Sir Arthur Hardinge, 8 Oct., 1917, Hardinge Papers 34.

[14] Balfour (code name Falsterbo) to House (code name Brussa), 4 Oct., 1917, Wiseman Papers. The copy in the House Papers is dated 5 Oct., 1917, but the acknowledgment which House cabled to Balfour referred to the latter's message of the fourth. See House to Balfour, 5 Oct., 1917, Wiseman Papers.

[15] House to Wilson, 5 Oct., 1917, Wilson Papers, Series 2.

[16] Telegram from Wiseman to Balfour, 7 Oct., 1917, Wiseman Papers.

[17] Telegram to H. M. Representatives, 8 Oct., 1917, CAB 23/16.

[18] Hardinge Papers 34.

[19] CAB 23/4/227/2.

[20] Telegram from Cecil to House, 3 Sept., 1917, House Papers.

[21] CAB 24/26/2015.

eventually decided to send a draft statement to the president as well as to leading Zionists and representative Jewish anti-Zionists.[22] On 16 October, Wiseman reported Wilson's reaction to the declaration as follows:

Colonel House put formula before President who approves of it but asks that no mention of his approval shall be made when His Majesty's Government makes formula public, as he has arranged that American Jews shall then ask him for his approval which he will give publicly here.[23]

At the end of the month, the War Cabinet finally authorized Balfour to make the famous declaration of sympathy with Zionist aspirations. In stating the case for approving such a statement, Balfour told the War Cabinet that it would enable Britain to carry on extremely useful propaganda both in Russia and America. As for the meaning of the words "national home," he had in mind "some form of British, American, or other protectorate. . . ." The foreign secretary explained that this "did not necessarily involve the early establishment of an Independent Jewish State, which was a matter for gradual development in accordance with the ordinary laws of political evolution."[24]

Another topic for consultation was the League of Nations. On 30 August, Viscount Bryce wrote to the prime minister, enclosing a memorial signed by seventeen "persons of weight" who wished to promote the idea. They proposed that the British government should arrange for a small body of persons drawn from Allied countries to study the subject and make practical recommendations. As a first step in this direction, it was suggested that the cooperation of specially qualified Americans might be obtained who would confer with British members and prepare preliminary drafts as a basis of discussion for the consideration of the Allied governments.[25]

A few days later, Lord Robert Cecil wrote to House about this project. "I am not," he remarked, "a very great admirer of or believer in Commissions of any kind, but I should be very glad if some machinery could be hit on which would direct some of our best brains to the consideration of this problem." Cecil's main concern was to prevent attempts to implement an impractical scheme. "I am very much afraid," he explained, "that, if anything like a complete system for the judicial or quasi-judicial settlement of international disputes be aimed at, it will infallibly break down and throw the movement back for many years."[26]

One wonders whether Cecil feared, in particular, that Wilson might promote an impractical scheme. Perhaps he reasoned that an impressive team of British experts could guide American advisers along feasible and reasonable lines and that these would in turn guide the president. The League of Nations was the British government's best chance of involving the United States in European security arrangements on a long-standing basis. Cecil was anxious not to see the opportunity ruined by excessive idealism.

Bryce's letter did not come before the War Cabinet until 19 October, whereupon the War Cabinet merely decided to "adjourn the matter" until it could be discussed "with the representative of President Wilson" who was soon expected in Britain.[27] The "representative" was Colonel House, whom Wilson had chosen to head an American war mission. Shortly before House accepted the task of leading the mission, it was announced that he had been entrusted by the president to form an organization which became known as the Inquiry. The United States government wanted to forestall speculation that these preparations were for an early peace conference.[28] When it was decided to send House to Europe, the U. S. government also tried to prevent speculation that the mission was connected with the peace movement. They insisted that the conference which the mission would attend be called a "war conference."[29] The British government fully agreed with this desire, but they nevertheless wanted to take advantage of the opportunity to consult House informally on questions of peace. House looked more than ever like the essential link with Wilson. Wiseman wrote to Drummond on 4 October that House's responsibility for preparing the American case for the peace conference was "a natural step towards making him chief American delegate." He also thought that House's influence with the president was stronger than ever. Moreover, House was receptive to the idea of British-American cooperation. He had made Wiseman almost his private secretary. Wiseman mentioned in his letter to Drummond that he thought House showed him everything he received and discussed practically everything with him. "He feels very strongly," Wiseman wrote, "that England and America ought to work together, because as he expresses it, 'what is good for one is good for the other.'"[30]

[22] CAB 23/4/245/18. The declaration was cabled to House through Wiseman on 6 Oct., 1917. F.O. 371/3083/143082/200850.

[23] Telegram from Wiseman to Drummond, 16 Oct., 1917, F.O. 371/3083/143082/200850. It was not until the end of Aug., 1918, that Wilson publicly endorsed the Zionist movement with an expression of his "satisfaction" in the movement's progress since the declaration by Balfour. Baker and Dodd, 1927: 1: p. 243.

[24] War Cabinet minutes, 31 Oct., 1917, CAB 23/4/261/12. The declaration was published in the London *Times* on 9 Nov., 1917.

[25] CAB 24/28/2293. For an interesting account of the origins of this memorial, see Mason, 1970: pp. 88–100.

[26] Cecil to House, 3 Sept., 1917, Balfour Papers, Add. MSS. 49687.

[27] CAB 23/4/253/17.

[28] Spring Rice to Balfour, 5 Oct., 1917, F.O. 371/3077/2/205699.

[29] Telegram from Lansing to Page, 7 Nov., 1917, *Foreign Relations, 1917, Supplement 2,* 1: pp. 295–296; telegram from Spring Rice, transmitting message from Lord Reading to the prime minister, the War Cabinet and Balfour, received 16 Oct., 1917, F.O. 371/3086/196737/198775.

[30] Wiseman to Drummond, 4 Oct., 1917, F.O. 800/209.

These propitious factors were, however, frustrated by other aspects of the situation. The president had only reluctantly consented to send a representative to Europe, and he was still determined to avoid political entanglements with the Allies as much as possible. As far as peace terms were concerned, he shunned any well-defined commitments, preferring characteristically to preserve his options through the use of inspired but vague rhetoric. Another obstacle was what the president himself called his "one-track mind." As long as he was preoccupied with fighting the war, it was difficult to get him to concentrate on details of the peace settlement.[31] An American commission of experts might have avoided this particular problem, but on major political issues Wilson was inclined to insist on holding the reins when dealing with other governments.

Sir Eric Drummond encountered something of these difficulties when he consulted House about the idea of establishing an Anglo-American committee of experts to examine the League of Nations question. On 15 November, in a minute addressed to Balfour, Drummond reported on his conversation with House as follows:

It was clear to me that in his view it would be a mistake to set up any such Committee. He told me that the President thought it better that the Government of the United States should not in any way be committed to a cut and dried plan for the establishment of a League of Nations. The President hoped that if any nation showed an aggressive disposition, or clearly intended to go to War, Great Britain, the United States, France and perhaps some other Nations should come to an understanding between themselves as to what attitude they should adopt and that having come to a decision on this point they should then determine what steps should be taken to make it effective. Colonel House added that the President and he were discouraging in the United States discussions as to the League of Nations, etc., and that he had succeeded in employing a number of advocates of the League on various work immediately connected with the prosecution of the War.[32]

League enthusiasts in the British government were to meet similar objections throughout the war. The president avidly endorsed the League idea, but he did not cooperate in planning it in detail.

The British also talked with House about the question of economic discrimination against Germany after the war. In view of the importance of making the fullest use of the Allies' "economic lever" to counteract Germany's "territorial lever," a committee had been formed early in October to study the subject from the British point of view. This was considered a preliminary to a comprehensive agreement with France and the United States.[33] During late October and early November, two disasters to the Allies' war effort enhanced the British government's interest in the subject. The Bolshevik Revolution and Caporetto—the Italian defeat on the Isonzo—had brought them face to face with the possibility of France, America, and England fighting on by themselves. Balfour believed that, if such a situation developed, commercial warfare would be the only means of ending the fighting. By this he meant not only economic war measures during hostilities, but also the threat of "commercial disabilities when the war was over." On 8 November, soon after House arrived in England, Balfour made the following comment in a memorandum which considered these possibilities:

I gather from my conversation this afternoon with Colonel House that the President is prepared to go to any lengths in organising a trade war, to be used both before and after the conclusion of peace, if the peace is not, broadly speaking, satisfactory to America and the reasonable desires of her co-belligerents.[34]

Two days later House discussed the possibility of ending the war and the war's aftermath with the chancellor of the exchequer. "I told him," House recorded in his diary, "of the President's purpose to address Congress on the subject of economic freedom, and to threaten Germany with an economic war in the event she refused to be a party to a just and lasting peace." House added that Bonar Law "expressed unqualified approval." [35]

House and the British leaders discussed territorial war aims, as well. According to his diary, on 20 November, House "pinned [Lloyd] George down" about British objectives.

What Great Britain desires are the African Colonies, both East and West, an independent Arabia, under the suzerainty of Great Britain. Palestine to be given to the Zionists under British or, if desired by us, to be under American control. An independent Armenia and the internationalization of the Straits.[36]

On the following day, the British initiated another discussion. During the morning, British military authorities suggested to the War Cabinet that an announcement should be made that German East Africa would not be surrendered to Germany at the end of the war. The secretary of state for the colonies endorsed the proposal. He said that it would safeguard the natives against subsequent reprisals by the Germans. Walter Long also suggested that many lives might be spared if the natives who were with the Germans could be

---

[31] Wiseman mentioned this explanation later in the war. See Wiseman to Cecil, 18 July, 1918, Wiseman Papers.

[32] CAB 24/32/2667.

[33] War Cabinet minutes, 9 Oct., 1917, CAB 23/4/247/8. For manifestations of the British government's interest in securing America's cooperation, particularly in reference to securing control of raw materials, see CAB 23/4/265/19; CAB 23/4/273/16; CAB 23/4/283/17.

[34] F.O. 371/3086/218315/218315.

[35] House Diary, 10 Nov., 1917. Published in Seymour, 1928: 3: p. 228.

[36] House Diary, 20 Nov., 1917. Published in Seymour, 1928: 3: p. 235. Balfour remarked in a letter to Frederick Dixon on 16 Nov., that he personally thought that an autonomous Armenia should be placed under the sole protection of the United States, if America would assume the responsibility. F.O. 800/211.

induced to desert. Balfour had a more complicated approach to the problem. He first pointed out the three main arguments in favor of not returning the colonies to the enemy:

(*a*) Could we . . . afford to allow Germany the possession of good submarine bases such as Dar-es-Salam, after the war?

(*b*) Could we allow the native population to be retransferred against their will to German domination?

(*c*) Could the civilised world as a whole regard with equanimity the avowed and expressed intentions of Germany to create a large and well-disciplined black army in the heart of Africa which would be in a position to threaten not merely the whole of that continent, but white civilisation also?

On the other hand, the foreign secretary saw one difficulty. Britain had to face the accusation that the "Allies, and more particularly Great Britain, were out for plunder and further territorial acquisitions." Balfour thought that the Cabinet should consider the proposal for internationalization of the German colonies in Africa. This would prevent the establishment of a German naval and military menace and, at the same time, would make the raw materials there available to the world. The question was adjourned until the next day, pending a meeting which the prime minister and Balfour were to hold with Colonel House that afternoon.[37]

House was not cooperative. The War Cabinet minutes of 22 November betray the British government's annoyance:

. . . The Prime Minister and the Secretary of State for Foreign Affairs reported to the War Cabinet that Colonel House was resolutely opposed to the issuing of any Proclamation announcing that German East Africa would not be returned to the Germans at the end of the war. All the arguments bearing on the shortening of the duration of the campaign in East Africa, with all its hardships involved for the white troops and suffering for the population, as well as the locking up of shipping had not been able to weigh with him as against the inconvenience such a declaration would cause to President Wilson. This applied no less, in Colonel House's opinion, to a merely negative Proclamation saying that the country was not to be given back to the Germans than to a positive one stating that we meant to retain it. Colonel House was not opposed to our keeping the country eventually, and thought it was in our interest not to tie our hands publicly at this moment.[38]

The secretary of state for the colonies protested that the United States must be interested in the menace to the world's peace which would result from the creation of a great black army in Africa. It was suggested that some public statement might be devised which would reassure the natives without tying the hands of the government or embarrassing Britain's allies; the War Cabinet felt, however, that, in view of House's

attitude, they must refrain from making an announcement at that time as to their war aims in East Africa.

The more general question of making a further declaration of war aims was related to this incident. At the War Cabinet meeting on 21 November, Sir Edward Carson observed that the pacifists were benefiting by the lack of definiteness in Britain's declared war aims. The War Cabinet felt that this also should be discussed after the prime minister and Balfour had their interview with House.[39]

The presidential adviser's remarks on this subject were also negative. House wrote in his diary:

We . . . went into the question of war aims. Maps were brought and Mr. Balfour started in with his ideas of territorial division. I did not allow him to go far when I spoke of the futility of such a discussion. I thought what we agreed upon today might be utterly impossible tomorrow, and it seemed worse than useless to discuss territorial aims at this time. They both caught the point and agreed to drop the discussion.[40]

Once again he shunned a detailed discussion. House had decided it would be pointless to try to get the French and British to specify their terms. He had observed in his diary on 16 November that "Great Britain cannot meet the new Russian terms of 'no indemnities and no aggression' and neither can France." When he met with Balfour and Lloyd George, what he thought was then "necessary and pertinent . . . was the announcement of general war aims. . . ."[41] House maintained this attitude at the Inter-Allied Conference in Paris which got under way at the end of the month.

As the winter drew near, the Russian question became increasingly critical. On 30 November, the principal Allied leaders and Colonel House considered making a statement to Russia with regard to war aims. The Bolsheviks were determined to leave the war immediately—by a general peace if possible, by a separate peace if necessary. Balfour conveyed to the inter-Allied discussion the advice from the British ambassador in Petrograd that the Allies should release Russia from her obligation not to make a separate peace. The French leaders raised objections to this proposal, and Baron Sonnino emphatically argued that no diplomatic action should be taken. House responded that some statement should be made to counteract a recent speech by the German chancellor which promoted peace negotiations between Russia and Germany. According to Hankey's notes of this discussion, "*Colonel House* suggested that the statement could be so drafted as to hearten everyone, including the smaller Powers."[42]

[37] War Cabinet minutes, 21 Nov., 1917, CAB 23/4/279/3.

[38] CAB 23/4/280/8. For House's version of his conversation with Lloyd George and Balfour, see House Diary, 21 Nov., 1917. See also *Foreign Relations, 1917, Supplement 2,* 1: p. 344.

[39] CAB 23/4/279/3.

[40] House Diary, 21 Nov., 1917.

[41] *Ibid.* On 25 Nov., House remarked in a telegram to the President: "I am refusing to be drawn into any of their controversies, particularly those concerning war aims of a territorial nature. We must, I think, hold to the broad principles you have laid down and not get mixed in the small and selfish ones." *Foreign Relations, 1917, Supplement 2,* 1: pp. 317–318.

[42] CAB 28/3/35.

After this meeting, he cabled for the president's approval of the following resolution:

The Allies and the United States declare that they are not waging war for the purpose of aggression or indemnity. The sacrifices they are making are in order that militarism shall not continue to cast its shadow over the world, and that nations shall have the right to lead their lives in the way that seems to them best for the development of their general welfare.

House added that the British had agreed to vote for the resolution when he submitted it to the conference.[43]

Wilson approved of the resolution on the following day. In his telegram he commented that it would be unfortunate "for the conference to discuss peace terms in a spirit antagonistic" to his address of January (the "Peace without Victory" speech). "Our people and Congress," he asserted, "will not fight for any selfish aim on the part of any belligerent, with the possible exception of Alsace-Lorraine, least of all for divisions of territory such as have been contemplated in Asia Minor." Wilson went on: ". . . It will be obvious to all that it would be a fatal mistake to cool the ardour of America."[44] The British almost certainly intercepted these telegrams between House and the president. One wonders whether Wilson assumed that his cables would be read by his "associates." The wording of the telegram cited here suggests that he perhaps intended it for foreign eyes.

Meanwhile, the Russian ambassador in Paris had been consulted about the question of a declaration to Russia. He subsequently produced some draft statements which took the line that the Allies would discuss their war aims as soon as Russia had a "decent" government. They were designed to strengthen the hand of "Moderates" in Russia who might oppose the Bolsheviks. When the inter-Allied discussions of this problem were resumed on 1 December, Balfour criticized the draft statements on the ground that they implied the Allies were being forced to discuss their war aims. House expressed general agreement with the British foreign secretary and introduced his own resolution. He made it clear that it was impossible for the United States to associate itself with any of the other drafts.[45] Discussing the revision of war aims, he argued, would involve material considerations embodied in treaties to which the United States had not adhered. That is, the United States government would not promise to revise war aims which it had not endorsed. House also conveyed the argument that the forces of public opinion behind the president believed that they were making war to achieve idealistic and not materialistic war aims, and that nothing should be done which would jeopardize this belief.

It was agreed that, if the United States did not endorse a declaration, it would be at best worthless and could possibly make a bad impression. On the other hand, the conference did not think House's draft resolution was adequate. House reported to Wilson that "England passively was willing [to accept it]."[46] But according to Hankey's notes of the discussion, "any declaration in which the United States could associate itself was found to be emasculated and characterless."[47] The Allied leaders, in fact, felt that, if a resolution were to be of value to their friends in Russia, it must include a promise to discuss the revision of war aims.

The dilemma was insoluble. Lloyd George attempted to splice part of one of the Russian ambassador's drafts to House's resolution. "It seemed to suit [Lloyd] George," House wrote in his diary, "but it did not suit me."[48] Balfour concluded that it would be better for each government to send its own declaration to Russia. This did not receive immediate assent, but further discussion made it increasingly clear that agreement on any joint declaration was impossible.

The American attitude remained the main obstacle, but it was not the only important source of difficulty. The question of making any further declarations of war aims had very recently been seriously complicated for the British government by Lord Lansdowne's famous letter to the *Daily Telegraph*, which was published on 29 November, 1917. Lansdowne's letter advocated a reconsideration of Allied war aims and suggested that certain assurances would promote peace negotiations on an acceptable basis: (1) that the Allies did not want Germany to be annihilated as a great power; (2) that they did not want to impose any form of government on Germany other than what the German people wanted; (3) that except as a war measure, the Allies did not want to deny Germany her place among the great trading communities; and (4) that they were prepared to enter into an international pact to settle disputes peacefully.[49] The letter brought a storm of criticism down upon Lansdowne. Though controversy developed as to the meaning of the letter, there was a predominant feeling that its publication had been unfortunate. Certainly this was the view which Lloyd George took at Paris. Hankey's detailed notes of the discussion about a statement for Russia read as follows:

Mr. Lloyd George said that the more he thought the matter over the more alarmed he became at the idea of at-

---

[43] Telegram from House to Wilson, 30 Nov., 1917, *Foreign Relations, 1917, Supplement 2,* 1: p. 328.

[44] Telegram from Wilson to House, 1 Dec., 1917, *ibid.,* p. 331.

[45] CAB 28/3/35(a). Hankey and his staff produced two summaries of the discussion which took place on 1 December: a preliminary general summary and a much more detailed set of notes. The latter gives a confused impression on first reading. It seems to suggest that House would not associate the U.S. with his own resolution. The wording of his resolution makes it clear that this impression is wrong.

[46] Telegram from House to Wilson, 2 Dec., 1917, Seymour, 1928: 3: pp. 284–285.

[47] "Note of the Progress of the Paris Conference," CAB 28/3/35(a).

[48] House Diary, 1 Dec., 1917. Published in Seymour, 1928: 3: p. 284.

[49] Reprinted in Dickinson, 1919: pp. 84–89.

tempting to make any joint declaration at all. Even in Great Britain it was more difficult to make any announcement of our consent to discuss war aims after Lord Lansdowne's letter. . . . If we were to publish a document here it would be regarded as a support to Lord Lansdowne's point of view. This made any declaration much more difficult. What he feared was that, from the point of view of the war, a rot would set in. Hence, he was impressed with Mr. Balfour's suggestion not to make a public declaration other than Colonel House's which, however, did not touch the question of war aims; but that each nation should tell its own Ambassador to let it be known in Russia that we were ready to discuss war aims. It should be left to the discretion of each Ambassador to let this be known in the way which he considered best.[50]

It was agreed that the Allies should adopt this suggestion. The decision, which actually represented the failure to agree on a brief joint statement, was soon followed by a strong movement in the direction of relatively elaborate, independent declarations of war aims.

4. WILSON'S SPEECH OF 4 DECEMBER AND ITS PLACE IN THE LANSDOWNE CONTROVERSY

On 1 December, 1917, House cabled to the president: "I hope you will not think it necessary to make any statement concerning foreign affairs until I can see you. This seems to me very important." House wrote on a copy of this cable that he had in mind the president making a statement of war aims. "I tried to get this done at Paris, but failed," he added. "The next best thing was for the President to do it." Charles Seymour accepted these remarks at face value.[51] Yet, it seems incredible that House could have considered the very vague draft resolution which he had proposed at Paris as an adequate statement of war aims. Even if the Allies had adopted his declaration, House would probably have wanted Wilson to make a separate statement. In the meantime, of course, he did not want the president to broach the subject of war aims without his advice. Wilson, however, did not wait. "Sorry," he replied on 3 December, "impossible to omit foreign affairs from address to Congress. Reticence on my part at this juncture would be misunderstood and resented and do much harm."[52] He delivered an important speech to a joint session on the following day, 4 December.

The president began his remarks on war aims with the premise that America's object was "of course, to win the war," and he declared that the country would not be diverted until victory was achieved. Nevertheless, he thought it worth asking: "When shall we consider the war won?" He said that it was necessary for the government to say plainly what the war was for and the part they meant to play in its settlement. "We shall regard the war as won," he went on, "only when

the German people say to us, through properly accredited representatives, that they are ready to agree to a settlement based upon justice and reparation of the wrongs their rulers have done." He added that their wrong to Belgium must be repaired and that their power over the great empire of Austria-Hungary, over the hitherto free Balkan states, over Turkey, and within Asia, must be relinquished. In calling for the liberation of various peoples from Prussian domination, the president specifically disclaimed any wish "to impair or to arrange the Austro-Hungarian Empire." (He was not going to compromise the chances of a separate peace for the sake of the principle of national self-determination.) "It is no affair of ours," he said, "what they do with their own life, either industrially or politically. We do not . . . desire to dictate to them in any way," he maintained. "We only desire to see that their affairs are left in their own hands, in all matters, great and small." As for the people of the Balkan peninsula and the Turkish Empire, America hoped to secure their rights and fortunes against "oppression or injustice and from the dictation of foreign courts or parties."

Much later in his speech, without previous warning, Wilson advised Congress to declare the United States to be in a state of war with Austria-Hungary. He argued that Austria-Hungary was "for the time being not her own mistress but simply the vassal of the German Government." The Central Powers, he said, must be regarded as one.[53] Wilson acknowledged that this "logic" would also lead to declarations of war against Turkey and Bulgaria, since they, too, were instruments of Germany. "But," he explained unconvincingly, "they are mere tools" and did not yet obstruct America's "necessary action." Actually Wilson asked for a declaration of war primarily to bolster Italian morale and to satisfy a rising demand for it by the American public.[54] His problem was to declare war and promote a separate peace at the same time.

As well as trying to divide the Central Powers, the president continued his efforts to separate the German government from the German people. He denied that he was meddling in Germany's domestic affairs. "We intend no wrong against the German Empire," he declared, "no interference with her internal affairs." This assertion, of course, ignored the fact that his war policy demanded a transformation in the character of the German government.

---

[50] CAB 28/3/35(a). For the impact of the Lansdowne letter on these deliberations, see CAB 23/13/290A/2. See also, *Foreign Relations, 1917, Supplement 2*, 1: p. 353.

[51] Seymour, 1928: 3: p. 284.

[52] Published in Baker, 1939: 7: p. 389.

[53] One wonders with Victor Mamatey how Austria, as a helpless tool of Germany, could be expected to separate herself from Berlin. See Mamatey, 1957: p. 66. The appeal for a declaration of war on Austria-Hungary came so abruptly that Spring Rice thought Wilson must have decided on it only at the last moment. Spring Rice to Balfour, 7 Dec., 1917, F.O. 800/209.

[54] For an account of this decision, see Mamatey, 1957: pp. 155–160.

The president developed the theme that once the necessary victory was achieved, America would press for a peace settlement which granted "full, impartial justice" for enemies and friends alike. "No one," he maintained, "is threatening the existence or the independence or the peaceful enterprise of the German Empire." Yet, his speech did contain some threat to the German people. He no longer fully exonerated them. In fact, he suggested that they had permitted themselves to be deceived and mastered. Moreover, he warned that, if complete victory over the German autocracy were not achieved, Germany would be "shut out from the friendly intercourse of the nations." If the German people continued "to live under ambitious and intriguing masters . . . it might be impossible to admit them to the partnership which must henceforth guarantee the world's peace."

Wilson went on to threaten German trade explicitly. He said:

It might be impossible, also, in such untoward circumstances to admit Germany to the free economic intercourse which must inevitably spring out of the other partnerships of a real peace. But there would be no aggression in that; and such a situation, inevitable because of distrust, would in the very nature of things sooner or later cure itself, by processes which would assuredly set in.

This statement confirmed what House had told the British in regard to America's attitude toward economic discrimination against Germany after the war.

The president presented his declarations as specific interpretations of what he had said to the Senate during his "Peace without Victory" address. He still claimed that America's entrance into the war had not altered her attitude toward its settlement. In particular, he referred to his comments in January about free pathways upon the sea and equal rights to unmolested access to those pathways. More generally, Wilson said that he was thinking of all nations, great and small, present enemies as well as associates. "Justice and equality of rights can be had only at a great price," he declared. "We are seeking permanent . . . foundations for the peace of the world and must seek them candidly and fearlessly." Characteristically he concluded: "As always, the right will prove to be the expedient." [55]

In London one of the most noteworthy aspects of the president's speech was his reference to the possibility of economic discrimination against Germany after the war. During the latter part of January, Sir Edward Carson, who was chairman of the Economic Offensive Committee, quoted the president's statement on postwar economic relations in a War Cabinet memorandum, and declared that he was "in perfect accord" with what Wilson had said. Indeed, he asserted that the president had expressed the "guiding motive" of the British government's "preparations" for the reconstruction period. [56]

The usefulness of Carson's remarks as a sweetner of British-American relations was not overlooked. In the following spring a paper by Lord Eustace Percy was circulated to the War Cabinet which mentioned that Carson's "memorandum was shown to certain American officials in Washington" during March, and that it "came to them as a complete and agreeable surprise." This revelation was part of the British government's effort to allay American suspicions that British intentions were "sinister and selfish." Percy suggested that it was only by making assurances that Britain's aims were "unselfish and no other than those enunciated by the President himself, that Lord Reading is able to lead the administration at Washington on to a joint consideration of economic policy." [57] Wilson's adoption of the principle that postwar economic discrimination against Germany might be necessary was sufficiently imprecise to make this kind of reassurance and flattery possible without readily revealing the limitations of his sympathy with the British point of view. On closer examination, at least a difference of emphasis remained, if not a conflict, between the president's and the British government's outlook. Wilson tended to regard the question of postwar economic discrimination almost exclusively in terms of securing a satisfactory peace settlement. The British government, on the other hand, generally thought that even in the event of a satisfactory peace, restrictive policies would be necessary and desirable. In this situation, the vagueness of Wilson's rhetoric served the cause of Anglo-American harmony very well. It fostered some useful confusion and permitted the British to indulge in some congenial prevarication.

The president's speech of 4 December is also interesting because it became involved in the controversy over Lord Lansdowne's letter to the press. Lord Robert Cecil was very impressed by parallels between Wilson's address and Lansdowne's observations. He even went to the trouble of sending Balfour newspaper clippings of the respective statements, arranged side by side to illustrate their similarites. [58] This was part of Cecil's own campaign to promote a more sympathetic treatment of Lord Lansdowne. He also wrote to the prime minister on 5 December, suggesting that Lansdowne had been misinterpreted as desiring peace on any terms. Cecil explained:

In effect, he [Lansdowne] argues that we ought to restate our war aims: that undoubtedly some of those which we put forward in the Wilson note have become obsolete, and that we should remove the impression that we desire

---

[55] Baker and Dodd, 1927: 1: pp. 128–129.

[56] Memorandum by Carson, 21 Jan., 1918, CAB 24/4/190.

[57] F.O. 800/214. Percy's memorandum was not dated. It was circulated to the War Cabinet by Balfour and was printed for the War Cabinet in May, 1918.

[58] Cecil probably sent the document to Balfour around 6 Dec., 1917. Balfour Papers, Add. MSS. 49738.

the political annihilation of any of our enemies. This is in substance, also, what President Wilson said yesterday: indeed, if you compare closely the substantive demands made by Lansdowne and Wilson, my impression is that you will find comparatively little to choose between them, apart from two important exceptions. Wilson, though he has weakened on his reply to the Papal Note as to no peace with the Hohenzollerns, still does say that any peace with them might be followed by economic war, or, at any rate, by exclusion of Germany from the partnership of nations. It is not, however, very clear what he means, and I think myself that he is merely getting ready to admit the possibility of a peace with the Hohenzollerns, though he wished to say as you said, with far greater judgment, if I may be allowed to say so, that it would be much easier to make a peace with a democratic Germany.

The other great difference between the two pronouncements is that, as far as I can understand him, Wilson has definitely abandoned all idea of breaking up Austria-Hungary. All he asks is that Austria-Hungary shall be freed from Prussian influence, and while declaring war with that Power, he apparently offers peace with her on almost any terms, provided she will break with Prussia.

You will find no counterpart of this in Lansdowne's letter. . . .[59]

Lloyd George did not agree with Cecil's analysis. According to C. P. Scott's diary for 16 December, Lloyd George said "there was all the difference in the world between Lansdowne and Wilson because Wilson postulated victory and Lansdowne did not."[60] Two days earlier, the prime minister had publicly taken a slightly different line, though not without tongue in cheek. In a speech at Gray's Inn, he referred to the startled reaction to the Lansdowne letter on the part of those who wanted "an upright and enduring peace and not a humiliating surrender." He continued:

I now understand that all our anxieties as to this epistle were groundless, that Lord Lansdowne had not intended in the least to convey the meaning which his words might reasonably bear; that all the time he was in complete agreement with President Wilson, and only meant to say exactly the same thing as the American President said in his recent great speech to Congress. Now the government are in full agreement with that speech. Mr. Asquith, I am not surprised to see, is also in agreement with it. The British nation is undoubtedly in agreement with it, and as Lord Lansdowne has also declared that he agrees with it, things which agree with the same thing agree with one another. I therefore take it that the interpretation placed on Lord Lansdowne's letter, not merely by strong supporters of the Allied case, but also by its opponents, in this country, in America, and in France, and now also, I observe, in Germany and in Austria, was not in the least that which Lord Lansdowne desired to give to it. I do not desire to force a controversy if none exists, for national unity is essential to success. But I might be forgiven for saying that if Lord Lansdowne simply meant to say exactly the same thing as President Wilson, it is a great misfortune that he did not carry out that intention. I was attending the Allied Conference in Paris at the time that his letter appeared. It was received there with painful amazement. However, it is satisfactory to know that Lord

Lansdowne was misunderstood both by his friends and by his critics, and that the whole weight of his authority and influence may be reckoned on the side of the enforcement of what I call the Wilson policy.[61]

Lloyd George then went on to argue the familiar case that victory was absolutely necessary if justice and permanent peace were to be achieved. The Prussian criminals had to be punished or the world would be subject to the terror of successful bandits.

On the same day that Lloyd George delivered this speech, Wiseman cabled further congenial remarks to House, who had by then returned home. "President's speech to Congress enthusiastically received in England," he observed. "It expresses perfectly British sentiment and is excellent antidote to Lansdowne Letter which is now generally recognized as unfortunate blunder."[62] Wiseman undoubtedly assumed that House would pass this flattering comment on to the president.

Despite Lloyd George's public identification with the president's address, it was suggested in the House of Commons that the British government's statements actually contrasted with Wilson's. Balfour again denied this:

They [the British and American statements] seem to me to be absolutely identical in spirit, and I do not think there has been in the whole history of the world more powerful State documents than those which have been issued from time to time by the President of the United States of America.[63]

During the course of debate on 19 December, Arthur Ponsonby accused the government of hiding behind President Wilson's reply in regard to the pope's note. Balfour retorted that he presumed the accusation meant "no more than that when a statement of policy has been admirably made by the head of a great Republic with whom we are carrying on the War . . . very often it is not necessary that it should at once be copied by everyone who may agree with it on this side of the Atlantic." He added, on the other hand, that, if Ponsonby meant that explicit statements of British policy had not been made, he was profoundly mistaken and was unfairly ignoring the statements on record. Balfour's own note of January, 1917, which commented on the Allies' reply to President Wilson, was one example.

After Ponsonby had accused the British government of hiding behind the president, he had added a very sour assessment of British policy statements. "President Wilson makes a speech," he said, "and all we can get from the War Cabinet are variations of the knock-out blow theme, disparaging remarks about the League of Nations, and hints that the economic war is still

[59] Lloyd George Papers, F/6/5/10. The last remark quoted is questionable. Lansdowne advocated suspending judgment on the rearrangement of South Eastern Europe.
[60] Wilson, 1970: p. 319.

[61] Scott, 1921: pp. 210-215.
[62] Telegram from Wiseman to House, 14 Dec., 1917, Balfour Papers, Add. MSS. 49687.
[63] *Parliamentary Debates,* Commons **100**: cols. 2009-2010 (19 Dec., 1917).

part of the policy of His Majesty's Government." [64] Lloyd George was provoked by what he perceived as the point of this and other remarks in the debate. On the following day, 20 December, he rhetorically asked in the House of Commons whether the honorable members who had participated in the debate were merely seeking to criticize ministers or were actually trying to find out exactly what the country's war aims were. "I am told," he said, "that I never said anything which in the least traveled in the same direction as President Wilson. I failed to see in any speech delivered yesterday a single word about what I said at Glasgow." [65] He then proceeded to reiterate some of the points he had made in late June. Lloyd George's tone was more moderate than it had been on 14 December, though he still argued that the temper of the Prussian military caste must be destroyed before the world could live in peace. "That is why," he declared, ". . . we say— whether it is President Wilson or my right honourable friend, Mr. Asquith, or myself—that victory is an essential condition." [66]

5. THE BRITISH AND AMERICAN DECLARATIONS OF WAR AIMS, JANUARY, 1918

The pressure upon the British government for a more definite statement of war aims continued to mount until 5 January, when the prime minister delivered the most complete official British statement made during the war. Various factors had brought matters to a head. The War Cabinet had recently sent General Smuts to Switzerland for a meeting with Count Mensdorff, who urged the Allies to restate their war aims. Lloyd George's principal private secretary, Philip Kerr, who had accompanied Smuts to Switzerland and who had interviewed an Egyptian intermediary about conditions in Turkey, also reported that a restatement would be useful.

Another impetus came from a speech by the Austro-Hungarian foreign minister, which was delivered on Christmas day at the recently convened conference at Brest-Litovsk. On behalf of the Central Powers, Count Czernin accepted, with various qualifications, Trotsky's proposals for a general peace. Lloyd George felt very strongly that a reply to Czernin was necessary and the War Cabinet agreed. [67] The Allies had been embarrassed during December by the Bolshevik's publication of the secret treaties, which seemed to support accusations that the Allies' war aims were imperialistic and added weight to the argument that a restatement of aims was imperative. This consideration was force-

fully put to the prime minister in a joint letter from the head of the Trades Union Congress, C. W. Bowerman, and the leader of the Parliamentary Labour party, Arthur Henderson. [68]

Lloyd George's reply was evasive, but he was undoubtedly anxious to satisfy organized Labour at this time. [69] The government needed to comb out more men from industry to reinforce the western front. The war aims statement was, of course, delivered to trade-union leaders. The decision to address this particular audience obviously reveals something of the importance attached to Labour's views, though it does not necessarily imply that Parliament was being ignored. Parliament was in recess. [70]

An essential element in this decision was the evidence that the Labour movement actually favored war aims which were substantially in agreement with the aims that the War Cabinet was prepared to announce. In his *War Memoirs* Lloyd George recalled: "The Parliamentary Committee of the Trade Union Congress and [the Executive Committee] of the Labour Party had already formulated their peace proposals on December 16th. They did not differ," he observed, "in any material respect from those which we were putting forward." [71] His account has been questioned, but it is actually quite accurate for Lloyd George. [72] The Labour peace proposals were circulated as a "Memorandum on War Aims" on 17 December. [73] A special conference of the British Labour movement accepted the memorandum on the twenty-eighth. Lloyd George also had an interview with a deputation from the British Labour party which reinforced the impression that Labour's views coincided with those of the government. [74]

One other factor may have been in the minds of British leaders. House had undoubtedly made it clear to them that the president might make a major statement on war aims. This was probably not decisive, but it may have spurred the British government to action. Wiseman later stressed this interpretation, [75] and there were several possible motives which lend it plausibility. The British may have wanted to anticipate Wilson's declaration in order to steal some of his thunder. Moreover, if their statement followed the

---

[64] *Ibid.*, col. 2006.
[65] See p. 54 above.
[66] Scott, 1921: pp. 216–220.
[67] War Cabinet minutes, 31 Dec., 1917, CAB 23/13/308A/3; War Cabinet minutes, 3 Jan., 1918, CAB 23/5/312/8; Hankey, 1961: 2: p. 737; Lloyd George to H. M. the King, 27 Dec., 1917, Lloyd George Papers, F/29/1/53; Cecil to Balfour, 27 Dec., 1917, Balfour Papers, Add. MSS. 49738.

[68] See C. W. Bowerman and Arthur Henderson to Lloyd George, 20 Dec., 1917, Lloyd George Papers, F/27/3/22.
[69] Lloyd George to C. W. Bowerman and Arthur Henderson, 27 Dec., 1917, Lloyd George Papers, F/27/3/23.
[70] The War Cabinet minutes of a meeting on 3 Jan., 1918 record: "It was generally agreed that if the House of Commons had been sitting, that would be the proper place for the Prime Minister to make a statement." CAB 23/5/313/1. *Cf.* Taylor, 1964: p. 35.
[71] Lloyd George, 1936: 5: p. 39.
[72] Taylor, 1957: p. 156 and 156n.
[73] See London *Times*, 18 Dec., 1917.
[74] War Cabinet minutes, 31 Dec., 1917, CAB 23/4/308/9.
[75] Wiseman to House, 20 Mar., 1933, and Wiseman's "Notes for Dr. Seymour," 19 Dec., 1927, Wiseman Papers.

president's, it might appear that they had been forced by him into making a moderate statement. Perhaps, in part, Lloyd George's speech was also, as Victor Mamatey has suggested, "an effort to steer him [Wilson] along safe channels."[76] The importance of such considerations remains a matter for speculation.

There is, however, definite evidence in the War Cabinet minutes that the British leaders had the president in mind when they decided upon making an independent statement. When they agreed that a reply, couched in moderate terms, must be made to Czernin's peace move at Brest-Litovsk, it was obvious that a joint Allied document would be "extremely difficult to draft." A joint statement would also be "apt to lose all its effectiveness and individuality and to become merely a cumulative statement of every country's claims." The War Cabinet minutes of 31 December record that

Lord Robert Cecil pointed out there were considerable advantages in President Wilson's method of issuing statements entirely on the responsibility of the United States Government, although it would be more courteous for us at least to inform our Allies of the purport of our statement before it was issued.[77]

On 3 January, 1918, the prime minister, after reiterating the disadvantages of consulting the Allies, also concluded that the War Cabinet "ought to adopt President Wilson's plan of an independent statement."[78]

This step was, of course, adopted. The British were true to the president's method in all its essential aspects. With perhaps one exception, Britain's Allies were not given an opportunity to offer criticism of the statement prior to publication. Special care was taken, however, to explain the statement to the president. On the afternoon of 5 January, the War Cabinet decided:

That a telegram should be sent by the Foreign Office to the British Ambassador, Washington, directing him to notify the United States Government for the personal information of the President, that for the last week or two the Prime Minister and the War Cabinet have been in negotiation with the trades in regard to the release of the Government from certain pledges made earlier in the war, such release being indispensable to the development of our manpower for military purposes. The negotiations had reached a point at which success turned mainly on the immediate publication of a statement on War Aims by the Government. After consulting the leaders of the Opposition and the Labour leaders, the Prime Minister made an important national statement of War Aims to the Trades Unionist Conference that morning. The British Ambassador should explain that there was not time to consult our Allies in regard to the text of the statement, which, however, they would find to be in accordance with President Wilson's declarations.[79]

This explanation had the advantage of referring to a

domestic problem, which made an independent statement seem more justifiable.

The Foreign Office promptly carried out the War Cabinet's instructions. The telegram to Washington also contained the following remarks:

Should the President himself make a statement of his own views which in view of the appeal made to the peoples of the world by the Bolsheviki might appear a desirable course, the Prime Minister is confident that such a statement would also be in general accordance with the lines of the President's previous speeches, which in England as well as in other countries have been so warmly received by public opinion. Such a further statement would naturally receive an equally warm welcome.[80]

Meanwhile, House had cabled to London on the same day that the president felt "he must presently make some specific utterance as a counter to the German peace suggestion, and that . . . the utterance must be in effect a repetition of his recent address to Congress, in even more specific form than before." The president hoped that no statement was in contemplation on the British side "which would be likely to sound a different note or suggest claims inconsistent with what he [Wilson] proclaims the object[s] of the United States to be." The cable, which had actually been drafted by Wilson himself, explained: "The President feels that we have so far been playing into the hands of the German Military Party, and solidifying German opinion against us, and he has information which seems to open a clear way to weaken the hand of that Party and clear the air of all possible misrepresentation and misunderstandings."[81]

The president's famous address was delivered on 8 January. It was by and large in harmony with Lloyd George's statement, though there were some important differences.[82] The president's first point read as follows:

Open covenants of peace, openly arrived at, after which there shall be no private international understanding of any kind, but diplomacy shall proceed always frankly and in the public view.[83]

The British speech contained no reference to open diplomacy. In a Foreign Office minute about Wilson's address, Sir Ronald Graham, an assistant under-secretary of state, commented: "As regards the old bug bear of 'secret diplomacy' never has it come in for so much general abuse or general use as at the present moment."[84]

Wilson's second point also had no counterpart in

---

[76] Mamatey, 1957: p. 175.
[77] CAB 23/5/308A/3.
[78] CAB 23/5/312/8.
[79] CAB 23/5/315/2. If Balfour had not been ill early in Jan., perhaps Wilson would have been informed sooner.

[80] Published in Seymour, 1928: 3: p. 340. This passage does not appear on the Foreign Office copy. See F.O. 371/3435/593/3754.
[81] Telegram from House to Drummond, 5 Jan., 1918, Balfour Papers, Add. MSS. 49687. See also Seymour, 1928: 3: p. 339n.
[82] According to House, the president momentarily thought that the British statement was so similar to his own that he should abandon his plans to address Congress. See Seymour, 1928: 3: p. 341.
[83] Scott, 1921: pp. 234–239.
[84] F.O. 371/3486/4441/4441.

Lloyd George's statement. It read:

Absolute freedom of navigation upon the seas, outside territorial waters, alike in peace and in war, except as the seas may be closed in whole or in part by international action for the enforcement of international covenants.

The British regarded this as the most disagreeable of the Fourteen Points.

The president's third point was as follows:

The removal, so far as possible, of all economic barriers and the establishment of an equality of trade conditions among all the nations consenting to the peace and associating themselves for its maintenance.

Near the end of his address, Wilson added that the United States did not wish to fight Germany "either with arms or with hostile arrangements of trade if she is willing to associate herself with us and the other peace-loving nations of the world in covenants of justice and law and fair dealing."[85] The British statement did not contradict the president's point as far as permanent trade arrangements were concerned, but it did reflect their greater interest in preparing for the reconstruction period. Lloyd George said:

The economic conditions at the end of the war will be in the highest degree difficult. Owing to the diversion of human effort to warlike pursuits, there must follow a world shortage of raw materials which will increase the longer the war lasts, and it is inevitable that those countries which have control of the raw materials will desire to help themselves and their friends first.[86]

This meant, in effect, that there would be discrimination against Germany for a period after the war even if Germany capitulated unconditionally.

In his fourth point, Wilson called for the following: "Adequate guarantees given and taken that national armaments will be reduced to the lowest point consistent with domestic safety." The British statement was more prudent. Lloyd George said: "We must seek by the creation of some international organisation to limit the burden of armaments. . . ."

The president's fifth point read as follows:

A free, open-minded, and absolutely impartial adjustment of all colonial claims, based upon a strict observance of the principle that in determining all such questions of sovereignty the interests of the populations concerned must have equal weight with the equitable claims of the government whose title is to be determined.

The British statement leaned further than Wilson in the direction of the principle of "consent of the gov-

erned." Lloyd George stated:

With regard to the German colonies, I have repeatedly declared that they are held at the disposal of a conference whose decisions must have primary regard to the wishes and interests of the native inhabitants of such colonies. . . . The governing consideration . . . in all these cases must be that the inhabitants should be placed under the control of an administration acceptable to themselves, one of whose main purposes will be to prevent their exploitation for the benefit of European capitalists or governments.

Unlike Wilson, of course, Lloyd George had not referred to "all colonial claims."

The president's sixth point dealt very sympathetically with Russia. He declared:

The evacuation of all Russian territory and such a settlement of all questions affecting Russia as will secure the best and freest cooperation of the other nations of the world in obtaining for her an unhampered and unembarrassed opportunity for the independent determination of her own political development and national policy and assure her of a sincere welcome into the society of free nations under institutions of her own choosing; and, more than a welcome, assistance also of every kind that she may need and may herself desire. The treatment accorded Russia by her sister nations in the months to come will be the acid test of their good will, of their comprehension of her needs as distinguished from their own interests, and of their intelligent and unselfish sympathy.

Lloyd George's statement took a harder line, which reflected a sense of betrayal. Harold Nicolson later summarized it very succinctly: "If Russia deserts her Allies they cannot help her."[87] In case serious peace negotiations did materialize, the prime minister obviously intended that Allied concessions would be made chiefly at Russia's expense.[88]

Wilson's point seven dealt with the Belgium question.

Belgium, the whole world will agree, must be evacuated and restored, without any attempt to limit sovereignty which she enjoys in common with all other free nations. No other single act will serve as this will serve to restore confidence among the nations in the laws which they have themselves set and determined for the government of their relations with one another. Without this healing act the whole structure and validity of international law is forever impaired.

The president made no explicit reference to reparations. In calling for the complete political, territorial, and economic restoration of Belgium's independence, Lloyd George added a demand for "such reparation as can be made for the devastation of its towns and prov-

---

[85] On 25 Jan., after an interview with the president, Wiseman cabled: "He feels that control of raw materials which England and America have will be weapons of enormous value at a Peace Conference and he is prepared to use them to the full if necessary to bring the German military party to reason." F.O. 800/223/U.S./2. Wiseman sent a more detailed report to Drummond by bag which added that Wilson "had no doubt the Senate would quickly ratify any Peace terms he submitted." Lloyd George Papers, F/60/2/42.

[86] Scott, 1921: pp. 225–233.

[87] CAB 24/5/203. Nicolson prepared a tabular summary of the two speeches.

[88] This is one of the few important aspects of the British statement which can be attributed exclusively to Lloyd George. The main body of the prime minister's speech was contributed by Smuts and Cecil. See, Rothwell, 1971: pp. 149–152. In typical contrast, Wilson's address was substantially his own work, though he listened to House's advice and relied in parts on a memorandum which the Inquiry had produced. See Gelfand, 1963: pp. 134–153.

inces." He said that this was no demand for war indemnity such as Germany imposed on France in 1871. It was not an attempt to shift the cost of warlike operations onto another belligerent. Rather it was a vindication of the public law of Europe which Germany had breached. "Unless international life is recognized by insistence on payment for injury done in defiance of its canons," he argued, "it can never be a reality."

The president's eighth point was less emphatic than his observation on Belgium.

All French territory should be freed and the invaded portions restored, and the wrong done to France by Prussia in 1871 in the matter of Alsace-Lorraine, which has unsettled the peace of the world for nearly fifty years, should be righted, in order that peace may once more be made secure in the interest of all.

In reference to Alsace-Lorraine, the British statement declared: "We mean to stand by the French Democracy to the death in the demand they make for reconsideration of the great wrong of 1871. . . ."

As far as the ninth point was concerned the American and British statements were very similar. Wilson said: "A readjustment of the frontiers of Italy should be effected along clearly recognizable lines of nationality." Lloyd George stated: "We regard as vital the satisfaction of the legitimate claims of the Italians for union with those of their own race and tongue."

The British and American statements were also in accord on the more general question of the nationalities within the Austro-Hungarian Empire. Referring to Wilson's address of 4 December, 1917, Lloyd George said:

Though we agree with President Wilson that the breakup of Austria-Hungary is no part of our war aims, we feel that unless genuine self-government on true democratic principles is granted to those Austro-Hungarian nationalities who have long desired it, it is impossible to hope for the removal of those causes of unrest in that part of Europe which have so long threatened its general peace.

Wilson's tenth point brought him closely in line with this position. He declared: "The peoples of Austria-Hungary, whose place among the nations we wish to see safeguarded and assured, should be accorded the freest opportunity of autonomous development."

The eleventh point dealt with thorny problems of the Balkans.

Roumania, Serbia, and Montenegro should be evacuated; occupied territories restored; Serbia accorded free and secure access to the sea; and the relations of the several Balkan States to one another determined by friendly counsel along historically established lines of allegiance and nationality; and international guarantees of the political and economic independence and territorial integrity of the several Balkan States should be entered into.

Lloyd George also demanded the restoration of Serbia, Montenegro, and the occupied part of Rumania, but he went further in regard to Rumania.[89] The British intended "to press that justice be done to men of Roumanian blood and speech in their legitimate aspirations." On the other hand, the prime minister made no reference to Serbia's access to the sea.

Wilson's twelfth point read as follows:

The Turkish portions of the present Ottoman Empire should be assured a secure sovereignty, but the other nationalities which are now under Turkish rule should be assured an undoubted security of life and an absolutely unmolested opportunity of autonomous development, and the Dardanelles should be permanently opened as a free passage to the ships and commerce of all nations under international guarantees.

This harmonized closely with the British position. Lloyd George said:

While we do not challenge the maintenance of the Turkish empire in the home lands of the Turkish race with its capital at Constantinople, the passage between the Mediterranean and the Black Sea being internationalized and neutralized—Arabia, Armenia, Mesopotamia, Syria, and Palestine are in our judgment entitled to a recognition of their separate national condition.

The president's declaration about Poland was much less vague than the previous two points. The thirteenth point stated:

An independent Polish State should be erected which should include the territories inhabited by indisputable Polish populations, which should be assured a free and secure access to the sea, and whose political and economic independence and territorial integrity should be guaranteed by international covenant.

Lloyd George merely said: "We believe . . . that an independent Poland, comprising all those genuinely Polish elements who desire to form part of it is an urgent necessity for the stability of Western Europe." He made no reference to Poland's access to the sea.

The president's fourteenth point was, from his perspective, the most important. "A general association of nations must be formed," he declared, "under specific convenants for the purpose of affording mutual guarantees of political independence and territorial integrity to great and small States alike." Lloyd George's statement regarding the League of Nations was much more reserved. He said:

We are confident that a great attempt must be made to establish by some international organisation an alternative to war as a means of settling international disputes. . . . We must seek by the creation of some international organisation to limit the burden of armaments and diminish the probability of war.

The British statement did not suggest making any guarantees of political independence or territorial integrity.

[89] The British government later received information that Wilson's speech had "a very serious effect in Roumania." It seemed to have stimulated demands in Rumania for immediate peace. Drummond to J. T. Davies, private secretary to the prime minister, 23 Jan., 1918. Lloyd George Papers, F/3/3/1.

At the end of his address to Congress, Wilson made one further point—one which was not numbered. He declared that the United States did not presume to suggest alterations in Germany's institutions, but he added that it would be necessary, before entering into any "intelligent dealings" with her, to know whether her spokesman represented the Reichstag majority or the military party. Thus, in this speech he did not deny that he would interfere with Germany's internal affairs. He merely denied that he would dictate their constitution. All he demanded was a shift of power within Germany's existing constitutional structure. Lloyd George, delivering the British statement, again took the line that the democratization of Germany would make it easier to conclude a peace with her, but that it was a question for the German people to decide.

The British government and the American administration were full of praise for each other's statements. On 6 January, House cabled to the prime minister: "Congratulations and felicitations over your great speech."[90] He added that it was a long step in the right direction and was warmly approved in America. On the same day, Spring Rice cabled that the president had read the prime minister's speech with satisfaction and had no criticism to offer.[91] In his speech to Congress, the president publicly praised the prime minister's statement for its "admirable candor" and "admirable spirit." On 10 January, after a private conversation with Wilson, Spring Rice sent a telegram to the Foreign Office which reported that Wilson "was much pleased" with the prime minister's statement and believed his own speech would meet with the approval of the British government.[92]

Wilson clearly wanted the British to express their approval of his address. On the same day, Spring Rice also sent a "personal and secret" telegram saying that he gathered that the "President would have been glad of an expression of opinion from H. M. Government about his speech."[93] Before this message arrived, Balfour more than reciprocated Wilson's praise in a speech at Edinburgh. The Foreign Office's reply to Spring Rice on 12 January pointed out Balfour's flattering remarks, but in case a further message seemed desirable, the ambassador was authorized to express the prime minister's gratitude for the presi-

dent's declaration and his happiness at finding their respective peace policies "so entirely in harmony."

The praise was purposely general and vague. In a further passage marked "private," the telegram stated: "You will no doubt realize that there are certain obstacles to a more precise endorsement, and there are naturally some slight divergencies between the two speeches."[94] Obviously the British wanted to minimize the differences.

During the friendly exchange of praise between the two governments, Spring Rice was enduring a personal crisis. His government had finally recalled him, and he retreated to Canada to nurse his grievously wounded pride. He died there a month later. Meanwhile Colville Barclay, counselor of the British Embassy, communicated the substance of the Foreign Office's message to the president on 17 January and reported Wilson's cordial reply:

It has been a matter of genuine gratification to me to find my own programme of peace so entirely consistent with the programme set forth by Mr. Lloyd George, and the speech of Mr. Balfour, to which Sir C. Spring Rice was kind enough to call attention, has afforded me the deepest satisfaction.[95]

Wilson, too, wanted to minimize any disagreements.

Occasionally declarations of British-American unanimity were extravagant. In his "Fourteen Points" address, Wilson declared that there was "no confusion of counsel among the adversaries of the Central Powers, no uncertainty of principle, no vagueness of detail." This was a remarkable claim. Differences and doubts were apparent then just as they are in retrospect. For example, Lloyd George, after delivering a second speech to trade-union leaders on 18 January, was asked whether the views on freedom of the seas which Wilson had expressed were the views of the British government. If they were not the same, the questioner wanted to know what the government's views were. This confronted the prime minister with an interesting task. He had to avoid contradicting Wilson without endorsing freedom of the seas.

Actually, the president had made it fairly easy for him. Wilson's point two had a clause in it which mitigated the demand for absolute freedom of navigation in both peace and war. He had added: "except as the seas may be closed in whole or in part by international covenants." In the Foreign Office, Sir Ronald Graham observed that the reservations in point two "appear to mitigate its force considerably."[96] The vagueness of Wilson's qualification clearly meant that there was room to maneuver. Moreover, the closing

[90] Lloyd George Papers, F/60/2/38. House's message was reported in the London *Times*, 8 Jan., 1918.

[91] F.O. 371/3435/593/4061. The British ambassador's telegram was received on the seventh. His information was apparently based on a conversation with House. The cable ended with the statement that the "President would no doubt be grateful for any hints as to attitude of Labour Party in England and France." The Foreign Office took note of this and arranged for memoranda on the Labour Movement to be sent to Washington for the president. Their main theme was that the great majority of Labour were in favor of active prosecution of the war. F.O. 395/22/37233/37233, 43315, 66909.

[92] F.O. 371/3435/593/6381.

[93] F.O. 800/209.

[94] *Ibid.*

[95] Telegram from Barclay, 17 Jan., 1917, F.O. 800/209. For further congenial remarks by Wilson, see Wiseman's cable of 25 Jan., 1918, reporting an interview with the president. F.O. 800/223/U.S./2. See also the more detailed report which Wiseman sent by bag. Lloyd George Papers, F/60/2/42.

[96] See the minutes in F.O. 371/3486/4441/4441.

of the seas to enemy commerce had not been ruled out. The president reinforced this impression in his conversation with Spring Rice on 10 January. The British ambassador reported that Wilson's statement "about freedom of the seas was to be interpreted in the sense that all restrictive measures should be based on a formal agreement of nations brought into conformity with modern conditions." The president felt that the "old rules of blockade were plainly inapplicable now but no one nation should be allowed to be sole and arbitrary interpreter." This remark was not without some sting, but it nevertheless allowed for restrictive measures. Furthermore, the president was not entirely unsympathetic to the British position. According to Spring Rice, he commented that the British Empire, in contrast to the German Empire, was a union of free peoples and that "Great Britain had to keep a strong fleet for preservation of means of subsistence and also for police purposes." [97]

In response to the trade unionist's question about freedom of the seas, Lloyd George exploited the loop holes in the president's position. He said that he wanted "to know what 'freedom of the seas' means." Did it mean freedom from submarines or Britain's starvation? "After all," he observed, "we are in a very different position from America, or Germany or France, or any other continental country." As an island, Britain must carefully scrutinize "any proposal which might impair her ability to protect her lines of communication across the seas." He went on: "Freedom of the seas is a very elastic term. There is a sense in which we would rejoice to accept it, but we must," he said, "guard very carefully against any attempt to interfere with the capacity to protect our shores and our shipping that has alone enabled us even to exist up to the present moment."

Later the prime minister was asked to indicate what steps would be taken to consolidate the respective war aims of America and the Allies in order to present a unified front to the Germans. Lloyd George replied that they had hoped to consolidate war aims at the conference in Paris two months earlier, and he blamed their failure on the absence of representatives of the Russian government. He also asserted that, if there were any doubt about the Allies' war aims which had been stated by the president and himself, it would be desirable to meet, but so far they had had "nothing but complete assent." [98]

Since Wilson was willing to cooperate with this kind of verbal maneuver in the interest of waging an all-out war against Germany, potentially divisive issues were successfully evaded. Freedom of the seas would be the subject of a tense diplomatic confrontation only after Germany was beaten. This was one of the implications of Wilson's policy of maintaining unity with the Allies in order to secure a peace through victory.

6. MORE FLIRTATIONS WITH AUSTRIA-HUNGARY

The new German chancellor, Count George von Hertling, and the Austro-Hungarian foreign minister, Count Czernin, both replied to Wilson's Fourteen Points in concerted speeches on 24 January. They agreed with the general non-territorial points, but neither accepted the particular territorial points which would affect their respective countries adversely. Hertling argued that Russian and Polish questions concerned only Russia, Poland, and the Central Powers. He was evasive about restoring Belgium, and rejected any cession of Alsace-Lorraine. He also foresaw difficulties in settling colonial questions according to Wilson's principles, though he demanded a reconstruction of colonial possessions. [99] In regard to the questions directly affecting Austria-Hungary, Czernin did not commit his government to the evacuation of Italy, Serbia, Montenegro, and Rumania; he refused to make any concessions to Italian claims, and he rejected foreign interference in the monarchy's internal nationality problems. On the other hand, he expressed agreement with Wilson on Poland, and his speech sounded friendlier and more reasonable than the German chancellor's—especially to American ears. Czernin wanted to pursue general peace negotiations by beginning with an exchange of ideas with the United States. He asserted:

Let Herr Wilson employ the great influence which he doubtless possesses over all his allies so that they shall for their part state the conditions upon which they are ready to talk. If he does so he will have rendered the inestimable service of getting general peace negotiations in motion. [100]

The impact of this proposal was heightened by reports that Czernin, before delivering his speech, had intimated that the president had already received his reply. [101]

Entente leaders prepared an official response on 2 February. The third session of the Supreme War Council, meeting at Versailles, agreed on a declaration which contained the following passage.

The Supreme War Council gave the most careful consideration to the recent utterances of the German Chancellor and of the Austro-Hungarian Minister for Foreign Affairs, but was unable to find in them any real approximation to the moderate conditions laid down by all the Allied Governments. This conviction was only deepened by the impression made by the contrast between the professed idealistic aims with which the Central Powers entered upon the present negotiations at Brest-Litovsk, and the new openly discussed plans of conquest and spoli-

---

[97] Telegram from Spring Rice, received 11 Jan., 1918, F.O. 371/3435/593/6381.
[98] Scott, 1921: pp. 240–245.

[99] Ibid., pp. 246–254.
[100] Ibid., pp. 255–261.
[101] Mamatey, 1957: p. 196n.

ation. Under the circumstances the Supreme War Council decided that the only immediate task before them lay in the prosecution with the utmost vigour . . . of the military efforts of the Allies until such time as the pressure of that effort shall have brought about in the enemy Governments and peoples a change of temper which would justify the hope of the conclusion of peace on terms which would not involve the abandonment, in [the] face of an aggressive and unrepentant militarism, of all the principles of freedom, justice, and the respect for the Law of Nations which the Allies are resolved to vindicate.[102]

This statement was published on 4 February, 1918.

On the same day, Wiseman cabled to Balfour that the president was "not altogether pleased" with the message.[103] This was something of an understatement. Wilson was undoubtedly angry. Though the declaration created the impression that the United States government was a party to it, he had not been consulted. Wilson had given his blessing to the Supreme War Council, and had appointed a military representative, General Tasker H. Bliss; however, he did not seat a political delegate. House had attended the second session as his representative in December, 1917. After that, Arthur Hugh Frazier of the United States Embassy in Paris monitored the meetings but did not participate in the Council's deliberations.[104] House would not attend again until the end of the war. In this way Wilson tried to avoid compromising his independent diplomatic position while still promoting military cooperation. He felt that he could not allow the Supreme War Council to make political statements which might seem to have the approval of the United States. Frazier was told to make it clear that the Supreme War Council must not make such statements unless the president himself approved of them. Furthermore, Lansing addressed a letter to Lord Reading, who had replaced Spring Rice as ambassador, warning that political statements by the Supreme War Council might make it necessary to review American participation in the organization.[105]

The president also emphatically disagreed with the Supreme War Council's interpretation of Count Czernin's speech. This emerged in public on 11 February, when Wilson again addressed Congress. He drew a sharp distinction between the addresses of Czernin and Hertling. The president described Hertling's speech as "very vague and very confusing." It was, he said "certainly in a different tone from that of Count Czernin, and apparently of an opposite purpose." Moreover, Wilson was very gentle at the beginning of his address when refuting Czernin's intimation that

his views were communicated to Washington before they were made public. He said that he was "sure" the foreign minister had been misunderstood.[106]

The president did not deny that Czernin's speech had deficiencies, but he was inclined to excuse them. He thought Czernin "would probably have gone much farther had it not been for the embarrassments of Austria's alliances and of her dependence upon Germany." Wilson stated that the test of whether it was possible to go further in the comparison of views was, after all, simple and obvious. He then listed the four vague principles known as his Four Supplementary Points: (1) that each part of the peace settlement must be based upon its essential justice; (2) that peoples and provinces are not to be bartered about as pawns, even in the great balance of power game, now forever discredited; (3) every territorial settlement must be made in the interest of the populations concerned; and (4) that all well-defined national aspirations shall be accorded the utmost satisfaction possible without introducing or perpetuating elements of discord that would be likely to break the peace. The president suggested that these principles were accepted everywhere as imperative "except among the spokesmen of the military and annexationist party in Germany."[107]

On 12 February, after Wilson's speech had appeared in the British press, Lloyd George acknowledged that there was a great difference between the tone of the Austrian speech and the German speech, but he maintained that there was little difference in substance. He found nothing in either speech which indicated a readiness to make peace on acceptable terms.[108] Balfour took a similar line in a muddled speech on the following day.[109]

The difference of opinion between Wilson and the British government caused some public comment, but the irritation was rapidly mollified. After a long interview with the president on 15 February, Lord Reading reported that no mention was made of the different views of Czernin's speech. He had discussed the matter with Lansing who attributed no importance to it, and Reading thought that raising the matter with Wilson would be inadvisable.[110] Several days earlier, the new British ambassador had attempted to smooth relations by extravagantly praising Wilson's speech in a conversation with House. As Reading un-

---

[102] CAB 28/3/44.
[103] Lloyd George Papers, F/60/2/37.
[104] Trask, 1961: pp. 39 and 46.
[105] Reading cabled the text of Lansing's letter to the Foreign Office on 19 Feb., 1918. F.O. 371/3431/41/32763. The protest, which had been sent to the French and Italian ambassadors in identic terms, also referred to action by the Inter-Allied Council on War Purchases and Finance in regard to recognition of the Bolshevik authorities.

[106] Ambassador Page was instructed to reassure the British that the United States was not talking to the Central Powers behind their backs. See Lansing's telegrams to Page, 29 Jan. and 1 Feb., 1918, *Foreign Relations, 1918, Supplement 1, 1*: pp. 51–52 and 67.
[107] Scott, 1921: pp. 265–271.
[108] *Ibid.*, pp. 271–273.
[109] *Ibid.*, pp. 273–277. See also Balfour's gingerly criticism of Wilson in the House of Commons on 27 Feb., 1918, p. 286.
[110] F.O. 371/3486/4556/30373.

doubtedly expected, House duly conveyed the flattery to the president.[111]

It was, of course, no time for the British and American governments to dwell upon their differences. Moreover, their public statements about Czernin's speech seemed to imply a greater difference of opinion than actually existed. Charles Seymour long ago pointed to some irony in the Supreme War Council's deliberations. The Allied leaders suggested that their declaration, which proved irksome to the president, was meant to promote Wilson's policy of detaching the German people from their rulers.[112] During the Supreme War Council meeting on 2 February, Lloyd George explicitly debated this particular point with Baron Sonnino. Wilson has often been criticized for his excessive faith in the power of words, but here Lloyd George professed a similar confidence. The procès-verbal of the meeting states: "He was inclined to believe that a statement to the effect that our aim was to do away with militarism would divide the enemy nations rather than consolidate them." Furthermore, the British prime minister argued not only in terms of political propaganda, but also of personal conviction. He asserted "that the point was no [sic] rhetoric, but facts. . . . Peace could never be made until that [unrepentant military] class was overthrown." Sonnino, on the other hand, argued that such declarations would only bind the enemy closer together. Milner, who accompanied Lloyd George at the meeting, agreed with the Italian foreign minister, but he did not want to labor the point as they were obviously in the minority.

The whole episode had begun with a well-intentioned miscalculation. Lloyd George advocated issuing the troublesome declaration because he wanted to avoid the difficulty of formulating a joint declaration of war aims. He also argued that it would be impossible to formulate such a joint statement without consulting President Wilson, which would cause too much delay. This was the context in which the British prime minister reminded his colleagues that the speeches by Hertling and Czernin had shown that the enemy had no intention of relaxing their claims.[113]

The British government was certainly not opposed to the idea of attempting to detach Austria from Germany. At the inter-Allied meetings in Paris at the end of November, 1917, Lloyd George had secured, with the support of Colonel House, permission to try to ascertain informally what Austria-Hungary's peace terms might be.[114] This had been followed by the interviews between General Smuts and Count Mensdorff in Geneva on 18 and 19 December. On 2 January, 1918, Drummond cabled a message from Balfour to the president, which briefly reported the substance of these conversations. The British representative (Smuts was not named in the telegram) had refused to discuss the question of a general peace, and the Austrian held out no hopes of a separate one. Nevertheless, the British representative's statement that the destruction of Austria was no part of British war aims had been received "with much satisfaction." Furthermore, his expression of Britain's strong desire to see the various nationalities of the Hapsburg empire "given an opportunity for autonomous development" was said "to reflect opinion in the 'Highest Quarters.'" Balfour's message to Wilson also reported Austria's wish to renew these conversations. He added that it was "a wish with which the British Government will probably comply." [115]

On 18 January, the War Cabinet discussed a cable from Berne which stated that Czernin would meet Lloyd George in Switzerland if the latter agreed. A mission by the prime minister at that time was ruled out, but the question remained as to whether Smuts should meet Czernin. The War Cabinet decided that, subject to Balfour's concurrence, a reply should be sent to Berne offering to arrange for Smuts to meet the Austrian foreign minister.[116]

When the subject was discussed again in the War Cabinet on 28 January, no action had yet been taken on this decision. Balfour had asked that the matter be postponed until after a visit by Signor Orlando. The Italian Premier had agreed that conversations with Austria "should continue," but by the twenty-eighth, Count Czernin had complicated the situation. The War Cabinet minutes observe that the Austro-Hungarian foreign minister had delivered the speech "in which he had rather suggested a conversation with President Wilson's representatives." Lloyd George doubted whether, in these circumstances, "the moment was favourable for approaching the Austrian Government." This led to further delay. It was decided "that a telegram should be sent, informing President Wilson that we should like to resume the conversations, and inquiring whether in his opinion this was desirable." [117]

This decision was also not carried out by the time the War Cabinet returned to the subject on 4 February, 1918. The secret minutes explain that "Mr. Balfour had drafted a telegram, but, in the Prime Minister's absence at Versailles, the War Cabinet had not thought it right to pursue the matter." Meanwhile, however, another telegram from Switzerland had been

---

[111] House Diary, 11 Feb., 1918.
[112] Seymour, 1928: 3: p. 361.
[113] CAB 28/3/44.
[114] House Diary, 29 Nov., 1917.

[115] Telegram to House from Drummond, 2 Jan., 1918, Balfour Papers, Add. MSS. 49738. Victor Mamatey has noted that Balfour's reference to "an opportunity for autonomous development" was echoed in the Fourteen Points. See Mamatey, 1957: p. 175.
[116] CAB 23/16/325A.
[117] CAB 23/16/331A. See also CAB 23/16/357A.

received, which added impetus to the idea of further talks with Austria. The British minister in Berne reported that Count Skrzynski, counsellor of the Austrian Legation there, had alluded to the possibility of a separate peace between Austria and the Entente.[118] Skrzynski also emphasized that America could be useful in bringing about peace. Lloyd George, now back in London, drew the War Cabinet's attention to this cable and pointed out that it corresponded in some respects with the views of Count Horodyski, a pro-Allies Pole with Austrian connections. The latter had talked with the prime minister and Hankey at Versailles. He had suggested that Austria was near to revolution and that Czernin's overture to Wilson should be exploited. Horodyski did not think that peace discussions were likely to result in a separate peace, but he argued that they could delay the employment of Austrian troops on the western front until revolution broke out.[119]

Lloyd George was understandably attracted by this argument. The British government's greatest source of anxiety at this time was the transfer of enemy troops from the eastern to the western front and the impending enemy offensive which this movement foreshadowed. In the War Cabinet meeting of 18 January the prime minister had, in fact, expressed similar reasons for pursuing talks with Austria-Hungary.[120] On the other hand, Lloyd George was still not immune to bouts of wishful thinking that Austria-Hungary might be lured into a separate peace. This was apparent in his remarks on 4 February about urging the United States to pursue the matter. The War Cabinet minutes continue:

> The Prime Minister pointed out two reasons in favour of conversations between America and Austria:
> (1) It was easier for Austria to make peace with the United States than with anyone else owing to the number of Austrian subjects in that country.
> (2) It was easier for the Italians to yield to the pressure of the U. S. A. than to anyone else in regard to their extravagant war aims.

The advantages of Wilson's position were noted repeatedly in London. In the Foreign Office, for example, Harold Nicolson later observed:

> Although it will be all-important to secure the early defection of Austria, yet the problem is one of infinite complexity, and it is questionable indeed whether a solution could be secured by any one but President Wilson, who is unhampered by engagements to Italy, and whose prestige rests on a basis at once more solid and more spiritual than that of the older belligerents.[121]

Implicit in the British attitude was the realization that it would be easier for them to violate their treaty commitments if Wilson took a strong lead.

The idea of talks between Austrians and Americans was not, of course, endorsed without reservations. Some doubt was expressed in the War Cabinet "as to whether besides Col. House, the United States could find a suitable person to conduct the negotiation." This doubt probably stemmed not only from the British government's conviction that America was critically short of diplomatic ability, but also from their knowledge that Wilson was very reluctant to trust anyone with important negotiations. Such qualms, however, were not decisive. The War Cabinet decided that Balfour should draft, for Lloyd George's consideration, a telegram to Wilson "intimating that the British Government had reason to believe that some advantage might be gained from a conversation between representatives of the Governments of Austria and the United States of America."[122]

A suitable cable was approved by Lloyd George on 6 February and sent to the president through Colonel House. The telegram transmitted Skrzynski's remarks almost verbatim as they had been reported from Berne. Balfour described the information as coming "from a source in touch with Count Czernin" and it was virtually assumed that he had acted under instructions. Czernin was understood to want a separate peace, but he wished "to find a pretext for breaking with Germany" such as having his hand forced by the "Austrian nation." The Austrian public was "wearied" by the slow progress of the peace negotiations with Russia. The emperor, fearing "the 'Red Wave,'" favored a "speedy peace," and tension between Austria and Germany was greater than ever. Continuing with Skrzynski's suggestions, the telegram stated:

> If Austria could be given to understand that in concluding a separate peace she would obtain from America the financial assistance which is absolutely indispensable to her, public opinion would be strong enough to impose such a peace even on partisans of a war to the end. The expediency of America acting as an intermediary between Austria and the Entente is specially emphasized.

Though Balfour appreciated Wilson's advantages, he was clearly apprehensive about the dangers involved. The telegram politely urged the president to proceed very carefully, if the matter were pursued. The recent intimations about a separate peace might be designed "to divide the Entente powers." While Balfour did not want Czernin to feel that his message to the British had been ignored, he feared any show of haste in approaching the Austrians. He pointed out that mere rumors of negotiations on the basis of one undivided Austria not only caused great alarm in Italy, but were used by Austrian diplomats as proof

---

[118] Telegram from Sir H. Rumbold, received 3 Feb., 1918, F.O. 371/3113/2002/21231. This document was brought to the author's attention by Fest, 1970.

[119] CAB 23/16/338A. For Hankey's notes of Horodyski's remarks, see F.O. 371/3440/21235/21235.

[120] CAB 23/16/325A.

[121] Memorandum by Nicolson, 10 Mar., 1918, F.O. 371/3440/40497/40497.

[122] War Cabinet minutes, 4 Feb., 1918, CAB 23/16/338A.

that the Entente had abandoned the cause of the subject nationalities under Hapsburg rule. These were, Balfour acknowledged, considerations which were as familiar to the United States government as to the British, and, "though they show the extreme delicacy of the questions to be solved, they indicate that of all the Allied Powers America is in the best position to solve them." [123]

Thus, the British encouraged Wilson to approach the Austrians well before his address to Congress of 11 February, in which, as we have seen, he publicly courted Czernin. He had also received other enticing news from Switzerland. On 3 and 4 February, Professor Heinrich Lammasch, a prominent Austrian, met George D. Herron, an American living in Switzerland who was widely believed to have the confidence of President Wilson. Lammasch said that the emperor sincerely wanted peace and was prepared to reform his empire, granting autonomy to subject nationalities. Lammasch wanted the president to promote the emperor's efforts by recognizing Austria's readiness for peace and by demanding autonomy for the nationalities. [124]

A week after Wilson's speech of 11 February, Emperor Karl addressed a message to the president through the King of Spain. The emperor said that the president's and Czernin's speeches had materially cleared the European situation and that the time had apparently come when a discussion between one of the emperor's representatives and one representing Mr. Wilson might clear the way to a general peace. The emperor's message differed markedly from the recent overtures made in Switzerland. His position, which was outlined with reference to the president's "four principles," amounted essentially to a proposal of general peace on the basis of the *status quo ante*. He avoided the question of the subject nationalities, with two uncompromising exceptions. He suggested that the satisfaction of certain national demands would only cause future trouble, and he offered to prove that Austria's Italians did not want to be part of Italy.

The British were actually the first to inform the Americans of this message. It was intercepted and deciphered by British Intelligence, who passed it on to Ambassador Page. He cabled it to Washington on 20 February. [125] While waiting for the Spanish to transmit the emperor's message to him, Wilson decided to consult Balfour. He personally drafted a cable inviting "any comments or suggestions. . . ." [126]

The Spanish ambassador in Washington did not deliver the Austrian emperor's message until 25 February. The president said afterward that he had difficulty composing his face and appearing surprised. [127] On the following day, Wiseman cabled a message to Balfour warning that the president did not want to delay an answer and that both Wilson and House were inclined to encourage further discussion. "I have begged them," Wiseman added, "to await your view. . . ." [128]

Balfour replied to the president on 27 February. He had been able to follow developments closely. The Foreign Office had even received an account of the conversation between Lammasch and Herron from Switzerland. [129] Balfour pointed out the difference between the official Austrian message conveyed through Spain, which he attributed to Czernin's hand, and the personal policy of Emperor Karl conveyed by Professor Lammasch. He asserted that the proposals sent through Spain were known to the German emperor and represented his policy. "They amount to success for the Central Powers," Balfour observed, "and can hardly be reconciled with public declarations of [the] President on the subject of Peace terms." The proposals conveyed by Lammasch were much more in harmony with the president's principles, but the British foreign secretary noted two serious objections. The scheme outlined by Lammasch ignored Italy, and it could "alienate the subject races of Austria whom [the] President desired to benefit." Balfour stressed the danger of demoralizing the Italians or discouraging anti-German sentiments among Austria's Slav population. On the other hand, he observed that some risks had to be run, and suggested that if the president wanted to pursue the matter, it might be worth-while to ascertain whether the Lammasch conversations really represented the emperor's views. [130]

Actually, Balfour's advice was unnecessary as far as the Austrian overture through Spain was concerned. Wilson had drafted a cautious reply to the emperor's message before Balfour's telegram of 27 February arrived in Washington. The president's letter politely rejected the Austrian suggestion of secret discussions until the emperor expressed his views more clearly and definitely. [131]

House briefly informed Balfour of this step in a cable which Wiseman transmitted on 1 March. He stated blandly that they had waited until Balfour's telegram of 27 February arrived before reaching a decision. The president was "glad to find (as he fully anticipated)" that Balfour's view agreed substantially

[123] Telegram to Wiseman from Drummond, 6 Feb., 1918, Balfour Papers, Add. MSS. 49687. A copy dated 7 Feb. is in the P.R.O. See F.O. 800/222/Aus/1.

[124] Mamatey, 1957: pp. 219–224; *Foreign Relations, 1918, Supplement 1, 1*: pp. 82–105.

[125] *Foreign Relations, 1918, Supplement 1, 1*: pp. 126–127; Page Diary, 20 Feb., 1918.

[126] Telegram from House to Balfour, 24 Feb., 1918, House Papers.

[127] Baker, 1939: 7: p. 566.

[128] Wiseman to Drummond, 26 Feb., 1918, F.O. 800/222/Aus/3.

[129] Telegram from Sir Horace Rumbold, 13 Feb., 1918, F.O. 371/3113/2002/27390.

[130] F.O. 800/222/Aus/4.

[131] Mamatey, 1957: pp. 229–230.

with his own. House reported that Wilson replied to the message from Spain "in a way which will not close the door to further discussion, but rather develop and probe what the Emperor of Austria has in mind." House also tried to reassure the British. He declared that, if any further conversations took place, the United States would simultaneously redouble her war efforts. Moreover, he stated that Wilson had no intention of allowing the United States to be committed to any further steps unless the Central Powers were prepared to translate general principles into frank and concrete assurances.[132]

Shortly before House's cable was received, the War Cabinet showed that they were in need of reassurance about the idea of Wilson pursuing peace negotiations with Austria. Their earlier doubts had mushroomed. During a secret meeting on 1 March, the prime minister expressed his apprehension about the president's intervention in the question. In Lloyd George's view, "President Wilson was not making a success of his war administration." The United States seemed behind hand in their raising of men, construction of aircraft, shipbuilding, the provision of railway material for France, and the organization of American railways. In such circumstances he feared that the president might want to end the war on conditions which the British could not accept. Lloyd George added that the Austro-Hungarian proposals conveyed through the King of Spain revealed that Wilson's four principles could be interpreted in a hostile sense. Balfour interjected that "they were really platitudes, which could equally easily be interpreted in our [Britain's] favour."

Lloyd George went on to suggest that, if Colonel House came to Europe to discuss peace with Austria, the world would learn of it. The negotiations would be tantamount to a peace conference. The prime minister wanted to tell the president that the British government considered any such conversations dangerous, and that, meanwhile, they would probe Austrian overtures to ascertain the real position. Robert Cecil warned that once the British stated they "were going to hold conversations with Austria, President Wilson would insist that he was the man to do it." (Cecil should have added that Balfour had, with the prime minister's approval, recently told President Wilson that he was the best man to do it.)[133]

Bonar Law wondered whether they were not jeopardizing Austria's apparent willingness to make a separate peace. He had in mind a particularly enticing overture which had recently been received. On 23 February, the British minister in Berne had reported an offer by Skrzynski to furnish a written declaration by Czernin to the effect that Austria would only discuss her own affairs in conversation with England,

America, and the Allies.[134] This seemed to imply that she would discuss a separate rather than a general peace. The British prime minister had replied to Skrzynski through an intermediary that such a message might be helpful. Bonar Law suggested to the War Cabinet that Wilson should be informed that they had received this approach and that they would pursue it.

Cecil favored a more devious course of action. He proposed merely trying to obtain a written message as described by Skrzynski. This was the only chance of remaining undiscovered. "If we sent anyone [to Switzerland]," he explained, "we must tell President Wilson." After considerable discussion, the War Cabinet decided simply to inform their minister in Berne that they awaited further news.[135]

Another encouraging telegram from Switzerland was received on 4 March. It reported that Skrzynski had asked whether the Entente would enter into *pourparlers* for a separate peace if the Austro-Hungarian government declared that they would only discuss questions affecting Austria. Moreover, Skrzynski had intimated that Czernin wanted to conduct the talks himself.[136]

The War Cabinet considered this development on the following day. One of the key points of discussion was whether Britain could enter into conversations with Austria without notifying President Wilson. Once again Balfour championed consultation with Washington. The president, he urged, "should be told everything." Wilson was keeping the British government informed, and once the president thought they were acting behind his back, he would tell them nothing. In opposition to Balfour's argument, it was pointed out with some justification that Wilson had not actually told them "what answer he had given to the King of Spain." This presumably referred to the fact that they had only been sketchily informed.

Apparently it was assumed that Balfour actually wanted to let the president handle the investigations of Austria's position.[137] For it was argued that they should not permit Wilson to stop them from pursuing their own inquiries. Eventually, the War Cabinet agreed that the president should be kept informed "with complete candour" and that reciprocity should be invited from him. They also decided that Philip

---

[132] F.O. 800/222/Aus/5. Published in Seymour, 1928: 3: pp. 378–379.
[133] See pp. 80–81 above.

[134] Telegram from Sir Horace Rumbold, received 24 Feb., 1918, F.O. 371/3113/2002/35034.
[135] CAB 23/16/357A.
[136] Telegram from Sir Horace Rumbold, received 5 Mar., 1918, F.O. 371/3113/2002/40495.
[137] Hankey was certainly attuned to such a suspicion. On 2 Mar., 1918, he wrote to the prime minister, complaining angrily about the Foreign Office's delay. "As to the idea of letting our political and diplomatic lead pass to Wilson," he added, "it is preposterous. We have all at stake; Wilson very little. But we shall automatically lose it if we don't look out." CAB 23/16.

Kerr should be sent immediately to Switzerland to ascertain the meaning of Skrzynski's latest message.[138]

The next day, 6 March, 1918, the foreign secretary tried to get Kerr's mission called off. The War Cabinet minutes recorded the effort as follows:

Sir Eric Drummond, who had been invited in Mr. Balfour's absence (through indisposition) to attend for the purpose, communicated some highly secret information in regard to the probable tenor of President Wilson's reply to Austria. He said that, in view of the satisfactory nature of this reply from our point of view Mr. Balfour considered it would be better to leave the matter for the present in the hands of President Wilson and not to send Mr. Philip Kerr to Switzerland as decided on the previous day.[139]

The highly secret information was almost certainly based on the text of the president's reply which British Intelligence intercepted when it was telegraphed from Madrid to Vienna.[140]

The alternative of leaving the matter to Wilson was attractive to Balfour for various reasons, some of which were devious. Actually, he was dubious about the president negotiating with Austria. As we have seen, for example, he warned him against any action which might discourage the Italians. In fact, during this phase of the war, Balfour was acutely concerned about the president's attitude toward Italy. Near the end of January, Wiseman had reminded the British government that Wilson was "not very much in sympathy with Italy's war aims." The president had heard that the Italian premier had gone to London to demand that the Allies live up to their secret treaties. Wiseman reported that Wilson wanted "to know what H. M. Government proposes to do about it."[141] In response to this message, Balfour wrote the president a letter describing his attitude toward the Treaty of London. The foreign secretary pointed out that Britain was obligated to uphold the agreement, but he clearly hoped that Italy could be induced to accept less than its full terms. He acknowledged objections to Italy's Adriatic claims, and he suggested that she might "not be ill satisfied" with securing "peace and 'Italia Irredenta.'" At the same time, he wondered "whether our difficulty may not be to induce her to go on fighting even for 'Italia Irredenta.'"[142] Evidently Balfour thought that Wilson might eventually help them discreetly to evade some provisions in the Treaty of London, but he feared that the president might help too soon and thereby alienate Rome before the Central Powers were defeated on the western front.[143]

The foreign secretary valued the idea of letting Wilson handle Austrian approaches chiefly as an argument to stop the Kerr mission. He profoundly doubted that Austria could be separated from Germany at that stage of the war. He preferred relying on the president, but this does not necessarily mean that he really approved of Wilson's pursuit of a separate peace. The president's communication with Austria could not be prevented, but, by endorsing the American reply to Austria, Balfour thought he might, at least, be able to postpone the British move. He was very suspicious of Czernin's intentions, as conveyed by Skrzynski, and had again warned that any British approach would be used to alarm the Italians. No doubt the foreign office's disapproval of the use of "amateurs" like Kerr also played a part.

On this occasion, Balfour was overruled. Though the War Cabinet agreed that the nature of Wilson's reply was satisfactory, they "unanimously" refused to change their decision of the previous day. They still did not see why their investigation of Skrzynski's messages should be stopped because Wilson was making his own inquiries, especially since the Austrian reply to Wilson might take a long time. It was also observed that the British Empire's interests should not be entrusted to another nation.[144] Beneath these explicit reasons, there was a general reluctance to follow the president's diplomatic lead as long as an alternative was readily available. A sense of rivalry with America for diplomatic leadership was seldom far from the surface.

Balfour cabled a message to Colonel House on 7 March, informing him that the War Cabinet had decided to send an emissary to Switzerland to explore recent approaches from Austria. He assured House that the emissary would not be empowered to negotiate and that he would keep House informed of the results. Balfour added that he did not think their action was inconsistent with or could be harmful to the president's exchange of messages with the emperor.[145]

Kerr was very sanguine about his prospects of arranging substantive negotiations with Austria, and Lloyd George was anxious to pursue the matter. In response to an encouraging cable which was received from Kerr on 12 March, the prime minister and Hankey drafted a reply which authorized Kerr to arrange a meeting between Smuts and Czernin. Hankey recorded in his diary that Lloyd George sent Drummond to see Balfour with the draft and that Drummond later said "he had a fearful tussle with the foreign secretary, whom he only persuaded to send the

---

[138] War Cabinet minutes, 5 Mar., 1918, CAB 23/16/359A.

[139] CAB 23/16/360A.

[140] See *Foreign Relations, 1918, Supplement 1*, 1: pp. 182–184. See also, Roskill, 1970: 1: p. 505.

[141] Wiseman to Drummond, 25 Jan., 1918, F.O. 800/223/US/2.

[142] Balfour to Wilson, 31 Jan., 1918, Wilson Papers, Series 2.

[143] Balfour made it clear to Ambassador Page that he feared

---

any premature mention of the "unfortunate treaty" with Italy. Page to Lansing, 27 Feb., 1918, *Foreign Relations, 1918, Supplement 1*, 1: pp. 140–141.

[144] CAB 23/16/360A.

[145] F.O. 800/222/Aus/6.

telegram on condition that he was allowed to tell President Wilson. . . ."[146] The foreign secretary cabled a message to House on the same day informing him of the British government's intentions and again assuring him that he would be kept fully informed.[147]

It soon became obvious, however, that Kerr's mission was completely futile, and on 22 March, Balfour sent another cable to House which stated:

Our messenger reports interview with Austrian Agent and change of attitude on the part of Czernin, who no longer proposed meeting with British statesmen on alleged ground that Allies are not so much interested in coming to real settlement with Austria-Hungary as in maneuvering to detach her from Germany.

This cable also reported that the Austrian agent wanted a commitment from the British to the effect that a separate peace would not be discussed at a future meeting.[148]

By this time the matter had been effectively closed by the beginning of Germany's great bid for victory in the West. A terrible blow had been struck on 21 March. Thereafter it became abundantly clear that diplomacy would have to await the results of the offensives. On 2 April, Czernin delivered a speech in which he declared that President Wilson did not want to separate Vienna from Berlin and knew that it would be impossible. He also expressed approval of Wilson's "four principles" as a basis for discussing a general peace. Czernin added that the question was whether the "President would succeed in his endeavor to rally his allies on this basis or not. . . ."[149] When a report of the speech came into the Foreign Office on 3 April, Sir Ronald Graham commented: "This finally disposes of all idea of a separate peace with Austria."[150] On the same day, Balfour cabled a memorandum to House which expressed Czernin's views of the conversations between the British messenger and Austrian agent. This memorandum made it abundantly clear that further talks would be fruitless. Balfour observed at the end of his telegram: "There is evidently nothing more to be done at present."[151] The season of peace talk was closed.

VI.   CRISIS AND VICTORY

Germany's advance on the western front gave her enemies a bad fright. There followed several months of acute anxiety and strenuous efforts to reinforce the western front. Yet, when the tide eventually turned

in midsummer, it moved rapidly against Germany. Indeed, the enemy was defeated before the Allies realized that they had won. The gigantic changes of military fortune forced the pace of poltical events and, in some cases, outran diplomacy.

1. THE HARDENING OF WILSON'S ATTITUDE

The impact of Germany's spring offensive was dramatic in America, and from the British point of view, advantageous. Reading reported to Balfour on 27 March that the battle had been a shock to the administration. His telegram observed:

They had hoped and believed that the effect of the President's speeches had been to strengthen the Liberal party in Germany and sap the morale of the army and the influence of the military party. Today they are very conscious of their delusion, and realise that there is no hope that speeches and propaganda will turn the German people against their military party or detach Austria from Germany. At last they face the fact that if Germany is to be beaten she must be beaten by force.[1]

On 6 April, the anniversary of America's entry into the war, President Wilson delivered a speech which reflected the change of mood in the country. He denounced Germany's military masters for the oppressive peace which they imposed on Russia at Brest-Litovsk and asked rhetorically whether America was not justified in believing that the German military leaders would do the same things along their western front if they were not confronted with armies which they could not overcome. Wilson also suggested that, if the German militarists, when they were finally checked, should propose equitable terms in the West, America could only conclude that they merely wanted to assure themselves a free hand in the East. He warned that a far-reaching German dominion stretching eastwards would force America and those who stood with her "to contest the mastery of the world" lest all of their ideals and principles be ruined.

The president claimed that he did not want to judge harshly "in this moment of utter disillusionment." He said that he was ready "even now" to discuss a just peace at any time it was sincerely proposed. "But the answer," he added, "when I proposed such a peace came from the German commanders in Russia. . . ." The speech ended with this belligerent declaration: "There is . . . but one response possible from us: force, force to the utmost, force without stint or limit, the righteous and triumphant force which shall make right the law of the world, and cast every selfish dominion down in the dust."[2] Lord Reading cabled on 7 April that the president's speech had been received in the United States with the "greatest enthusiasm."

[146] Roskill, 1970: 1: p. 507.

[147] Telegram to Wiseman, 12 Mar., 1918, Balfour Papers, Add. MSS. 49687. A copy in the P.R.O. is dated 13 Mar. F.O. 800/222/Aus/7.

[148] F.O. 800/222/Aus/8.

[149] Scott, 1921: pp. 298–308.

[150] F.O. 371/3435/593/58514.

[151] Telegram to Wiseman from Drummond, 3 Apr., 1918, Balfour Papers, Add. MSS. 49687.

[1] Telegram from Wiseman transmitting a message from Reading for Balfour, 27 Mar., 1918, F.O. 800/223/U.S./14.

[2] Scott, 1921: pp. 309–312.

He went on: "There is no criticism of it which certainly was not the case with speech of February 11th."[3]

During the spring the war spirit in America seemed to grow markedly stronger.[4] In Britain there was also some change in this direction. After three and a half years of slaughter, there was understandably not a dramatic resurgence of enthusiasm for the war, but the country's determination to win deepened. One manifestation of this development was a dramatic reduction in pacifist agitation.[5]

Important changes also developed on the diplomatic front, especially in policies toward Austria-Hungary and her subject nationalities. During April, Clemenceau and Czernin became embroiled in public recriminations which led to the French premier's publication of the famous Prince Sixtus letter. This document revealed that back in March, 1917, Emperor Karl had tried to interest France in peace negotiations by promising support for her "just claims" to Alsace-Lorraine and for the restoration of Belgium. Clemenceau's disclosure left the hapless monarch with no alternative to committing himself more deeply to the German alliance, which he did at a conference with the German emperor at Spa during May, 1918. President Wilson observed to Wiseman on 29 May that the French premier's action had permanently rivetted the Austro-Hungarian government to Germany. When Wiseman reported this to Drummond, he paraphrased the president's conclusions as follows:

Now we had no chance of making a separate peace with Austria, and must look to the other way—the way which he disliked most intensely—of setting the AUSTRIAN people against their own Government by plots and intrigues. We were not good at that work, and generally made a failure of it, but he saw no other way. He intended to support the Czechs, Poles, and Jugo-Slavs.[6]

On the same day Lansing issued a public declaration that the nationalistic aspirations of the Czech-Slovaks and Jugo-Slavs for freedom had the earnest sympathy of the United States government.[7]

The Allies were generally moving in the same direction. On 3 June, at the sixth session of the Supreme War Council, which was held at Versailles, two declarations were approved. The first "noted with pleasure" the statement which Lansing had issued and it expressed "earnest sympathy for the Nationalistic aspirations towards freedom of the Czech-Slovak and Yugo-Slav people." The second stated: "The creation of a united and independent Polish State with free access to the sea constitutes one of the conditions of a solid and just peace, and of the rule of right in Europe." The procés-verbal of the meeting observed that both declarations "were in accordance with the views of President Wilson."[8]

On 28 June, another statement was published which clarified America's anti-Austrian policy still further. Lansing declared the position of the United States government to be "that all branches of the Slav race should be completely freed from German and Austrian rule."[9] The president had, at this late stage of the war, finally committed himself to a policy toward the Austro-Hungarian Empire which was consistent with his reputation as a champion of national self-determination. Since the British had also decided to encourage the break-up of the Habsburg Empire, there was obviously no longer any question of pursuing a separate peace with Austria-Hungary. The British government went on to recognize the Czechoslovak National Council on 9 August. The United States took this step on 3 September.

When the Austro-Hungarian government launched a desperate peace move in mid-September, it received short shrift from the president. In response to Vienna's appeal to all belligerents for confidential conversations about the basic principles of a peace settlement, Wilson declared on 17 September that the United States would "entertain no proposal for a Conference upon a matter concerning which it has made its position and purpose so plain."[10]

Sir William Wiseman thought that the president's intransigence created an opportunity to improve the Lloyd George government's image. In his view the president's brusque action "alienated the semi-pacifist, socialist and advanced labour group." Wiseman promptly sent a telegram to Lord Reading, who had returned to London in August, suggesting that the prime minister now had a chance to show greater statesmanship by seizing on the suggestion of secret negotiations and insisting that the enemy governments must openly state their terms to the democracies.[11]

---

[3] F.O. 371/3491/61542/61813.

[4] For reports of this change, see the following: Telegram from Reading for Wiseman, 13 May, 1918, F.O. 800/223/U.S./43; Reading to Lloyd George, 5 May, 1918, Lloyd George Papers, F/60/2/59; report by Political Intelligence Department, 10 June, 1918, CAB 24/54/4830.

[5] Report circulated by the Home Secretary, 10 Apr., 1918, CAB 24/47/4199.

[6] Telegram from Wiseman to Drummond, 30 May, 1918, published in Fowler, 1969: pp. 271–275.

[7] *Foreign Relations, 1918, Russia* 2: p. 183n.

[8] CAB 28/4/66. Northcliffe, who was at this time directing British propaganda in enemy countries, complained to Balfour about the weakness of the declaration in regard to the Czecho-Slovaks and Jugo-Slavs. Northcliffe to Balfour, 6 June, 1918, F.O. 800/212. In reply, Balfour suggested: ". . . We can defend the declaration to our Yugo-Slav friends by saying (quite truly) that it was in strict conformity with Mr. Lansing's statement, and that American opinion will scarcely go beyond this at present." Balfour to Northcliffe, 8 June, 1918, F.O. 800/212.

[9] *Foreign Relations, 1918, Supplement 1*, 1: p. 816. See also, Mamatey, 1957: pp. 265–270. The president had not intended for this policy to be declared publicly in this way, but it was, nevertheless, an accurate statement of his position.

[10] *Foreign Relations, 1918, Supplement 1*, 1: pp. 306–310.

[11] Telegram from Wiseman to Reading, 17 Sept., 1918, F.O. 800/225. See also Fowler, 1969: pp. 221–222.

Reading cabled to the prime minister, who was visiting Manchester, that he was anxious to communicate with him before a formal answer was sent to Austria-Hungary.[12] Wiseman's suggestion, however, was not carried out. Both Reading and Lloyd George were ill in bed at this time, which delayed action on Wiseman's suggestion because Reading apparently dared not risk explaining it in a telegram. In any case, the suggestion probably came too late. As early as 16 September, Balfour had made a speech rejecting the Austro-Hungarian proposal.[13] His rejection was not as brief as President Wilson's, but it was no less emphatic and had no greater appeal to "semi-pacifist" or Labour sentiment. Moreover, on the fifteenth, Lloyd George himself had instructed Sir Eric Geddes to tell representatives of the press that the Austro-Hungarian proposal was insincere and unacceptable. He thought that it was designed to gain time for the Germans, to paralyze the Allies' armies and to create dissension in Allied countries.[14] After such statements, there was little point in explaining the rejection of the proposal further, though Lloyd George may have been attracted by Wiseman's idea. On 21 September, after returning to London and perhaps after hearing of Wiseman's suggestion, he remarked that the American reply was very brusque and that he thought a more reasoned answer was necessary.[15] Actually, he had expressed a similar sentiment to C. P. Scott as early as 18 September. The prime minister criticized both Wilson and Balfour for their haste in tossing the Austro-Hungarian proposal aside.[16] Yet, he did not act on these sentiments. In fact, he had expressed contradictory opinions in the space of a few days. On 16 September, Lloyd George had sent a telegram to Balfour stating that he had read his speech on the Austrian document with "great satisfaction," and that it struck "exactly the right note."[17] The prime minister was volatile as well as devious, so it may be that he merely changed his mind after sending this cable, but the fact that he had praised the foreign secretary's speech made it more difficult to advocate a markedly different reply. There was, in any case, no compelling need to cater to "semi-pacifist" sentiments. Perhaps the idea of responding to the enemy peace move with a more reasoned reply was simply lost sight of amidst rapid military and diplomatic changes. It was, for instance, during the latter half of September that Bulgaria collapsed.

2. THE QUESTION OF AMERICAN RELATIONS WITH BULGARIA AND TURKEY

During the spring and summer of 1918, British thoughts of detaching one of Germany's allies had turned more and more toward Bulgaria. The problem became entwined with another question, namely, whether the United States should declare war on Bulgaria. This, in turn, was tied to the possibility of taking the same action against Turkey. Demands in America for such steps were increasing, and early in May, Lansing asked the British for their opinions on the issue.[18] The Foreign Office replied on 17 May, recommending a declaration of war against both Bulgaria and Turkey. This would, it was argued, encourage friends and discourage enemies. The Foreign Office also suggested that, if America avoided making the declarations of war, the inference would be drawn by both friends and foes that she meant the various phases of the eastern question would be settled at the peace conference without her active intervention.[19] "His Majesty's Government would," it was added, "regard this as a great misfortune." This remark was not merely flattery. Harold Nicolson commented in an influential memorandum that America alone was "in a position to cut the Gordian knot with which our treaties have involved us."[20]

The Foreign Office's advice was followed by second thoughts. On 14 June, Balfour cabled to Wiseman that he now thought that, before America declared war on Bulgaria, she should warn the latter of her intention, adding that she would take action within a short period unless Bulgaria came forward with reasonable peace proposals. Balfour observed that the present moment was probably unfavorable for any effort to detach Bulgaria, but he suggested that, if the Allies were able to prevent the enemy from achieving any substantial victory on the western front, the situation might completely change in the next five or six weeks. He added that the enormous importance of eliminating Bulgaria from the war was obvious and that the United States could do more than any other power to secure that object. Balfour wanted Wiseman to place these suggestions before Colonel House.[21]

Despite repeated prodding by the British, the administration would not act. Late in August, Wiseman explained the president's views to the Foreign Office

---

[12] Telegram from Reading for the prime minister, 19 Sept., 1918, F.O. 800/225.

[13] London *Times*, 17 Sept., 1918.

[14] Geddes to Balfour, 15 Sept., 1918, and "Memorandum of Meeting with Press Editors," Lloyd George Papers, F/18/2/16.

[15] Riddell, 1933: p. 356.

[16] Wilson, 1970: p. 356.

[17] Telegram from Lloyd George to Balfour, 16 Sept., 1918, F.O. 800/199.

[18] Lansing to Page, 3 May, 1918, *Foreign Relations, 1918, Supplement 1*, 1: p. 222.

[19] *Ibid.*, pp. 232–233.

[20] See Nicolson's memorandum dated 7 May, 1918, F.O. 371/3492/81386/82373. See also his minute in F.O. 371/3448/163316/179302.

[21] F.O. 800/222/Bul/3. Actually, the idea of first threatening Bulgaria with an American declaration of war had already been suggested to the president in May by the military representatives with the Supreme War Council at Versailles. *Foreign Relations, 1918, Supplement 1*, 1: pp. 227–228.

as follows:

He has no sympathy for Bulgaria, nor does he believe in the so-called 'Traditional Friendship' with the U.S.A. He does not regard the Bulgarians as dupes of the Germans, with whom he classes them. While he admits that a declaration of war against Bulgaria might achieve certain political advantages, he is reluctant to declare a war which would be unaccompanied by any definite military action on the part of the U.S.A., considering such a situation empty and undignified.[22]

The Foreign Office documents mention various other reasons why the Americans were reluctant to declare war on Bulgaria, but the main problem seemed to be that the issue was linked to the question of declaring war on Turkey. Lansing told Reading that the United States could not declare war against Bulgaria, "a Christian country," without doing the same against Turkey, a Moslem power. Obviously the administration was reluctant to move against the Ottoman Empire because of American missionary and capitalist interests there. While he acknowledged such concerns, the American secretary of state also suggested that a declaration of war would end the propaganda benefits which flowed from the distribution of relief to the Armenians and Syrians. Upon learning this, Harold Nicolson commented that the Foreign Office would be glad to see the end of the relief schemes which merely brought food and money into Turkey.[23] The president ventured another reason which was less than convincing. He argued that American missionaries and others had prevented massacres and atrocities which would otherwise have occurred. Sir Ronald Graham thought that, on the contrary, Turkish manners would improve after a United States declaration of war. "In the Oriental," he maintained, "fear inculcates respect." Graham despaired of securing an American declaration of war against Turkey, but he advocated continuing efforts to secure an American move against Bulgaria.[24]

House was eventually persuaded to try to get the president to threaten Bulgaria with United States belligerency; however, this was not until mid-September which was very late in the war against that country. On 17 September, Balfour cabled Wiseman instructing him to inform the president most confidentially that a general offensive was about to take place on the Macedonian front. Balfour wanted Wilson to threaten a declaration of war immediately "so as to weaken Bulgarian morale and resistance before the offensive ma-

tures."[25] House conveyed this suggestion to the president with a brief summary of the case in its favor, but the advice came to nothing.[26] Wilson remained neutral in the conflict.

Bulgaria agreed to an armistice at the end of that month which practically amounted to complete surrender. The negotiations were carried out by the Allies' commander-in-chief on the Bulgarian front. The Bulgarian government had asked President Wilson to support its request for an armistice but Bulgarian representatives accepted the Allies' armistice terms at Salonika before Wilson's reply could be considered. Thus, the first of Germany's allies to leave the war did so without involving the president in the negotiations.

Nevertheless, the diplomacy surrounding Bulgaria's departure from the war revealed the inherent danger of Anglo-American antagonism. Wilson replied to the Bulgarian government's request on 27 September, that he would only urge an armistice upon the Allies if the Bulgarians left the armistice conditions to him for decision.[27] Wiseman undoubtedly feared trouble and put forward a reassuring interpretation of the president's action. He sent an urgent cable to Reading on the twenty-seventh suggesting that Wilson had avoided mentioning any particular armistice terms in order to avoid any possible embarrassment to the Allies.[28]

A minor incident proved that Wiseman's fears were justified. While the Bulgarians were pursuing an armistice, the United States minister at Sophia sent a note to the Allied commander, General d'Esperey, demanding mediation by President Wilson.[29] Clemenceau protested to Washington against such intervention, and Lloyd George privately expressed himself as being in general agreement with the French premier's action. Lord Reading and Balfour were at pains to avoid any British response which would be interpreted as a rebuff to Wilson. It was pointed out in a War Cabinet meeting on 1 October that there was no evidence the president would adopt the attitude of his minister at Sophia or that the minister was acting on instructions.[30] Two days later Balfour warned the War Cabinet that Wilson had entered the war for "great world objects" and it might be very important for them to work closely with the United States on settling peace terms. Hence, it would not be politic to associate themselves too closely with Clemenceau's

---

[22] Telegram from Wiseman to Drummond, 28 Aug., 1918, F.O. 371/3493/150195/150195.

[23] Telegram from Reading, 6 May, 1918, and Nicolson's minute dated 8 May, 1918, F.O. 371/3492/81386/81386.

[24] Telegram from Wiseman to Drummond, 28 Aug., 1918, and Graham's minute dated 3 Sept., 1918, F.O. 371/3493/150195/150195. For further American arguments reported to the Foreign Office, see also F.O. 800/222/Bul/4, 5.

[25] F.O. 371/3493/150195/158587. The telegram stressed that the information was most confidential. This was superfluous. The offensive actually began before the telegram was sent.

[26] House to Wilson, 18 Sept., 1918, Wilson Papers, Series 2.

[27] Lansing to Bliss, chargé d'affairs in the Netherlands, 27 Sept., 1918, *Foreign Relations, 1918, Supplement 1*, 1: p. 324.

[28] Telegram from Wiseman to Reading, 17 Sept., 1918, F.O. 800/225.

[29] Telegram from Lord Derby, 30 Sept., 1918, F.O. 371/3448/163316/165014.

[30] CAB 23/8/480/1.

protest. The foreign secretary added that in regard to armistice terms, President Wilson, who was not at war either with Bulgaria or Turkey, had no right to a voice, but that in questions of peace he had this right.[31] The president had, in fact, sent declarations to the Allies on 2 October that the United States regarded every question which concerned the Balkans as an essential part of the general peace settlement. In effect, Wilson was claiming a voice in settling the peace terms even though he had no voice in the armistice negotiations.[32] The prime minister agreed to bear Balfour's points in mind, though not without reiterating his sympathy with Clemenceau's attitude.[33]

After discussing the Bulgarian situation, Balfour explained to the War Cabinet the situation in regard to Turkey. Turkey was obviously tottering. Damascus had fallen on 1 October, and her position was deteriorating rapidly. The prime minister raised the question of whether it would be better to conclude peace with Turkey right away without first negotiating an armistice. By concluding peace, the Allies would wrest the captured territories from the Turks and the enemy would have no say in their subsequent disposal. Lloyd George went on to point out that, if President Wilson raised questions of self-determination, he could then be told that he must deal with the Allies and not Turkey. Similarly, if Palestine were to be given to the United States, the prime minister wanted the British and the Allies to be able to hand it over instead of the Turks.[34]

Balfour feared that Lloyd George was risking trouble unnecessarily. He was not worried that President Wilson would make embarrassing demands for "self-determination" in the Middle East. At any rate he had shown considerable confidence about this during a meeting in April of the recently established Eastern Committee, which dealt with Middle East policy. The minutes record:

Mr. Balfour expressed the belief that President Wilson did not seriously mean to apply his formula outside Europe. He meant that no "civilised" communities should remain under the heel of other "civilised" communities: as to politically inarticulate peoples, he would probably not

say more than that their true interests should prevail as against exploitation by conquerors.[35]

The foreign secretary did not reiterate this during the War Cabinet meeting of 3 October, but he did warn that, if the prime minister were to raise the question of a separate peace with Turkey in Paris, he would find himself led into extremely complicated discussions in connection with the Sykes-Picot Agreement.[36] Lloyd George agreed with this, but still suggested that he might sound Clemenceau on the question.[37]

Balfour then raised the subject of whether it would be desirable to urge President Wilson to threaten the Turks that America would declare war on them if they would not negotiate. He doubted, however, that Wilson would accept such advice. Lloyd George had reservations for another reason. He pointed out that the president might claim that it was his threat rather than British arms which had brought Turkey to terms, and this would give Wilson a voice in the Turkish settlement to which he was not entitled. Lloyd George argued that from the point of view of British prestige, they should preserve their claim to a predominant voice in theaters where the Allies' position was due to British arms. Balfour accepted this and the idea of urging Wilson to threaten Turkey was finally dropped.[38]

3. CABINET DISCUSSIONS OF TERRITORIAL TERMS AND THE LEAGUE OF NATIONS

On the western front the military tide had turned by early August. Between 21 March and 15 July, the Germans had launched five offensives. Their advances had been enormous by the standards of the western front, and in London there had been gloomy thoughts about the possibility of Britain and the United States fighting on without the continental Allies. Milner wrote to the prime minister on 9 June, 1918, suggesting that Lloyd George send the president a message through Reading in order to find out what America would do in case of the collapse of the Continental campaign against Germany. "Unless he [Wilson] can be shaken out of his aloofness," Milner wrote, "and drops 'co-belligerency' or whatever halfway house he loves to shelter himself in, for out and out alliance—he is in practice already a long way on the road—I don't see how the new combination can have sufficient cohesion and inner strength."[39]

The predominently French counterattack in the Aisne-Marne battle during July was successfully com-

[31] CAB 23/14/482A/5.

[32] Lansing to Page, 2 Oct., 1918, *Foreign Relations, 1918, Supplement 1*, 1: p. 334. On 10 Oct., the Foreign Office learned of a rumor in Washington that peace terms had been settled with Bulgaria. F.O. 800/222/Ger/14. Balfour promptly sent a reassuring denial to the Embassy in Washington and suggested that Wiseman be given a copy of it to use as he saw fit. F.O. 371/3442/62451/169743. Several weeks later, the Foreign Office informed the United States Government that Britain had always shared the views expressed in the American note of 2 Oct., 1918. Laughlin to Lansing, 6 Nov., 1918, *Foreign Relations, 1918, Supplement 1*, 1: p. 474. The French and Italian foreign ministers had agreed to this statement being made. CAB 28/5/86.

[33] CAB 23/14/482A/5.

[34] CAB 23/14/482A/6.

[35] CAB 27/24/5/5. See also page 146 above.

[36] CAB 27/14/482A/5. See also Hankey's diary for 3 Oct., 1918, in Roskill, 1970: 1: pp. 606–607.

[37] Lloyd George did, in fact, bring up the question of settling terms of peace with Turkey when he met with Italian and French leaders in Paris on 6 Oct., but the inter-Allied conference only agreed on armistice terms. CAB 28/5/77.

[38] CAB 23/14/482A/7.

[39] Milner Papers 145. See also Amery to the prime minister, 19 June, 1918, Lloyd George Papers, F/2/1/25.

pleted by 6 August, and the British relieved the threat to Amiens on 8 August. By then the Germans had manifestly begun to loose their grip. At long last the Allies had started to push them slowly back towards the Rhine. After years of stalemate, a quick victory in 1918 still seemed most improbable, but at least the crisis was clearly passed by mid-August. With American troops arriving in France at the rate of 250,000–300,000 a month, some measure of victory in 1919 or 1920 did not seem to be a fanciful expectation.

It was in this strategic situation that the Imperial War Cabinet resumed its consideration of war aims on 13 August.[40] Balfour opened the deliberations with a lengthy statement. He observed that Britain was committed to support French claims to Alsace-Lorraine and that Britain was bound to support Italy's claims as agreed in the Treaty of London, unless Italy herself renounced them. He thought that Austria should be broken up largely on national lines, though he foresaw difficulties, particularly in regard to the Sudeten Germans. In some cases they must, he suggested, "throw ethnology to the winds." Balfour went on to observe that Britain was committed to establish a united Poland with some kind of access to the sea. The Brest-Litovsk settlement would have to be destroyed. In the Balkans, they could not offer any Greek or Serbian territory to Bulgaria and this would make the settlement there difficult. Any approach to Bulgaria required caution. In regard to the Ottoman Empire, the foreign secretary asserted that Palestine ought never to be restored to Turkish rule. What ought to happen to Palestine was, however, another question.

The Middle East question led to the most interesting part of the discussion as far as Anglo-American relations are concerned. Balfour said that he would like to associate the Americans in any protectorate, though he was unsure that, if this were done, the French and Italians could be excluded. The prime minister observed that there was a good deal to be said for inducing America to take charge of Palestine on her own. One advantage would be that the whole power of America would be interposed between Egypt and "anything that might come from the north." Balfour replied that he would have no jealousy of America taking that job, but he thought she would not be anxious to do it and would regard it as a bribe. Lloyd George, on the contrary, thought the American public would be pleased, though President Wilson would probably shrink from it a little. Moreover, in response to a suggestion that the American public did not know much about Palestine, the prime minister argued that they would get more imperialistic as the war continued. Balfour agreed that this was worth considering.

The foreign secretary went on to the subject of Mesopotamia. He pointed out that the British had pledged to hand it over to an Arab State, but he was sure that in one form or another Britain must be in control there. In particular, Britain must assure herself of oil supplies from Mesopotamia. Turning to the question of the German colonies, Balfour referred to various memoranda which had been circulated to the Cabinet on the subject. He reiterated that he was opposed to restoring any of the colonies to Germany and that Australia, New Zealand, and South Africa should retain the captured colonies which were adjacent to them. Balfour was thinking of South-West Africa and the captured colonies in the Pacific south of the equator. There was a consensus on these particular points. The main disagreements concerned the remaining German African colonies. Early in May, 1918, Balfour had recommended either giving these colonies to Britain's allies or establishing a condominium, despite its admitted drawbacks. This suggestion had been made partly because the military situation during May had strongly implied that some compromises would be unavoidable. Balfour had reasoned that giving up some of this territory to powers other than Germany would improve Britain's negotiating position in regard to other questions more vital than African colonies.[41] Yet, even after the military situation had dramatically improved, the foreign secretary persisted in his desire to limit Britain's gains in order to appear disinterested. Hence, during the Imperial War Cabinet meeting on 13 August, he urged that they should try to avoid coming out of the war with an increase in territory compared to which everybody else's gain would sink into insignificance. In short, he wanted some alternative to Britain's acquiring these colonies.

Sir Robert Borden, the prime minister of Canada, expressed his general agreement with this attitude, but he went further than Balfour in regard to the United States. He argued that the more they could induce the United States to undertake just responsibilities in world affairs, the better it would be for the world and for the British Empire. He was ready to have virtually any of the German colonies pass under the control of the United States. The chief difficulty would be to induce the Americans to depart from their traditional policies.

Lord Reading asserted that the idea of the United States acting as a trustee in Palestine would appeal to Americans in view of their idealism and the importance of their Jewish population. As for the German colonies, Reading said that as the war progressed America would be increasingly against returning territory to Germany.[42] In fact, he thought that there was already

---

[40] CAB 23/43/W.C. 457, I.W.C. 30; CAB 23/7/457/7. During the summer of 1918, Imperial War Cabinet meetings were also classified as War Cabinet meetings. Two different sets of minutes were kept. One is very detailed; the other is relatively brief.

[41] CAB 24/53/4774.

[42] This idea was quite well established. Back in Jan., 1918, an important Colonial Office memorandum by Sir George Fiddes had been circulated by Walter Long which suggested

a majority against restoring the colonies, and that the president himself did not want them to be handed back. Reading recalled that the arguments against returning Germany's colonies which Australia's Prime Minister Hughes had put forward during a recent visit to America had been well received.[43] On the other hand, Reading intimated that the American attitude might change if Germany became truly democratic. He also stressed that so long as President Wilson was at the head of affairs, America would not stand for the direct annexation of territories by herself or other powers. Reading's main point was that in order to avoid difficulties with the United States, Britain should try to secure her aims by some way short of annexation.

The prime minister quoted from a speech which the president had made to foreign press correspondents for their private guidance only. Wilson allegedly said that America's position at the Peace Conference could be summed up as follows: "We come here asking nothing for ourselves and we are here to see you get nothing." [44] Reading doubted that these were the president's exact words, but Lloyd George thought that it was very much like what the president would say and that it expressed what the British had to keep in mind. The prime minister's main point was that they first had to see that Wilson got something—say Palestine and one of the German African colonies—and then the rest followed, that is, Britain could have trusteeships elsewhere. He was thinking in terms of Britain taking Mesopotamia, Samoa, and New Guinea, and of South Africa controlling South-West Africa.[45]

The discussion on war aims continued intermittently for several days. On 14 August, General Smuts criticized the program outlined by Balfour on the grounds

that it assumed the complete defeat of the enemy, which, in his opinion, was not justified by the existing military situation. In the remaining months of the war Smuts made persistently mistaken assessments in this pessimistic direction. His argument in mid-August was that the Allies would be unlikely to reach a decisive victory in 1919 and it would be unwise to fight on into 1920. The British army would shrink progressively and they might find themselves reduced at the end of the war to the position of a second-class power compared with America and Japan. Smuts did not want to insist on all the terms which Balfour had sketched and he wanted Britain's military and diplomatic efforts to be directed towards Germany's allies. As far as the German colonies were concerned, however, Smuts was opposed to returning them. He proposed that the captured colonies in Central Africa should be retained territorially, but suggested that their economic life could be administered by an international development board, on which Germany could be represented. Smuts feared that the United States might cause more trouble than Germany when peace was settled, and he suggested making America the president of the development board in order to conciliate her and to prove Britain's unselfish objectives.[46]

On 15 August, Lord Curzon criticized the views of Smuts. He pointed out that the military situation had greatly improved, and he believed that the prospect of the war ending with Japan relatively strong was less serious than the prospect of Germany being predominant. A decisive victory was essential. Moreover, he had been informed by a "personal friend of the President" that Wilson meant to go on until German militarism was destroyed.

When he came to the subject of Palestine, Curzon said he accepted the idea of a trusteeship being offered to America though he clearly believed British rule would be superior. Moreover, he doubted that the United States would be willing to take over Palestine.[47] Curzon said that he had been informed that the president would join international schemes to police the captured territories, but he would not assume the administration of them. Curzon and Lloyd George both indicated that this would be unsatisfactory. Indeed, Curzon would have preferred putting up with America administering Palestine on her own to a joint administration, which would, in his view, necessarily include the French and Italians.

In regard to East Africa, Curzon was reluctant to hand it over to any other power. He said that the salvation of "dark places" consisted of having them

---

that as the United States gained personal experience of what war with Germany really meant, she should be drawn more and more to Britain's view. CAB 24/37/3174.

[43] When Reading had first reported this in June, he stated that Wilson was sympathetic to the suggestion that it was vital to Australia's security that Germany should not have territory in the Pacific. F.O. 800/222/Dom/6. One attractive propaganda tactic consisted of relating the colonial question to the Monroe doctrine by suggesting that the doctrine's justification was that it prohibited powerfully armed European nations from interfering with the peaceful development of new-world nations. This was obviously an argument more suitable for the Dominions to put forward, and it was widely suggested that Dominion statesmen—especially Smuts—should visit the United States. See Smuts to Reading, 14 Aug., 1918, and enclosure, F.O. 800/223/U.S./74.

[44] Lord Burnham, the proprietor of *The Daily Telegraph*, had sent a copy of the speech to Balfour, who passed it on to the prime minister. See Lloyd George Papers, F/5/8/7.

[45] CAB 23/43/W.C. 457, I.W.C. 30; CAB 23/7/457/7. Given a choice between Palestine and East Africa, Lloyd George preferred to keep the former. See Louis, 1967: p. 112. Later Hankey recorded in his diary for 6 Oct., 1918, that Lloyd George "had some subtle dodge for asking America to take Palestine and Syria, in order to render the French more anxious to give us Palestine, so that they might have an excuse of [for] keeping Syria." See Roskill, 1970: 1: p. 609.

[46] CAB 23/43/W.C. 458, I.W.C. 31; CAB 23/7/458/7. See also memorandum by Smuts, 11 July, 1918, CAB 29/1/25.

[47] One wonders whether it was not in the backs of some British ministers' minds that America would probably not accept any proffered trusteeship, and thus, that making an offer would probably gain Britain some credit without costing her anything. See Louis, 1967: p. 115.

under British rule, and he deprecated the idea of passively receiving only what President Wilson might offer them. Curzon added that, while he was in favor of America extending her responsibilities where it was generally convenient, he was not anxious to set up American colonies everywhere in proximity to Britain's.

In the remaining discussion there were wide differences of opinion as to what territory America should govern. Austen Chamberlain, who had become a member of the War Cabinet several months earlier, supported the idea of putting the Americans in charge of Palestine. On the other hand, Barnes, Montagu, and Massey, the prime minister of New Zealand, expressed arguments against it. Lloyd George pointed out that the alternative was to give the United States great slices of Africa. Reading, however, doubted that the Americans would agree to administer East Africa. The discussion of territorial terms quickly tailed off at this point and ended on a ludicrous note. Lloyd George pointed out that America had millions of Negroes, and Borden suggested that if the Americans could be convinced that it was practical to ship all their Negroes to East Africa they would agree. Lloyd George asserted that America had been glad to get their labor, to which Borden replied that they had been a great trouble.[48] No definite policy decisions were reached, but the discussion of war aims during mid-August did clearly show that the British government seriously considered buying American consent for British conquests by encouraging the United States to take over a large part of the captured territories.

One of the other subjects considered by the Imperial War Cabinet was the question of whether or not to publish a report by the Phillimore Committee. This was a group appointed by the Foreign Office to study the League of Nations question. It began its deliberations at the end of January, 1918, under the chairmanship of an imminent jurist, Sir Walter Phillimore.[49] It is worth noting that Lloyd George, in his book about the peace settlement, stated that this committee was formed shortly after he became prime minister. The fact that this was not done until a year later weakens, though it does not totally invalidate, his point that the British government was doing detailed work on the League of Nations question long before the United States government.[50]

In February, 1918, the Foreign Office asked Wiseman to ascertain whether the Americans had formed a similar body with which the British committee might collaborate. Wiseman reported that the United States government had not yet formed a committee, but added that they were considering doing so and would "heartily

welcome" Britain's cooperation.[51] On Wiseman's advice, Cecil then wrote to Colonel House. The president's adviser, however, replied evasively that practical cooperation was impossible because American studies had not proceeded sufficiently far.[52]

During March, the Phillimore Committee presented an "Interim Report" to the foreign secretary which included a draft convention for a League of Nations.[53] On 17 May, 1918, with the War Cabinet's approval, Cecil dispatched six copies of the report to Wiseman, and requested him to give two copies to House so that one could be given to the president.[54] House did not, in fact, transmit a copy to the president. Wiseman explained that Wilson "was too busy to deal with it."[55] The Foreign Office, however, subsequently sent a copy to Lord Reading in Washington who communicated it to the president on 3 July. In his acknowledgment of the report, the president said that he had given it a hurried examination, but that he would go over it more carefully and comment on it.[56] Cecil later learned from Wiseman that the president sent the copy of the report to House with a letter asking him to prepare a reply.[57]

Meanwhile House had written to Cecil in June, outlining his own rather hazy ideas about the League of Nations.[58] After reading the letter, Cecil wondered whether House had looked at the Phillimore proposals, and on 15 July, he cabled Reading, asking whether House's letter should be taken as a reply to that document.[59] The ambassador answered that House's letter was, in fact, a reply to the Phillimore Committee's proposals. Wiseman, on the other hand, cabled almost simultaneously that it was not so much a reply to the report as an expression of House's views on the subject generally.[60] The president's adviser naturally wanted the League of Nations to be based largely on an American plan, so he deliberately ignored the British scheme as much as possible.[61]

Cecil replied to House's letter on 22 July. One of the points he made is of particular interest. House had stated that the members of the League should

[48] CAB 23/43/W.C. 459, I.W.C. 32; CAB 23/7/459/9.

[49] Note by Robert Cecil, 29 Jan., 1918, CAB 24/40/3489.

[50] Lloyd George, 1938: 1: pp. 605–607. The prime minister's role in establishing the Phillimore Committee was actually not a very positive one. See Mason, 1970: pp. 88ff.

[51] Telegram from Drummond to Wiseman, 9 Feb., 1918, F.O. 800/222/LoN/1; telegram from Wiseman to Drummond, 12 Feb., 1918, F.O. 800/222/LoN/2.

[52] Seymour, 1928: 4: pp. 6–7. See also Fowler, 1969: p. 205.

[53] F.O. 371/3439/13761/53848.

[54] CAB 23/6/412/7; F.O. 371/3439/13761/92255.

[55] Wiseman to Cecil, 18 July, 1918, F.O. 800/222/LoN/9.

[56] Reading forwarded a copy of the president's reply of 8 July, 1918. F.O. 371/3439/13761/128240.

[57] Telegram from Wiseman to Cecil, 17 July 1918, F.O. 800/222/LoN/8.

[58] House to Cecil, 24 June, 1918, CAB 24/59/5256.

[59] F.O. 371/3439/13761/124252.

[60] Telegram from Reading for Cecil, 17 July, 1918, F.O. 371/3439/13761/125255; telegram from Wiseman for Cecil, 17 July, 1918, F.O. 800/222/LoN/8.

[61] See House to Wilson, 14 July, 1918, published in Seymour, 1928: 4: p. 24.

agree to guarantee each other's territorial integrity. Cecil was reluctant to accept this principle. He wrote:

I am sure we ought to guarantee so far as it can be done, the observance of all treaties, and as a corollary we ought to provide means for their periodical renewal, but I do not know that territorial integrity should be specially singled out from other treaty obligations and as it were crystallized for all time.[62]

On the twenty-fourth, Reading cabled that the president was in substantial agreement with House's letter. As far as a guarantee of territorial integrity was concerned, this was certainly true. Wilson had specifically advocated it in his Fourteen Points. Reading's cable also stated: "The President hoped nothing would be done which would even informally bind His Majesty's Government before there had been full opportunity for interchange of views [between the United States and British governments]." Wilson had been at work on a paper regarding the Phillimore Committee report, Reading added, but he had been too busy to complete it.[63]

These delays were frustrating to Cecil. He was, as he admitted to the Imperial War Cabinet on 13 August, "violently in favour" of the Phillimore scheme. He was also anxious that the field should not be left to amateurs, lest the idea of the League of Nations should be ruined by faddist schemes. Cecil suggested publishing the Phillimore report, not as the views of the British Cabinet, but merely as a basis for discussion. He felt that the president might not object, if this intention were made clear. Lord Reading insisted that the president was anxious that they should not publish anything until he had submitted a memorandum on the Phillimore report. Cecil acknowledged that they must not antagonize the president in a matter of this kind, but he nevertheless thought that they should try and see whether Wilson would object to its publication merely as a basis for discussion. Cecil doubted whether the question should be left to the Americans because the Americans had not been able to give much time to the problem, and because they did not know "the immensely difficult atmosphere in which any scheme must be launched in Europe."

The prime minister offered two objections to publication. The first was that, although they might deny that the report was the government's scheme, everybody would take it as such. Consequently, he did not think it should be published without a "sort of Second Reading," that is, without a thorough discussion by the Cabinet. His second reason was that publication of the report might create an atmosphere of public discussion which would distract the people's minds away from the decisive victory which would be the only sure basis of any League of Nations. He feared that during November or December, when peace talk began, the Germans

might say with disastrous effect, that they generally accepted the British scheme.

The meeting seemed inclined against publication, and Lord Reading argued that the Cabinet should not even commit themselves to the "Second Reading" of a plan until they had received the president's views. He thought they would receive them in two or three weeks. Cecil remarked irritably that it was only too evident that some of his colleagues did not want the scheme put forward.

The Cabinet did, on the other hand, have one particular reason for being somewhat reluctant to postpone publication of the Phillimore report. There was some suspicion that the president wanted to publish a plan before the British government. When Bonar Law asked Reading whether this was Wilson's desire, Balfour interjected that it would be "natural" rather than improper. Reading, however, did not think the president would do such a thing, and he insisted that it would be improper for Wilson to prevent the British from publishing until he could publish his own plan.[64] Actually, Reading was not so sure that the president would refrain from publishing his own scheme before submitting it to the British. On 14 August, he cabled to Wiseman for reassurance on this point. He also remarked that he was having some difficulty in postponing publication of the Phillimore report.[65] The Cabinet was perhaps quite worried that Wilson was going to jump on the public platform first.

On 16 August, Wiseman sent a long telegram reporting an interview with the president. Wilson stressed his opposition to public discussions about the League. He explained that he did not want to see the question embroiled in controversy. The president told Wiseman that the Phillimore report had "no teeth," but he had not yet worked out his own ideas in detail, and he still refused to appoint an expert committee to study the question. On the other hand, he agreed with Wiseman that it would be necessary to find common ground with the British and said that he would be glad to discuss the question with anyone that the British government cared to send to him.[66]

Reading sent a copy of the telegram to Lloyd George, together with a letter warning that it was imperative that Cecil should know how seriously Britain's relations with the United States "might be embarrassed by premature public discussions based upon the Report of a Committee appointed by the Government."[67] On 20

[62] Cecil to House, 22 July, 1918, CAB 24/59/5256.
[63] F.O. 371/3439/13761/129429.

[64] CAB 23/43/W.C. 457, I.W.C. 30. For a more detailed account of Cecil's maneuvers to secure publication of the Phillimore report, see Mason, 1970: pp. 187ff.
[65] Telegram from Reading (code name "Swift") to Wiseman, 14 Aug., 1918, F.O. 800/225.
[66] Published in Fowler, 1969: pp. 278–280.
[67] Reading to Lloyd George, 19 Aug., 1918, Lloyd George Papers, F/43/1/14. Wiseman's telegram had mentioned that Wilson believed that the prime minister would share his views. Reading suggested that the president's impression was

August, Lloyd George wrote to Bonar Law asking him whether he had seen Wiseman's telegram. The prime minister observed:

It is clear from this that President Wilson does not take Robert Cecil's view about the League of Nations. We must take care that Cecil does not rush us into a premature pronouncement that would get us into trouble not merely with the French but with the Americans as well.[68]

Meanwhile, Cecil projected a dramatic image across the Atlantic. He portrayed himself as a committed supporter of the League ideal who was surrounded by its cunning opponents. On 19 August, he wrote to Wiseman dwelling on the need for a League of Nations and warning of immense obstacles. He asserted:

All the European bureaucracies will be against the idea, including probably the bureaucracy of this country. Nor must it be forgotten that the heresies of Militarsim have unfortunately extended beyond the limits of Germany, and all the militarists will be against the idea. Finally there will be many people who will fear that the Germans may use the League for their own purposes. . . . All these people are working already, more or less secretly, against the idea.

Cecil went on to explain very briefly that he wanted to publish something on the League question "in order to create and focus public opinion, and make it vigorous."[69] Wiseman showed the letter to Wilson, and House later sent a message to Cecil that the president was highly gratified to find that Cecil shared his convictions and principles in regard to the League.[70]

Despite Cecil's enthusiasm and protests, the British government acted in accordance with the president's wishes. Reading cabled Wiseman on 19 August that it was certain that Wilson's views would have great weight and that he did not anticipate any difficulty in preventing publication of the report until some time after his return to America, when he would have had an opportunity of discussing it with the president.[71]

Wilson was spared this discussion. Reading did not return to America until after the war was over. Wilson, in fact, had no detailed exchange of views with the British about the League until he went to Europe for the peace conference.

4. SUSPICIONS ON THE EVE OF VICTORY

As the military tide turned in the Allies' favor, the British realized that their efforts to promote Anglo-American cooperation were marred by some ominous signs of rivalry and antagonism. Responding to an anxious enquiry from Reading concerning the perceptible increase in friction, Wiseman pointed out that cooperation had generally been complicated by the president's adopting the stance of an "associate" rather than an ally. He also observed that Wilson was becoming "more arbitrary and aloof" and that sometimes he seemed to treat foreign governments hardly seriously. The "real danger point," in Wiseman's opinion, was "in trade questions." He noted that both nations found "it difficult to give way to each other's views and policies without apparently sacrificing their interests and principles."[72] There was, in fact, abundant evidence of mutual suspicions in many facets of British and American activities which had important implications for postwar trade. Shipbuilding, supply arrangements, finance, the transport of troops across the Atlantic, and administration of the blockade were all affected.[73]

The British generally resented the inroads which American business was making into their trade relations, and the Americans were annoyed at British attempts to regain lost ground. In this context, Wilson expressed displeasure about a speech by Lloyd George regarding postwar economic policy. On 31 July, the British prime minister told a deputation from the National Union of Manufacturers: "The longer the war lasts the sterner must be the economic terms we impose on the foe." Referring to the reconstruction period, he also said that in postwar trade, the Allies ought to see that the people who have been fighting together should be served before the enemy.[74]

Several weeks later, Wiseman cabled that the president had understood the Allies "would not officially resort to the punitive trade policy advocated by the Paris [Economic] Conference." The telegram continued: "He was disturbed therefore on reading . . . of the Prime Minister's speech . . . which seemed to recommend the crushing of Germany's trade after the war." According to Wiseman, the president fully appreciated the value of the economic weapon, which he

based on Lloyd George's speech of 7 Aug. in which he had stressed that victory over the Prussian military caste was essential to the establishment of a successful League of Nations. See *Parliamentary Debates*, Commons 109: cols. 1427–1428. Lloyd George himself had pointed out to the Imperial War Cabinet that Wilson's speeches seemed to exclude Germany from the League until she became democratic "in the British sense." CAB 23/43/W.C. 457, I.W.C. 30.

[68] Lloyd George Papers, F/30/2/41.

[69] Published in Cecil, 1949: pp. 142–144.

[70] Telegram from Wiseman to Drummond, 2 Oct., 1918, Balfour Papers, Add. MSS. 49687.

[71] Telegram from Reading to Wiseman, 19 Aug., 1918, F.O. 800/225.

[72] Telegram from Reading to Wiseman, 28 Aug., 1918, and telegrams from Wiseman to Reading, nos. 731 and 732, 5 Sept., 1918, F.O. 800/225.

[73] War Cabinet minutes, 4 Sept., 1918, CAB 23/14/469A; telegram from Wiseman to Reading, 31 Aug., 1918, F.O. 800/225; memorandum by Political Intelligence Department, Aug., 1918, CAB 24/60/5318; Balfour to Geddes, 27 Aug., 1918, Lloyd George Papers, F/3/3/31; War Cabinet minutes, 9 Oct., 1918, CAB 23/8/483/13. The British also realized, of course, that the problems were aggravated at this time by American suspicions that they were being pushed into a dubious policy of intervention in Russia. CAB 23/7/473/4; CAB 23/7/475/7.

[74] London *Times*, 2 Aug., 1918.

wanted to use in order to bring Germany to her senses and to ensure the observance of a just peace. On the other hand, Wiseman explained that Wilson was convinced that threats of punitive trade measures only strengthened the hand of the militarists in Germany. The president thought that the Allies should adopt the line that they had no desire to deny Germany her fair share of the world's commerce and that it was Germany's militarists who were ruining her trade by prolonging the war and obliging the Allies to maintain the blockade. This protest was not merely a disagreement about propaganda tactics, nor was the difference of opinion simply a conflict between punitive trade policies and enlightened, liberal trade policies. The disagreement reflected different basic attitudes toward the postwar economic question which in turn reflected differences in national interests. Wilson was thinking almost exclusively in terms of using discriminatory policies as a political weapon to be employed only so long as it was necessary to secure agreement to a satisfactory peace.[75] As far as the postwar world was concerned, the administration primarily wanted to open up the world's markets to American trade, arguing in favor of making markets accessible to all countries on equal terms in the confidence that America's great economic strength would enable her to compete successfully. The United States was much less concerned than the Allies with the problems of reconstruction. The British government placed much more emphasis upon the need for preferential policies to guarantee essential supplies and to promote economic recovery.

Wiseman's cable did not make this difference clear. The whole question of postwar trade policy was clouded by doubt and confusion. Wilson's policy still lacked definition, and contradictory interpretations were possible. Wiseman had reported on 5 August, 1918, that American press opinion was divided as to America's attitude towards the economic question. The president's reply to the pope of August, 1917, and his message to Congress of December, 1917, were being quoted in support of divergent views.[76] A further complication was that the administration wanted to avoid the subject at a time when the American public's interest in postwar economic discrimination was increasing. Wiseman had cabled on 7 August that the State Department evidently felt that the "hearty support" which the American public opinion seemed to give to Lloyd George's remarks might force the administration to declare their

policy before they were ready.[77] He may have felt that the British government would be tempted to appeal to the American public over Wilson's head, for in a later message Wiseman specifically warned against any semblance of such a maneuver.[78]

Evasion and vague generalities were the safest course as far as British-American relations were concerned. Obviously provoking the president was dangerous. Wiseman's cable of 20 August concluded with a warning from House that, if the Allies persisted with statements similar to the prime minister's speech, Wilson would feel obliged to publicly dissociate the United States from the policy.[79] The president's attitude was undoubtedly one of the major reasons why the British government repeatedly postponed its statement on economic policy until after the war.

Meanwhile, House played upon Wilson's suspicions in order to encourage him to commit the Allies to as much of his peace program as possible. He argued that as the Allies succeeded, the president's influence would diminish, and he portrayed Lloyd George along with Clemenceau and Sonnino as "hostile" to American aims. Though he did not actually consider Lloyd George as irremediably reactionary, House believed that reactionary views were dominant in the British government. On the other hand, he thought that the British people were warmly sympathetic to the president.[80]

This assessment of the situation was very persuasive to Wilson. He did not accept House's advice concerning the need to put forward a specific covenant for a League of Nations, but he felt compelled to try publicly to elicit from the Allies some commitment to his principles. The attempt was made in a speech opening a Liberty Loan drive on 27 September. While the president ruled out any compromise with the governments of the Central Powers, he also declared that there should be no compromise of the principles for which America was fighting. Moreover, he main-

---

[75] The Political Intelligence Department had perceived this aspect of the president's attitude to some extent. A report dated 26 July, 1918, stated: "He will hardly look at the 'economic weapon' from an economic standpoint. The haft of the weapon may be economic, but its point will be political." CAB 24/57/5018.

[76] Telegram from Wiseman for Arthur Murray (code name Arrow), 5 Aug., 1918, F.O. 800/225.

[77] Telegram from Wiseman for Reading, 7 Aug., 1918, F.O. 800/225.

[78] Telegram from Wiseman for Reading, no. 731, 5 Sept., 1918, F.O. 800/225.

[79] Telegram from Wiseman for Reading, 20 Aug., 1918, F.O. 800/225. Wiseman later reported further evidence of Wilson's sensitivity on the economic question. The president had learned that Prime Minister Hughes of Australia intended to visit the United States and to advocate a policy of economic retaliation against Germany. He warned that, if Hughes made a speech on that subject, he would repudiate the policy publicly. Moreover, the State Department urged that "Hughes shall be persuaded to abandon his tour and if he passes through the U. S. on his way home he should not make any public speech or statement." An even colder reaction to the Hughes visit had been contemplated. Wiseman noted that Wilson had initially been inclined to refuse him an American visa. Telegram from Wiseman to Reading, no. 723, 31 Aug., 1918, F.O. 800/225.

[80] Seymour, 1928: 4: pp. 64–66; House Diary, 20 Aug., 1918.

tained that the governments associated against Germany must be willing to pay the necessary price for a lasting peace. That price was impartial justice in every item of the settlement no matter whose interest was crossed. The associated governments must, he said, also be willing to create an effective League of Nations, which would guarantee the fulfillment of the peace agreements by those whose promises had proved untrustworthy. The League should, he thought, be established as an essential part of the peace settlement rather than before or after the peace conference. Wilson then went on to list five "particulars" which should be the basis of the settlement. The first repeated the importance of "impartial justice." Secondly, he said that no special interest could be made the basis of any part of the settlement which was not consistent with the common interests of all. Thirdly, there could be no alliance or understandings within the League of Nations. Fourthly, there could be "no special, selfish economic combinations within the League and no employment of any form of economic boycott or exclusion" except as an economic penalty exercised by the League itself. Fifthly, all international agreements and treaties must be made public knowledge in their entirety.

Wilson concluded his speech with an invitation to Allied leaders to speak as frankly as he had tried to speak. He hoped that they would feel free to say whether he was mistaken about the issues involved or his purpose with regard to the means of obtaining a satisfactory settlement. Unity of purpose was as imperative as unity of command in the battlefield. "With perfect unity of purpose and counsel," he said, "will come assurance of complete victory." [81]

Lord Robert Cecil promptly sent a telegram to Colonel House asking him to convey to the president his personal deep appreciation of the speech. Cecil praised it as "the finest description of our war aims yet uttered. . . ." [82] Wilson thanked Cecil for his message, but what he really wanted were public endorsements by the Allied governments. [83]

Balfour replied publicly to the president's speech during the opening of a War Savings Campaign at the Guildhall on 30 September. The British foreign secretary said that he understood the president's main theme to be that the world must come to some arrangement by which malefactors or would-be malefactors would be kept in order, if it were to be sure of having peace. The first proposition was that an effective League of Nations must be brought into being. The second proposition, as he understood it, was that this must be done when the peace was being forged by the victorious powers. Balfour said that he was personally very much of Wilson's mind that to allow the occasion to pass would be to lose one of mankind's great opportunities "to put international relations on a sound, lasting, and moral footing."

The foreign secretary described these propositions as the "two great pillars of the policy to which he [Wilson] has given eloquent expression." Balfour then went on to put forward his own favorite theme in regard to the place of the League of Nations in the peace settlement. "Evidently," he said, "something yet further is required." He warned that the new international machinery must not be asked to do the impossible. If you create an international machinery for securing peace, he believed, "you must so arrange the map of Europe and the world that the great occasions for wars will not overwhelm you." Balfour referred to a long list of evils which must be put right before the League of Nations set to work. He mentioned the German domination of Russia, the century of wrong to Poland, the subordinated peoples in the Austrian Empire, the instability of the Balkans, the "bloody sway" of the Turk, the unredeemed Italians, the threatened domination of Greece by the Central Powers, and the condition of Serbia, France, and Belgium. "You must," he said, give the League a "clean slate to work upon." It followed, therefore, that in order to make the League of Nations possible complete victory was absolutely necessary. Balfour indicated that it would not be enough for Germany to make a few constitutional modifications and subscribe to the admirable propositions which President Wilson had from time to time laid down. Germany could not be a member of the League of Nations until she found herself in a position when, though left powerful and prosperous, all her dreams of world domination were torn to pieces. [84]

Balfour had said, in effect, that he supported Wilson's advocacy of the League, but only in conjunction with Britain's other war aims. This did not directly contradict what Wilson had said, but it had a different emphasis and tone. Moreover, it clearly reflected a recurring fear in London that the president might underestimate the importance of concrete territorial and military terms in his eagerness to secure a peace based upon his glittering principles. The foreign secretary's speech was certainly not the kind of official endorsement which Wilson was seeking.

[81] Scott, 1921: pp. 399–405.

[82] Published in Seymour, 1928: 4: p. 72. At a War Cabinet meeting on 2 Oct., Cecil mentioned that the American chargé d'affaires had asked him to express the British government's reaction to Wilson's speech. Cecil thought that in reply to this request they should propose a special Allied conference—perhaps meeting in Washington—to prepare a definite scheme for the League of Nations. Reading reiterated that the president first wanted to discuss the question with the British government, and the War Cabinet proceeded with the assumption that Reading would exchange views with Wilson when he returned to Washington. CAB 23/8/481/9.

[83] Wilson's message was transmitted by House through Wiseman. Telegram from Wiseman to Drummond, 2 Oct., 1918, Balfour Papers, Add. MSS. 49687.

[84] Scott, 1921: pp. 407–409.

5. WILSON'S CORRESPONDENCE WITH GERMANY DURING OCTOBER, 1918

Germany gave Wilson another and better chance to commit the Allies to his principles. On 3 October, the German government sent a note to the president requesting him to invite all belligerents to take up peace negotiations on the basis of Wilson's message to Congress of 8 January, 1918 (the Fourteen Points speech) and his subsequent pronouncements, particularly the address of 27 September, 1918. The German government also urged the president to bring about an immediate armistice.[85] The note was signed by the new German chancellor, Prince Max of Baden and was transmitted by Switzerland. The Austro-Hungarian government appealed to Wilson in similar terms at the same time through the Swedish government.

After learning of the German move on the fifth, the British waited anxiously for Wilson's reply, while the president followed his usual practice of drafting his response without consulting the Allies.[86] Lloyd George was, at this time, in Paris conferring with the French and Italian governments, primarily about Bulgaria and Turkey. Wilson sent his reply on 8 October, and the Allies were not informed of its terms by United States representatives until the ninth, which was the same day that the president's note appeared in the press. General Sir Henry Wilson, who was then chief of the Imperial General Staff, exclaimed: "He really is the limit."[87]

President Wilson responded to Germany by seeking clarification on several points. He wanted to know first whether the German government accepted the terms he had laid down in his various speeches and whether the purpose of discussions would be only to agree upon practical details of their application. Secondly, the president stated that he would not propose a cessation of arms so long as the armies of the Central Powers were on the Allies' soil. The good faith of any discussion would depend upon the consent of those Powers to withdraw from invaded territory. Thirdly, Wilson asked whether the Imperial chancellor was speaking merely for the authorities of the empire who had so far conducted the war.[88]

At a conference of the three major Allied governments in the afternoon of 9 October, Clemenceau said that he thought Wilson's note was excellent. Lloyd George emphatically disagreed. He had, in fact, been angered by news of the president's note. He was not only irritated by Wilson's failure to consult the Allies,

but also by the content of the president's reply.[89] Lloyd George explained at the inter-Allied meeting that he believed the Germans were in a thoroughly bad way and predicted that Prince Max would readily accept Wilson's Fourteen Points. There were aspects of those points, Lloyd George observed, about which he would like to know more. He specifically noted British doubts about freedom of the seas and pointed out that the Fourteen Points made an uncertain allusion to Alsace-Lorraine.[90] He went on to say that he did not pretend to understand the president's question as to whether Prince Max's request emanated from the former rulers of Germany, but he did have definite and serious misgivings about Wilson's reference to an armistice. The British prime minister thought that Prince Max would also readily accept the evacuation of occupied territories as a condition of the armistice, and he feared that, if the Germans did do this and the Allies were to say nothing, the Germans could maintain that nobody had protested against it and that they were entitled to regard it as the Allied conditions of an armistice. Lloyd George had come to the conference armed with a draft telegram to Wilson which was designed to avoid this pitfall. The message made it clear that an armistice would involve more conditions than the evacuation of territory, that it must be drawn up by the military experts and that it should preclude the enemy from obtaining any advantage by withdrawing unpursued to a shorter, more defensible line. In advocating this cable, he also warned that once an armistice was declared, the Allies would not be able to start fighting again. Hence, it was essential to secure the evacuation of Alsace-Lorraine, the Trentino and Trieste as well as the evacuation of occupied territories.

When Clemenceau expressed concern that Wilson's susceptibilities not be offended, Lloyd George remarked that he was as eager as anyone else to avoid offending the president, but that he was even more anxious to avoid a German trap. Clemenceau was opposed to any public announcement at this time, but he agreed to a suggestion made by Baron Sonnino that they send a private telegram.

Lord Robert Cecil then warned that they must be careful not to imply that they accepted Wilson's proposals relating to matters other than the armistice, that is, to all of his Fourteen Points and other pro-

---

[85] Rudin, 1944: pp. 80 and 89.

[86] For British enquiries about Wilson's forthcoming reply, see F.O. 371/3444/157260/168439; Frazier to Lansing, 7 Oct., 1918, *Foreign Relations, 1918, Supplement 1*, 1: p. 344.

[87] Callwell, 1927: pp. 134–135.

[88] Scott, 1921: pp. 418–419.

[89] J. C. C. Davidson remembered a tirade about "honesty and fair dealing in international relations" which Lloyd George delivered (while standing on a golf tee) to an official of the United States Embassy in Paris. Davidson confused the occasion with Wilson's announcement of his Fourteen Points, but he caught the relish with which Lloyd George expressed his indignation. James, 1969: pp. 85–86. See also Hankey, 1961: 2: p. 854.

[90] See p. 75 above. Actually Wilson's "allusion" to Alsace-Lorraine was not significantly more "uncertain" than Lloyd George's demand for "reconsideration" of the question.

nouncements. Cecil mentioned freedom of the seas, of course, but he also referred specifically to Wilson's suggestion that he would not make peace with the Hohenzollerns. Cecil said that they should be very careful not to commit themselves to that.[91]

Various reservations were circulating among the British in regard to the idea of "no peace with the Hohenzollerns." One feeling was that it would not be worth while to prolong the war merely to change Germany's government. Lord Milner's views continued to be particularly definite on this topic. He especially feared that prolonging the war would promote the spread of Bolshevism and chaos. He thought that any attempt to dictate drastic changes in Germany's government might actually stiffen Germany's resistance, and, in any case, he considered such an attempt unnecessary, because a complete transformation was already in progress in Germany. Moreover, he believed that it was in the Allies' interest to see that there was a stable government in Germany to deal with.[92] Another reservation which was expressed at this phase of the war concerned a very interesting possibility. On 3 October, 1918, the Political Intelligence Department of the Foreign Office warned that Germany might turn the formula of "no peace with the Hohenzollerns" to its own advantage. A new, liberal German government might say that it had been given to understand that an agreed peace would be made easy for a liberal, democratic government, that it was such a government, and that it asked the Allies to redeem their pledges. If the Allies did not then waive certain demands, embarrassments and complications might follow. The memorandum concluded that it would be wise to return as quickly as possible "to the old and sound principles that the internal forms of government in one nation are not the concern of other nations."[93]

After Cecil's general warning about the idea of "no peace with the Hohenzollerns," the inter-Allied conference adjourned while the foreign ministers drafted a telegram to Wilson. Balfour did not attend the meetings in Paris because of illness, so Cecil acted in his place. When the conference reassembled, it approved a cable which politely embodied the main points which Lloyd George wanted to make. In addition, the meeting approved a telegram which was intended to alleviate some of the Allies' serious difficulties in cooperating with the president. Bonar Law had suggested earlier in the afternoon that, although President Wilson had not compromised the Allies yet, he might have placed them in a difficult position. He thought it would be wise to point out to Wilson that in view of the important decisions which had to be taken, it was desira-

ble that the president should send some person in whom he had complete confidence to join in the Allies' discussions.[94] This additional telegram stated tactfully that the purpose of the American representative would be "to keep the other associated Governments accurately and fully informed of the point of view of the United States Government."[95]

The text of both notes was cabled to Washington by Arthur Frazier of the United States Embassy in Paris on 9 October.[96] Copies of the two Allied messages to Wilson were also communicated to the president by the French ambassador in Washington on 10 October. A report of this interview indicated that Wilson's reception of the notes was friendly, and confirmed that he, in fact, did not regard his note to the German government as a statement of the only conditions of an armistice.[97]

The impression of amity and reassurance was not, however, long lived. The president, in fact, harbored acute suspicions and anger of his own. While the Allied leaders in Paris were waiting for Wilson's reply to the German note, they had discussed the terms of an armistice and had requested the advice of the military representatives on the Supreme War Council. General Bliss, the American representative, did not participate in the deliberations, but reported the recommendations to the president.[98] Wilson was furious. He thought that the Allies had not only discussed armistice terms without consulting him, but had agreed upon them. Allied officials in Washington and Balfour in London smoothed over the situation by explaining that the Allies were only making preparations, and that no decisions had been made.[99] The incident under-

[91] Procès-verbal of a conference held on 9 Oct., 1918, CAB 28/5/81.

[92] Gollin, 1964: pp. 569–574.

[93] CAB 24/65/5883.

[94] Bonar Law was more concerned than Lloyd George about the need to maintain smooth relations with Wilson. See Callwell, 1927: p. 133. The Foreign Office and Lord Reading, of course, were also very concerned. On 7 Oct., Cecil had sent an urgent cable from Paris to Drummond about the lack of an authoritative representative of the president in Europe. ". . . Lloyd George and Clemenceau," he observed, "vie with one another in scoffing at the President. . . ." To avoid misunderstandings, Cecil wanted Wilson himself to come to Europe. Balfour Papers, Add. MSS. 49738. Balfour pointed out to Cecil that it would be impossible for Wilson to leave the United States before the congressional elections in November. Telegram to Lord Derby for Cecil, 8 Oct., 1918, Balfour Papers, Add. MSS. 49738.

[95] CAB 28/5/81/Appendix II.

[96] Foreign Relations, 1918, Supplement 1, 1: pp. 353–354. For a report by Frazier of a conversation with Lloyd George and Bonar Law about British anxieties, see pp. 351–352.

[97] Telegram from Barclay, 10 Oct., 1918, F.O. 371/3444/157260/170667.

[98] Rudin, 1944: pp. 92–96.

[99] Telegrams from Barclay, received 10 Oct., 1918, F.O. 371/3442/62451/169742, 169743; telegram to Barclay, 10 Oct., 1918, F.O. 371/3442/62451/169743; War Cabinet minutes, 11 Oct., 1918, CAB 23/8/484/3; telegram from Reading for Wiseman, 12 Oct., 1918, F.O. 800/225; telegram to Barclay, 13 Oct., 1918, F.O. 371/3444/157260/171764; telegram from Wiseman for Reading and Drummond, 13 Oct., 1918, F.O. 800/225.

scored the need for an authoritative American representative in Europe.

The German government's second note further aggravated British-American relations. It fully accepted the points in Wilson's address of 8 January and in his subsequent addresses as the basis of peace. Worse from the British government's point of view, the German government said that it believed that the countries associated with the United States also accepted the position taken by the president in his addresses. Moreover, the German government, as Lloyd George predicted, declared its readiness to comply with the president's propositions regarding evacuation, and urged that a mixed commission should meet to make the necessary arrangements. Finally, the note declared that the present German government was supported by the will of the German people.[100]

When Lloyd George learned of the note late on 12 October, his anger at Wilson flared up again. He thought the president had placed Britain in a difficult situation.[101] The prime minister was staying at Danny Park, Lord Riddell's house in Sussex, at this time. On the following day Balfour, Bonar Law, Milner, Winston Churchill, General Wilson, Admiral Sir Rosslyn Wemyss, who was the First Sea Lord, Philip Kerr, and Hankey met in conference with the prime minister and discussed their next moves. The prime minister again hammered away at the point that the Central Powers must not be allowed to assume that the evacuation of occupied territories was the sole condition of an armistice. Milner suggested that Wilson had merely said that the enemy must evacuate the occupied territories before he would even propose an armistice, but the meeting readily agreed that they should suggest to the president that he make the position very clear.[102] The substance of a message was approved and promptly sent to Washington. The telegram urged Wilson to tell the German government publicly that he never contemplated granting an armistice merely on the promise of a German retirement from occupied territories, and that the associated powers would only consent to a cessation of hostilities on terms which, in the opinion of military and naval experts, rendered any resumption of hostilities by the enemy impossible.[103]

The British leaders meeting at Danny Park also agreed upon a telegram to Wilson concerning the German government's apparent acceptance of the president's Fourteen Points and other public utterances.

The cable stated:

With the general tenor of the President's policy we are in full accord. But it has to be observed (1) that these have never been discussed by the Associated Powers, (2) that certain of them are capable of various interpretations to some of which we should raise strong objection, (3) that there are probably other terms not referred to by the President (for example terms relating to outrages on shipping) which should be insisted on if full justice is to be done.

The reference to outrages at sea was intended to cover a British demand for compensation for the loss of merchant ships and reparation for the families of lost seamen. British anger about maritime atrocities had recently been heightened by the sinking of a passenger and mail steamer, the *Leinster*. The message to the president continued:

It seems to us that care must be taken lest the conditions of the armistice should be so framed as to deprive Allies of the necessary freedom of action in settling final terms in Peace Conference: and that the chief belligerent Powers should at once take steps to come to some agreement among themselves on doubtful points.[104]

In the discussion at Danny Park which led to this message, doubts were raised about various points. Freedom of the seas was once again the main focus of objections, but the prime minister also drew attention to the president's point number three which called for reduced economic barriers and equal trade conditions. Hankey's minutes record that Lloyd George said: "President Wilson was a Free Trader pure and simple and this was certainly a disputable point." Balfour replied: "What President Wilson failed to understand was that, however successful a League of Nations might be, there must be a transition period while it was being established."[105] The foreign secretary had touched one of the key differences between the outlook of Wilson and the British government. Wilson did not, in fact, share the British government's strong convictions about the necessity of having discriminatory trade policies during the period of reconstruction. On the other hand, the president's point three restricted the liberalized trade conditions to "nations consenting to the peace and associating themselves for its maintenance." In other words, Germany might be excluded from equal trading privileges until the League of Nations could be established and until she could be admitted to it. That could take considerable time after the war.

---

[100] Scott, 1921: pp. 420–421.

[101] Riddell, 1933: pp. 370–371.

[102] Draft notes of a conference at Danny Park, 13 Oct., 1918, CAB 24/66/5967.

[103] Telegram to Barclay, no. 6182, 13 Oct., 1918, F.O. 371/3444/157260/171765. Another cable urging essentially the same action was sent to Wiseman for House. Telegram from Reading to Wiseman, 13 Oct., 1918, F.O. 800/225.

[104] Telegram to Barclay, no. 6183, 13 Oct., 1918, F.O. 371/3444/157260/171765. Balfour simultaneously sent an additional cable (no. 6184) which reported information that the Germans were resolved to keep Alsace-Lorraine and all Polish areas. "Inference is," he pointed out, "that they hope both to accept President's terms and to dispute in Peace Conference over interpretation even of the conditions which seem to be most explicitly stated."

[105] CAB 24/66/5967.

When Balfour reported on the deliberations at Danny Park to the War Cabinet on the following day, 14 October, he apparently did not mention the president's point number three. He did, however, refer to another keen British interest, the fate of the German colonies. Like the question of freedom of the seas, the colonial question arising out of the Fourteen Points was, he observed, capable of wide variation in interpretation. The president's point number five, in fact, did little more than call for an impartial adjustment of colonial claims.[106] Cecil noted that while they had a great case made out against the return of the colonies to Germany, it was not so easy to make out a case for Britain keeping them. Lloyd George asked whether it was worth-while "suggesting to the American Government that they should send officers to the *ex*-German colonies" to inform the president about them directly. Balfour thought that this might be desirable if they could ensure the selection of "impartial and competent" officers. "This," he said, "would not be easy."[107]

Wilson replied to the second German note on 14 October. The president made it explicitly clear that "the process of evacuation and the conditions of an armistice" were matters to be decided by the military advisers of the United States and the Allies, and he declared that no arrangement could be accepted which did not safeguard and guarantee the present military supremacy of the United States and the Allies. Wilson's reply also told Germany to stop her outrages at sea and the destruction of cities and villages in Belgium and France from which the German armies were withdrawing. "The nations associated against Germany can not be expected to agree to a cessation of arms," he warned, "while acts of inhumanity, spoliation, and desolation are being continued which they justly look upon with horror and with burning hearts." Finally, Wilson stressed that the whole process of making peace would, in his opinion, depend upon the satisfactory character of the guarantees which can be given concerning the altered nature of the German government.[108]

This was a stiffer reply than Wilson's first note. The change of tone was greeted with some sarcasm at Downing Street and there was even some criticism of the note's strictness, particularly in regard to Wilson's uncompromising attitude toward the Hohenzollerns. There was also continued resentment of Wilson's failure to consult the Allies. On the other hand, as far as Wilson's remarks about armistice conditions were concerned, the note seemed more satisfactory, and the War Cabinet decided that there was no need for the Foreign Office to send any message with reference to the president's reply.[109]

It was the German government which once again provoked the British to give the president some direct advice. The third German note, dated 20 October, began as follows:

In accepting the proposal for an evacuation of the occupied territories the German Government has started from the assumption that the procedure of this evacuation and of the conditions of an armistice should be left to the judgment of the military advisors and that the actual standard of power on both sides in the field has to form the basis for arrangements safeguarding and guaranteeing this standard. The German Government suggests to the President to bring about an opportunity for fixing the details.[110]

This passage was discussed by the British Cabinet on 21 October. It was suggested that the German government still assumed that the evacuation only applied to the occupied territory and not to territory such as Alsace-Lorraine and the Trentino. It was pointed out that President Wilson's second note had not, in fact, definitely cleared up this matter. He said that the "process of evacuation and the conditions of an armistice" must be left to Allied and American military experts, but the question arose as to whether the president's phrase could be fairly interpreted in a way which would enable the military advisers of the associated governments to insist upon the evacuation of districts such as Alsace-Lorraine, the Trentino, Istria, and so on. It was felt that the Germans interpreted Wilson's phrase as applying only to the occupied territories. Vagueness on this point seemed dangerous. The correspondence between Washington and Berlin "might become damaging to public opinion in allied countries," and could be used in Germany to stiffen morale.

It was also observed that none of the German notes contained anything about naval terms of an armistice, although it was suggested that military terms might be interpreted as including naval terms. Other aspects of the German note were criticized, as well, but on the whole it was felt that, if satisfactory conditions of an armistice could be obtained, the remaining points would not in themselves justify prolonging hostilities.

The question was raised as to whether the Allied governments would be committed to the Fourteen Points if Wilson now accepted the German proposals. It was generally agreed that the Allies would not stand committed in that event. Moreover, according

---

[106] For a discussion of possible pitfalls in Wilson's fifth point from the British government's perspective, see the memorandum by the Political Intelligence Department on "President Wilson's Speeches as a basis of Negotiation," 12 Oct., 1918, CAB 24/67/6012.

[107] CAB 23/8/485/8.

[108] Scott, 1921: pp. 421–423. The substance of this reply had probably been formulated before the British notes of 13 Oct. were delivered to the president. See Baker, 1939: **8**: pp. 476–479.

[109] Roskill, 1970: **1**: p. 614; Callwell, 1927: p. 136; Jones, 1969: **1**: pp. 67–70; War Cabinet minutes, 15 Oct., 1918, CAB 23/8/486/5; Austen Chamberlain to his wife, Ivy, 16 Oct., 1918, Austen Chamberlain Papers, AC 6/1/319.

[110] Rudin, 1944: pp. 164-165.

to the War Cabinet minutes, "the view was expressed that President Wilson was not at all likely to agree to the German terms." The War Cabinet, however, felt that the president should be immediately notified of the British government's views about armistice conditions, and after considerable discussion, a draft telegram by Balfour was adopted.[111]

The message was sent to Washington in the early evening of 21 October. It pointed out that the Germans had not mentioned naval terms and that they were assuming that an undisturbed retreat to their frontier had been accepted in principle. "We are well aware," the telegram stated, "that this is not the President's view." It then explained that British experts believed that such a policy would give the Germans "time to reorganise, and a short and very defensible front." If peace negotiations broke down under such conditions, for example on questions like Alsace-Lorraine or Poland, the Allies would be compelled either to give way or to resume hostilities against an enemy who was in an improved position. The Germans would feel that they were fighting for their fatherland. Furthermore, what would inspire German troops, the telegram suggested, "would discourage ours; and all the fruits of victory would be lost." Any armistice must contain securities against the resumption of hostilities if peace negotiations break down, and probably also against violation of the final peace treaty. In the opinion of British experts, this required (a) the immediate occupation by Allied troops of some enemy territory, including at least Alsace-Lorraine, and (b) adequate precautions against the resumption of naval warfare. The telegram concluded by expressing the hope that the president would not commit himself on these vital questions without previous consultation with the Allies.[112]

Wilson replied to the German note on the twenty-third without consulting the Allies, but his answer satisfied the British as far as armistice conditions were concerned. Wilson agreed to take up the question of an armistice with the associated governments, but he made it clear that the only armistice which could be considered would leave the associated governments with an indisputable upper hand. The president's reply also indicated that he was transmitting his correspondence with the German authorities to the associated governments with a far-reaching suggestion. If those powers were disposed "to effect peace upon the terms and principles" expressed in his speeches, their military advisers, together with American advisers, should submit armistice conditions which would "ensure to the associated Governments the unrestricted power to safeguard and enforce the details of the peace. . . ." In conclusion, the president had some more harsh things to say about "those who have hitherto been the masters

of German policy," and he again said that America could only deal with the veritable representatives of the German people. If the United States had to deal with the military masters and autocrats, it must demand, not negotiations, but surrender.[113]

At a War Cabinet meeting on 24 October, Lloyd George said that he welcomed the terms of Wilson's reply and liked the tenor of the president's proposals. According to the minutes, he explained:

If Germany meant peace she would accept, and the acceptance would be equivalent to military surrender. If on the other hand, the Germans want to continue the war, they would now be compelled to continue the war upon a refusal to accept the armistice terms proposed by the Allies jointly.

General Wilson expressed his apprehension that the president's note would be construed as meaning that he would grant easier terms if he were dealing with a constitutional regime in Germany. The prime minister, however, thought that apprehension was unnecessary on this point, because the president had made it clear in the first part of his note that even if he were dealing with a constitutional regime, the armistice terms would amount in practice to military surrender. Austen Chamberlain, on the other hand, observed that, while there was no distinction in regard to armistice terms, a distinction was drawn in regard to ultimate peace terms.[114] Thereafter, being assured that the president's position was fully satisfactory as far as armistice conditions were concerned, the focus of the British government's concern turned to Wilson's peace program.

6. THE ARMISTICES WITH TURKEY AND AUSTRIA-HUNGARY

The president's Fourteen Points and subsequent declarations were, of course, bound up with Germany's request that Wilson promote armistice negotiations. In the remaining weeks of the war, they occupied a central place on the diplomatic stage and did, in fact, become an understood part of the agreement with Germany to stop the fighting. This was not, however, the case with the armistice agreements with Germany's allies, even though they also appealed to Wilson for negotiations on the basis of his Fourteen Points and other pronouncements. Indeed, a note from Turkey, which was transmitted through Spain on 14 October, appealed to Wilson in terms very similar to Germany's first note.[115] The British were anxious to get the Turks out of the war. They also wanted to keep negotiations with Turkey in their own hands as much as possible. On 17 October, the War Cabinet decided to send a telegram to the president saying that in his reply to the Turks, he should advise them to apply to one of the naval or military forces operating against

111 CAB 23/14/489A.
112 F.O. 371/3444/157260/175883.

113 Scott, 1921: pp. 434–436.
114 CAB 23/8/490/1.
115 *Foreign Relations, 1918, Supplement 1,* 1: pp. 359–360.

the Ottoman Empire. The War Cabinet specified that the telegram to Wilson should point out the advantages of concluding an armistice with the Turks quickly, including the effect on German morale and the opening of the Black Sea.[116] A cable in this sense was sent to Washington on the same day.[117]

The Allies had already agreed upon the terms of an armistice at the inter-Allied meetings in Paris between 6 and 8 October. It had also been decided to keep Wilson in ignorance of these proposed terms.[118] Balfour considered this decision unfortunate, though it was not "of vital importance" because only an armistice as opposed to a treaty was involved.[119] The Foreign Office subsequently urged that the president should be informed, and the War Cabinet as well as the French and Italian governments finally agreed.[120] The terms were handed to Wilson on the nineteenth by the French ambassador, who was the doyen of Allied ambassadors in Washington. On this occasion the president offered to advise the Turkish government to apply for an armistice and, if the Allies agreed, to state the Entente's armistice terms.[121] Before this suggestion could be acted upon, however, the Turks approached the British naval commander-in-chief at Mudros. On 23 October, the British informed Wilson that they had told their admiral at Mudros to negotiate an armistice.[122] It was not until 31 October that the United States government responded to the Turkish note. Lansing, by direction of the president, told the Spanish ambassador that the message from the Turkish government would be brought to the attention of the governments at war with the Ottoman empire.[123] Meanwhile, the armistice with Turkey had been signed on 30 October, and took effect on the thirty-first. Thus, Wilson had nothing to do with the armistice terms for Turkey, and the Allies made no promises concerning the president's peace program in the negotiations.[124]

The armistice with Austria-Hungary was also concluded without Wilson's Fourteen Points and other pronouncements being clearly part of the understanding. Even though Austria-Hungary had addressed an appeal to the president in concert with the first German note of 3 October, Wilson did not reply to it

until a fortnight later. The British were well aware that the president had changed his attitude toward the Habsburg Empire since the Fourteen Points were announced. He had endorsed the national aspirations of the Czechoslovaks and Jugo-Slavs and, indeed, during September had recognized the Czechoslovak National Council as a *de facto* belligerent government.[125] The British thus assumed that Wilson's policy was parallel to theirs. Their only anxiety was that the president might inadvertently appear to recognize the Austro-Hungarian government's right to represent the subject nationalities seeking independence. On 16 October, the Foreign Office sent a message to Colville Barclay, the counsellor of its Washington Embassy, telling him to put several considerations before Lansing verbally. The telegram referred to reports that Czech, Jugo-Slav, Polish, and Ukranian members had withdrawn from the Parliament in Vienna and observed that, if the reports were true, peace negotiations with Austria-Hungary could only apply to German Austria and the Magyar parts of Hungary, and not to the other nationalities. Thus, it was important that "the President should draft any reply which he may send to the note from [the] Austro-Hungarian Government in such a way as to exclude that Government using it as an admission of their claim to represent the Czechs and Slavs in any peace negotiations."[126]

The president proved to be more than reliable. When he replied to the Austro-Hungarian note on 19 October, he not only made it abundantly clear that he had revised the view expressed in his Fourteen Points; he also insisted that the Czechoslovak and Jugo-Slav peoples should be the judges of what action on the part of the Austro-Hungarian government would satisfy them.[127]

The tenor of this reply was so harsh that Lloyd George thought that Wilson was suggesting that there should be no armistice, but Balfour pointed out that "President Wilson's line was rather that he would not recommend an armistice to his Allies except on certain conditions."[128] It was again irritating not to have been consulted by the president, but his reply was clearly not embarrassing to the British.

On 29 October, the Allies, meeting again in Paris, discussed how they should proceed with the various requests for an armistice. Colonel House was present, acting as the personal representative of the president

[116] CAB 23/8/488/4.

[117] F.O. 371/3448/165564/173330.

[118] Telegram from Derby to Drummond for Cecil, 7 Oct., 1918, Balfour Papers, Add. MSS. 49738.

[119] Telegram from Drummond to Derby for Cecil, 8 Oct., 1918, Balfour Papers, Add. MSS. 49738.

[120] War Cabinet minutes, 11 Oct., 1918, CAB 23/8/484/3; telegram from Rodd, 12 Oct., 1918, F.O. 371/3448/165564/165564; telegram from Derby, 18 Oct., 1918, F.O. 371/3448/165564/171762.

[121] Telegram from Barclay, received 20 Oct., 1918, F.O. 371/3448/165564/175133.

[122] *Foreign Relations, 1918, Supplement 1,* 1: p. 384.

[123] *Ibid.,* p. 428; telegram from Barclay, 31 Oct., 1918, F.O. 371/3449/165564/181682.

[124] Rudin, 1944: pp. 191–192.

[125] Telegram from Reading to Wiseman, 8 Oct., 1918, F.O. 800/225; memorandum by Political Intelligence Department, 12 Oct., 1918, CAB 24/67/6012; telegram from Sir Eric Geddes to the prime minister, 13 Oct., 1918, Lloyd George Papers, F/18/2/23; telegram from Barclay, 14 Oct., 1918, F.O. 371/3444/157260/172682; telegram from Wiseman for Reading and Drummond, 16 Oct., 1918, F.O. 800/223/U.S./94.

[126] F.O. 371/3444/157260/173441.

[127] *Foreign Relations, 1918, Supplement 1,* 1: p. 368.

[128] Draft minutes of a War Cabinet meeting, 22 Oct., 1918, CAB 23/14/489B/3.

and as a special representative of the United States government. It was decided that the associated governments should consider terms of an armistice for both Germany and Austria and then forward them to Wilson. If he agreed, he should advise these enemy governments to send *parlementaires* respectively to Marshal Foch and to General Armando Diaz, the Italian commander-in-chief.[129] The Austro-Hungarian government, however, was not able to wait for this procedure to be carried out. The empire was crumbling politically and militarily. On 30 October, Orlando arrived in Paris with news that an Austrian officer had approached General Diaz asking for armistice terms immediately. The Italian commander-in-chief had told the officer to get proper credentials proving his authority to negotiate. Lloyd George eagerly wanted the talks with the Austrian general to be pursued. He stressed the great advantage of getting Austria out of the war before dealing with Germany and urged that they should act before President Wilson would have time to answer. House accepted this suggestion, believing that it would be easier to take up the Fourteen Points in connection with the German armistice rather than the Austrian one. Armistice terms were quickly formulated and dispatched to General Diaz on the following day.[130]

Meanwhile, the Austro-Hungarian government had addressed another note to Wilson accepting the president's conditions and urging him to promote an immediate armistice.[131] The note was delivered by the Swedish minister in Washington on 29 October. On the thirty-first, Lansing simply notified the Swedish representative that this Austro-Hungarian note would be submitted to the Allied governments. While Washington followed this cumbersome procedure, the armistice with Austria was agreed upon in negotiations at the Italian front.[132] Thus, another ally of Germany had concluded an armistice agreement without using Wilson as an intermediary, and no clear commitments were made to the Fourteen Points during the proceedings.

7. THE ARMISTICE WITH GERMANY

The main task of British diplomacy in arranging the German armistice was to make sure that the agreement secured their victory without (*a*) alienating the president and without (*b*) committing themselves to peace terms which were not in Britain's interest. This is not to say that there was not a large measure of agreement between Wilson and the British government. They agreed with most of Wilson's program.

Indeed, the British government considered much of his policy to be its own and resented suggestions to the contrary, particularly when it was implied that Wilson was morally superior to the Allies. This was another irritating aspect of the president's aloof position which added insult to his failure to consult the Allies about important diplomatic moves. Not only did he cultivate an image of being apart from the Allies, but he also projected an image of being above them—performing on a more statesmanlike level. The War Cabinet's sensitivity on this point was manifested clearly by their reaction to an article by the Washington correspondent of the London *Times* which appeared on 22 October. Strong objection was taken to a passage which observed that the president, according to his admirers, had always deprecated "an undue war mania, not because he is less determined than Lloyd George or M. Clemenceau to crush Prussianism, but because he believes it would militate against a fair and lasting peace." The article went on to suggest that Wilson stood for a peace with justice, "free from any taint of an old-fashioned, secret and revengeful diplomacy. . . ." Most galling of all, the article stated: "The Allies, it is now felt, have swung round to this view."

It was suggested in the War Cabinet that these remarks had been officially inspired in Washington, though Lord Reading observed that it would be more correct to say that they reflected the atmosphere at Washington. Lloyd George pointed out that much of what Balfour and he himself had said in public corresponded with Wilson's principles. The prime minister recalled that the British statement of war aims in January had anticipated the Fourteen Points by several days and that "Wilson's proclamation included practically only two new points, one dealing with Freedom of the Seas and the other with the Economic question." Lloyd George also referred to the statement of war aims which Balfour had made in January, 1917, before the Americans were in the war.

The War Cabinet decided that the prime minister's secretariat should arrange for the publication in *The Times* of a statement traversing the line in the offending article.[133] It appeared on the following day as a statement by a "well-informed" correspondent. The article cited various British pronouncements as proof "of the absence of 'war-mania' and of the practical identity of view which exists on both sides of the Atlantic."[134] In short, it maintained that the British government was as moral as Woodrow Wilson.

The areas of disagreement were, however, the main focus of attention. The British government was keenly aware that, if it simply accepted the president's pro-

[129] Notes of a conversation at the Quai d'Orsay, CAB 28/5/83.

[130] Seymour, 1928: **4**: pp. 104–106; notes of a conversation at the Quai d'Orsay, 30 Oct., 1918, CAB 28/5/84; House to Lansing for the President, 31 Oct., 1918, *Foreign Relations, 1918, Supplement 1*, **1**: pp. 430–431.

[131] *Foreign Relations, 1918, Supplement 1*, **1**: pp. 404–405.

[132] *Ibid.*, pp. 429–430. See also Rudin, 1944: p. 191.

[133] CAB 23/14/489B/2.

[134] London *Times*, 23 Oct., 1918.

nouncements when it entered into an armistice, it would restrict its freedom of action when the time came for settling peace terms. That is, unless reservations or qualifications were made, the British government might, on the one hand, be committed to carrying out all of Wilson's declared principles, a few of which aroused misgivings; on the other hand, it might be precluded from making demands at the peace conference which were not covered in the president's Fourteen Points and other statements.

On 25 and 26 October, the War Cabinet discussed these implications at great length. Once again the question of freedom of the seas was the main concern. Balfour mentioned during the course of the discussion that he had heard rumors that the French had had conversations with the Americans on the subject, and it was possible that these two nations would oppose Britain on the question. Sir Eric Geddes, the first lord of the admiralty, stated that he had received similar information when he was recently in America. British suspicions were easily aroused by such reports. Both Balfour and the prime minister believed that the Allies feared British sea power.[135]

The War Cabinet was uncertain about what Wilson's views actually were. Geddes, who had talked with the president during his visit to the United States, suggested that Wilson did not really want to press the issue very strongly and that he wished to leave it somewhat vague.[136] Lord Reading said that Colonel House was undoubtedly enamored of the doctrine. Moreover, though he had never discussed it with the president, Reading believed that Wilson agreed with his adviser.

Balfour, Geddes, and Reading all pointed out that the president thought of freedom of the seas in conjunction with the League of Nations.[137] This insight led to the formulation of the following argument: if the League of Nations developed into an effective instrument for securing international peace, it might well be that the right of blockade and the right of search at sea should never be used except as an international sanction controlled by the League, but until the League

had proved itself effective, the British government could not agree to the freedom of the seas doctrine.

The prime minister suggested that there were two ways of handling the question: (1) state that the freedom of the seas doctrine was unacceptable, but express willingness to debate it at the peace conference; (2) refuse even to discuss it. Lloyd George observed that the first method might "help the President's feelings," but he was, nevertheless, inclined to challenge the doctrine altogether. In any case, the War Cabinet was agreed that they must avoid committing themselves to freedom of the seas one way or another. The idea was anathema. Indeed, Smuts and Reading were so convinced that freedom of the seas was out of the question that they spoke of getting President Wilson out of his difficulties in regard to the issue.

Doubts had also arisen in London about the adequacy of the Fourteen Points on the subject of reparations to countries invaded by Germany or to the maritime powers which had suffered heavily from German submarines.[138] The president had merely provided for restoration of Belgium and occupied France.

Balfour had drafted a telegram to Wilson which was designed to make the British government's attitude clear about the shortcomings of the Fourteen Points, but it was eventually decided that it would be better to wait until the impending Allied conference in Paris and Versailles to declare the British position. It was felt that a telegram would be too slow, that they should first try to secure the support of Italy and France, and that it would be a great advantage to wait until they knew the atmosphere of the conference. This last reason reflects Lloyd George's extemporaneous (if not impromptu) approach to political conferences.

During the meetings on 25 and 26 October, the War Cabinet also discussed the basic question of whether or not it was really desirable to have an armistice at that time. The prime minister said that he had an open mind on the subject, but he was sometimes inclined to think that they should go on until Germany was smashed, forcefully occupied and put at the Allies' mercy in order to show the enemy that war could not be made with impunity. Balfour argued against this view. He said that, if the British could get the terms they wanted, Germany would be manifestly beaten and an attack across the Rhine would not mean greater defeat. Lloyd George raised the question of whether Germany should be lashed as France had been lashed. In this context Balfour read an extract from Wiseman's notes of a conversation with the president which stated that Wilson would be ashamed if any American troops destroyed a single German town.[139]

---

[135] CAB 23/14/491A; CAB 23/14/491B. See also Derby to Balfour, 23 Oct., 1918, Balfour Papers, Add. MSS. 49744.

[136] On 13 Oct., 1918, Geddes had cabled to the prime minister that Wilson's views on freedom of the seas were "obviously uninformed." Lloyd George Papers, F/18/2/23. For Wilson's account of his remarks to Geddes, see the House Diary, 13 Oct., 1918.

[137] Sir William Wiseman, who had returned to London when House departed for Europe, had supplied Balfour with memoranda based on conversations with the president which emphasized the relationship between the League and freedom of the seas. "Notes of an Interview with the President at the White House, October 16th 1918," F.O. 800/214; "The Attitude of the United States and of President Wilson towards the Peace Conference" (not dated), F.O. 800/214. Published in Fowler, 1969: pp. 283–296. Balfour, however, had realized the connection before reading the memoranda. See CAB 24/66/5967.

[138] CAB 23/14/491B; memorandum by Balfour entitled "The President's Message of Wednesday, October 23rd, 1918," Balfour Papers, Add. MSS. 49699; memorandum by Political Intelligence Department, 12 Oct., 1918, CAB 24/67/6012.

[139] CAB 23/14/491A; CAB 23/14/491B. For Wiseman's memorandum, see Fowler, 1969: pp. 283–290.

Smuts brought forward another argument for an early peace. He maintained that peace made at the present time would be a British peace. Britain was at the height of her power and prestige. If they prolonged the war, American power would increase and eventually the United States would dictate the course of events.[140] Reading took a similar view, suggesting that if they continued the war it might become more difficult for the British to hold their own. For this and other reasons, it was agreed that in the forthcoming conference in Paris, Lloyd George should pursue a "good peace" if that were "now attainable"—by which they meant a victory which secured Britain's main war aims.[141]

In Paris, the prime minister made it very clear that the British would not accept the Fourteen Points without reservations. On 29 October, during a conference with House, Etienne Pichon, the French foreign minister, and Sonnino, he took an almost adamant stand in regard to the freedom of the seas. According to Hankey's notes of the meeting, Lloyd George said that he would not accept Wilson's point two "under any conditions." He observed that the president's suggestion was to hand over the power of blockade to the League of Nations. The notes continue:

If Great Britain was fighting for life, no League of Nations could prevent her from applying a blockade. . . . He [Lloyd George] would like to see the League of Nations thoroughly established and proved before any discussion took place. Even after the establishment of the League of Nations he would only be prepared to begin discussing it. He was not prepared to discuss this question with Germany. . . .[142]

Hankey also recorded that when Colonel House threatened the Allies with the possibility of America making a separate peace, Lloyd George stood his ground. He maintained that it was impossible to agree to the president's second point. "If the United States of America was to make a separate peace," he said, "we should deeply regret it, but, nevertheless, should be prepared to go on fighting." He added that the British government also wanted to make it clear that reparations must be paid—including reparations to wives and children of every sailor illegally killed at sea. But apart from these considerations, the prime minister "had no objection to the President's fourteen points."

Lloyd George observed later in the discussion that the president's other clauses "were wide enough to allow us to place our own interpretation upon them. . . ." House had reinforced this view by explaining Wilson's attitude toward his point one, which advocated "open covenants of peace openly arrived at." The president's adviser made it clear that Wilson did not want to prohibit secret negotiations, but that he merely wanted to prohibit secret treaties. This was an impressive and welcome example of flexibility.[143]

Yet, the prime minister refused to rely on the vagueness of the Fourteen Points in regard to freedom of the seas and reparations. Explicit reservations would have to be stated, and, if possible, Lloyd George wanted to accomplish this in conjunction with Britain's allies. A suitable occasion was at hand. The Allies had to formulate an answer to the United States government's note which formally communicated to them the president's recent correspondence with Germany.[144] The prime minister suggested that a "reply should be sent to President Wilson" making it clear that reparation was included in the president's terms and that, as regards freedom of the seas, they "could not accept the interpretation which we understood Germany to put on it."

House suggested that the British, French, and Italian governments get together and draft their exceptions to the president's terms. Lloyd George and Balfour agreed. The British foreign secretary also expressed his anxiety that Germany should not succeed in driving a wedge between the associated governments. He was obviously apprehensive about the divisive trend of the discussion.[145]

Colonel House's account of this meeting also refers to Balfour's warning. He did so after observing that his own "statement [threatening the possibility of a separate peace] had a very exciting effect upon those present."[146] House was clearly promoting the impres-

[140] CAB 23/14/491B; memorandum by Smuts, 24 Oct., 1918, CAB 24/67/6091. W. K. Hancock wrote: "Smuts, no doubt, was arguing ad hominem and not with jingoistic intent; he proceeded at once to show that it was not the predominance of America but the fate of Europe which he had in the forefront of his mind." W. K. Hancock, 1962: 1: p. 494. This remark obscures the fact that Smuts clearly felt that British predominance was generally beneficial to the world and that American predominance would not be.

[141] CAB 23/14/491B. See also, Austen Chamberlain to Ida Chamberlain, 26 Oct., 1918, Austen Chamberlain Papers, AC 5/1/110. Quoted in Nelson, 1963: pp. 71–72.

[142] CAB 28/5/83.

[143] When House elucidated this as well as other points, he used an interpretive memorandum which had been drafted by Frank I. Cobb, editor of the New York World, and Walter Lippmann. House cabled this commentary to the president for his approval, and Wilson replied that it was a satisfactory interpretation, though he added that all details in the memorandum should be regarded as merely illustrative suggestions. See Seymour, 1928: 4: pp. 152–158 and 192–200. British Intelligence intercepted the Cobb-Lippmann commentary. Lloyd George Papers, F/60/1/7.

[144] For the American note, see F.O. 371/3445/157260/178262. Text published in Foreign Relations, 1918, Supplement 1, 1: p. 383.

[145] Notes of a conversation at the Quai d'Orsay, 29 Oct., 1918, CAB 28/5/83.

[146] House to Lansing for the president, 30 Oct., 1918, Foreign Relations, 1918, Supplement 1, 1: pp. 421–422. House also reported another threat which he had made earlier. He told the British privately that the President anticipated that their policy in regard to freedom of the seas "would lead to the greatest naval program by the United States that the world has ever seen." House to Lansing for the president, 30 Oct., 1918, pp. 423–424. See also, the House Diary, 28 Oct. and 1 Nov., 1918.

sion that he dominated events. He did not report that Lloyd George had stood his ground. In this respect his account of the conference differs markedly from Hankey's notes. Furthermore, Hankey's personal diary reveals an even sharper contrast. He observed that "House looked very sick" after Lloyd George's outburst regarding freedom of the seas. He also suggested that after Lloyd George "made it clear we were not to be bullied, things went better. . . ." Hankey's version is not, of course, conspicuously more impartial than House's report. He had a special interest in how Lloyd George performed. Hankey wrote that he had "coached" the prime minister for his outburst on freedom of the seas.[147]

The discussion about the president's peace program ended inconclusively on 29 October. It was eventually decided to meet again on the following day and consider the observations which the Allied representatives wished to make on the president's Fourteen Points with a view to a joint memorandum to be transmitted to Wilson together with the armistice terms.

Before the conference met again on the thirtieth, Lloyd George showed a British draft concerning the Fourteen Points to Clemenceau and House. Moreover, House learned that Clemenceau intended to submit an elaborate set of French objections to the Fourteen Points. Thereupon the president's adviser issued a prodigious warning. He told Clemenceau and Lloyd George that Sonnino would also have a memorandum and suggested that, if the Allies made many objections to Wilson's program, the president would go to Congress, explain what the Allies were fighting for and "place the responsibility upon Congress for the further continuation of the war by the United States in behalf of the aims of the Allies." House observed that when he said this, Lloyd George and Clemeneau "looked at each other significantly." He also reported that the French premier "at once abandoned his idea of submitting an elaborate memorandum. . . ."[148]

According to notes by Hankey, when Lloyd George subsequently submitted the British draft to the conference, he remarked that both the French premier and House had expressed their agreement. The draft declared the Allied government's willingness to make peace with Germany on the terms laid down in the president's address of 8 January, 1918, and in his subsequent speeches, subject to two qualifications.

They must point out . . . that clause two relating to what is usually described as the Freedom of the Seas, is open to various interpretations, some of which they could not accept. They must therefore reserve to themselves complete freedom on this subject when they enter the peace conference.

Further, in the conditions of peace laid down in his Address to Congress on the 8th of January, 1918, the President declared that invaded territories must be restored as well as evacuated and freed. The Allied Governments feel that no doubt ought to be allowed to exist as to what this provision implies. By it they understand that compensation will be made by Germany for all damage done to the civilian population of Allies and their property (by the forces of Germany?), by land, by sea, and from the air.[149]

Baron Sonnino agreed with the draft memorandum, "provided that it was clearly understood that the Austrian negotiations were not in any way compromised." The Italian foreign minister feared that the Fourteen Points might be applied to Austria-Hungary and he wanted to make an observation protecting Italy's claims. In particular, he was worried about Wilson's point nine, which only advocated a rectification of Italy's frontiers along clearly recognizable lines of nationality. Italy, of course, desired far more than that.

Lloyd George insisted that Sonnino's remarks were not relevant to the present discussion, which concerned only the armistice with Germany. Clearly the British prime minister wanted to keep the Allies' reservations in regard to the president's peace program to a minimum. No doubt he was also trying to avoid complicated and embarrassing questions involving the Treaty of London.

Meanwhile, Colonel House reported the text of the British draft to the president with a favorable recommendation. Indeed, he wanted it to be accepted without alteration.[150] Wilson's response, however, expressed some doubts. The president "sympathetically" recognized Britain's necessities with regard to the seas and he realized that freedom of the seas was a question "upon which there is need of the freest discussion and the most liberal interchange of views." He was not, however, sure that the Allies had definitely accepted the principle of the freedom of the seas. Wilson's reply went on to warn that he could not recede from the second of his Fourteen Points. It need not be discussed with the German government, he added, provided the associated governments agreed among themselves. The president also observed that the law governing blockade would have to be altered, though he mollified this remark with the assertion that there was no danger of blockade being abolished.[151]

[147] Roskill, 1970: 1: p. 623.

[148] House to Lansing for the president, 30 Oct., 1918, *Foreign Relations, 1918, Supplement 1,* 1: pp. 425–426.

[149] CAB 28/5/84. The original draft, which was composed by Philip Kerr, referred in the last line to damage done "by the invasion by Germany. . . . " This wording could have been used to exclude many British claims to reparations. Substituting the phrase "by the forces of Germany" was probably one attempt to avoid such an interpretation. Eventually the last line was amended to read: "by the aggression of Germany by land, by sea, and from the air." CAB 28/5/94. See also, Butler, 1960: pp. 72–74; Kerr to E. A. Walker, 18 Mar., 1931, Lothian Papers, GD 40/17/254; Kerr to Edgar Abraham, 22 Jan., 1934; Abraham to Kerr, 26 Jan., 1934; memorandum entitled "Reparation-Ships" by Edgar Abraham, Lothian Papers, GD 40/17/271.

[150] House to Lansing for the president, 30 Oct., 1918, *Foreign Relations, Supplement 1,* 1: pp. 425–426.

[151] Wilson to House, 31 Oct., 1918, *ibid.,* pp. 427–428.

House revealed a paraphrase of Wilson's reply during a meeting with Allied leaders at his Paris residence on 3 November. In the ensuing discussion, House at first tried to get the principle of freedom of the seas accepted. Lloyd George flatly refused. He said that, if he accepted the principle, it would only mean that in a week's time a new prime minister would be in Paris refusing to accept. Colonel House then suggested (according to Hankey) that "all he wanted was the principle that the question could be discussed." To this Lloyd George replied that the British government was willing to discuss the question in the light of new conditions which had arisen during the war.[152] Actually, House had been prepared in advance of the meeting to accept this compromise.[153]

During the afternoon, after consulting Balfour, Lloyd George sent a letter to Colonel House confirming his expression of readiness to talk about the question. Paraphrasing the president, he added that the subject "can only be dealt with satisfactorily through the freest debate and the most liberal exchange of views."[154] Thus, Colonel House succeeded in committing the British government to discuss the freedom of the seas, but Lloyd George had accomplished his essential task. He had avoided committing himself to this most disagreeable principle without alienating the administration.

In addition to the reservation regarding freedom of the seas and the clarification regarding reparations, the British commented on two other doubtful matters connected with the Fourteen Points. One concerned the question of the captured colonies. The president's point four, which called for an impartial adjustment of colonial claims, did not contradict the British government's position on this subject, but they nevertheless continued to be somewhat doubtful about it because it did not preclude the return of the colonies to Germany. Indeed, on 1 November, a War Cabinet meeting in London decided to send a telegram to the prime minister telling him that it should be made clear that the German colonies would in no circumstances be restored to Germany and that the claims of the Dominions to certain of them could not possibly be waived.[155] This was done despite the fact that Balfour had recently declared in a speech that "in no circumstances is it consistent with the safety, with the security, with

the unity of the British Empire, that the German colonies should be returned to Germany."[156] On 3 November, Lloyd George replied to the War Cabinet, informing them that he had made it clear to Colonel House that the British had "no intention of restoring Colonies to Germany, nor of taking away Colonies from [the] Dominions who . . . captured them." He added that while he could not say that House "assented to those views, he did not demur from [sic] them."[157]

House reported one of his conversations with Lloyd George about the colonies to the president. His telegram is particularly interesting because it shows that, when Lloyd George declared Britain's intentions, he also broached the idea of the United States undertaking responsibilities for some of the captured colonies. House wrote:

> In my private conversation with Lloyd George yesterday he said that Great Britain desired the United States to become trustee for German East African colonies. That Great Britain was unwilling that they should be turned back to Germany for the reason that the Germans had used such inhuman methods in their treatment of the natives. He said by right [South West] Africa and the Asiatic islands belonging to Germany must go to the South African Federation and to Australia respectively; that unless this was done Great Britain would be confronted by a revolution in those dominions.
>
> He added that Great Britain would have to assume a protectorate over Mesopotamia and perhaps Palestine. Arabia he thought should become autonomous. France might be given a sphere of influence in Syria.

The strategy behind the idea of an American trusteeship did not escape House. He went on: "My [opinion based on] his suggestion regarding German East Africa, is that the British would like us to accept something so they might more freely take what they desire."[158] Lloyd George had, indeed, made British intentions very clear.

The other clause which continued to bother the British was Wilson's point three, which called for the "removal, so far as possible, of all economic barriers and the establishment of an equality of trade conditions. . . ." Lloyd George's doubts about this clause seemed to increase as the conference in Paris proceeded. The questions which he asked House reflected, in particular, the British government's reluctance (a) to commit itself to share limited supplies of raw materials equitably with Germany and (b) to limit its freedom to establish preferential tariffs.[159] In London, the British War Cabinet was also uneasy about point three, and in a cable to the prime minister on 1 November, had urged him to avoid any commitment "to grant . . . 'most favoured nation' treatment

[152] CAB 28/5/92.

[153] House to Lansing for the president, 3 Nov., 1918, *Foreign Relations, 1918, Supplement 1,* 1: p. 448. It is interesting that on the day after reaching the compromise, House received some additional ammunition for his diplomatic battles. Wilson authorized him to say that if the Allies refused to accept the principle of freedom of the seas, they could count on the United States "to build up the strongest navy that our resources permit and as our people have long desired." Wilson to House, received 4 Nov., 1918, House Papers. House did not, of course, want to reopen the dispute.

[154] CAB 28/5/92. See also, House to Lansing, 3 Nov., 1918, *Foreign Relations, 1918, Supplement 1,* 1: pp. 455–456.

[155] CAB 23/14/495A/2; telegram for the prime minister, 1 Nov., 1918, F.O. 371/3445/157260/183157.

[156] London *Times,* 24 Oct., 1918.

[157] F.O. 371/3445/157260/182496.

[158] House to Lansing for the president, 30 Oct., 1918, *Foreign Relations, 1918, Supplement 1,* 1: p. 424.

[159] Procès-verbal of a meeting of the Supreme War Council, 1 Nov., 1918, CAB 28/5/88; notes of a conversation at the Paris residence of Colonel House, 3 Nov., 1918, CAB 28/5/92.

to enemy nations, which would prevent fulfilment of our obligations to assist in restoration of Allied territories, and prejudge our own economic policy in future."[160]

On 3 November, when the discussion at the conference in Paris turned to this subject, Lloyd George urged that the words "so far as possible" ought to apply to the whole of the president's clause. He explained that at present the qualifying phrase might be construed to apply only to the removal of economic barriers and not to the establishment of an equality of trade conditions. All difficulties would be removed, he suggested, if the words "so far as possible" were put at the beginning of Wilson's point three. Colonel House accepted this suggestion and undertook to call the president's attention to it.[161] The Belgian foreign minister wanted to add a further qualification regarding measures of restoration, but Lloyd George deprecated the suggestion because "he did not want to alter the Fourteen Points more than was absolutely essential." Thus, the British government protected its freedom of action regarding the postwar trade question as well as the question of the colonies, without adding to the memorandum of observations on the Fourteen Points to be addressed to the president. This had, of course, the advantage of keeping British differences with Wilson's program as inconspicuous as possible.

Further Italian and Belgian efforts to add reservations to the draft memorandum were also thwarted. In response to an attempt by the Italian prime minister to protect his government's claims, Lloyd George suggested that President Wilson should be asked to inform the German government that points nine through twelve did not affect Germany.[162] Obviously he was trying to placate the Italians without allowing them to take explicit exception to Wilson's pronouncements. In view of the fact that point twelve concerned the Ottoman Empire, Lloyd George may have, at the same time, thought that his suggestion might free him from any implied commitment to President Wilson's Fourteen Points when the peace terms with Turkey were eventually settled. Whatever his reasons, however, he had no desire to press his suggestion when Colonel House advised against saying anything to the president on the matter.

The Belgian minister, still anxious about securing compensation from Germany, also wanted to insert a phrase into the Allied memorandum that would cover compensations for "all damage caused by the war." Lloyd George feared that inserting these words would "tell Germany that she had to pay so huge an indemnity that it would be better for her to go on fighting." He also stated that he "was very averse to any altera-

tion in the memorandum."[163] At the end of the day, Britain's allies had added nothing to the draft which Lloyd George had submitted. It still contained only the reservation regarding freedom of the seas and the clarification that Germany would pay for all damage done to the civilian population.

On 4 November, a meeting of the Supreme War Council approved this memorandum to the president as well as the military and naval terms for the armistice with Germany. Colonel House promptly sent the memorandum and the armistice terms to Wilson.[164] On the following day, the president forwarded the memorandum to the Germans and informed them, as had been agreed in Paris, that Marshall Foch was authorized to receive properly accredited representatives of the German government, and to communicate the terms of an armistice.[165]

The armistice terms seemed stern to the British government. Certainly their acceptance by Germany would assure the Allies of military victory. When Lloyd George returned to London on 5 November and reported to the Imperial War Cabinet on the meetings in France, he was not sure that the German government would yield to the demands. The enemy was, however, incapable of effective resistance. Indeed, sick with war-weariness and defeat, Germany was being disrupted by revolution. The German government readily agreed to the armistice terms, after some minor modifications. The armistice took effect on 11 November, and the British celebrated their victory.

Meanwhile, an interesting turn of events in the United States had damaged President Wilson's position abroad. On 5 November, the day that he sent his final armistice note to the German government, the U. S. congressional elections took place, and the Republicans emerged with control of both the House of Representatives and the Senate. The British were, of course, well aware that a Republican Senate might cause trouble for the president over the peace settlement.[166] Moreover, the elections had cast a shadow on Wilson's authority to speak for America on questions of peace. The president himself had contributed to this impression. During the election campaign, he had appealed for the return of a Democratic Congress, suggesting that the election of a Republican majority would be interpreted abroad as a repudiation of his leadership. On 10 November, Lloyd George remarked to Lord Riddell: "The elections show that America is not behind Wilson."[167]

[160] F.O. 371/3445/157260/183157.

[161] CAB 28/5/92. House duly informed the president. See House to Lansing for the president, 3 Nov., 1918, *Foreign Relations, 1918, Supplement 1, 1:* p. 456.

[162] CAB 28/5/92. See also CAB 28/5/88.

[163] CAB 28/5/92.

[164] House to Lansing for the president, nos. 42 and 46, 4 Nov., 1918, *Foreign Relations, 1918, Supplement 1, 1:* pp. 460–468.

[165] Scott, 1921: pp. 456–457.

[166] Telegram from Barclay, 3 Nov., 1918, F.O. 371/3428/4555/182642; see also the F.O. minutes on a report by the British military attaché in Washington, received 11 Nov., 1918, F.O. 371/3428/4555/186827.

[167] Riddell, 1933: p. 380.

As far as his own position at the impending peace negotiations was concerned, Lloyd George was confident that he had not compromised British interests while in Paris. He did not go unchallenged on this point. At the Imperial War Cabinet meeting on 5 November, the Australian prime minister, W. M. Hughes, urged "the importance of entering a *caveat* that the Fourteen Points were not our [the British Empire's] Terms of Peace." He did not want "to be bound to the chariot-wheel of the Fourteen Points. . . ." Lloyd George replied that he had been carefully through Wilson's pronouncements and "he could not find a single point which we wanted that was not amply covered, with the exception of the points regarding the freedom of the seas and indemnities," and notice had been duly given on these matters.[168] Hughes was not content with this. In speeches, in a letter to *The Times,* and in a letter to the prime minister, he repeatedly suggested that the British had not done enough to protect and promote the empire's interests in regard to peace terms.[169] Wilson's point three dealing with economic policy particularly bothered him, and he wanted a definite provision regarding the Dominions' claims to the captured German colonies in the Pacific. Hughes was also angry about not having been consulted when, in his view, peace terms had been decided in Paris. In a letter to the Australian prime minister on 11 November, Lloyd George replied:

The Allies themselves at the Conference did not decide peace terms or do anything more than merely settle armistice terms, while satisfying themselves that the language of President Wilson's Fourteen Points together with that used in his subsequent speeches was wide enough to cover all that they intended to raise when the issues of peace came to be dealt with. The two points of the so-called Freedom of the Seas and Reparation were specifically raised in order to safeguard issues which might conceivably be prejudiced by President Wilson's terms. We also as you are aware safeguarded the posn. [position] as to raw materials.[170]

These remarks clearly express Lloyd George's view of the commitments which the British government had made to Wilson's peace program. In short, he had preserved plenty of scope for the British to secure their war aims at the peace conference.

This view contrasts sharply with an opinion which House expressed in a telegram to the president on 5 November. He cabled:

I consider that we have won a great diplomatic victory in getting the Allies to accept the principles laid down

---

[168] CAB 23/8/W.C. 497, I.W.C. 36. Hughes was the only Dominion prime minister present.

[169] London *Times,* 8 and 9 Nov., 1918; Hughes to the prime minister, 9 Nov., 1918, Lloyd George Papers, F/28/2/9.

[170] Lloyd George to Hughes, 11 Nov., 1918, Lloyd George Papers, F/28/2/9. L. S. Amery recalled in his memoirs that he "was deputed to explain to Hughes that nothing had really happened [at Paris], and that we were still quite free to enforce whatever peace terms we wished." Amery, 1953: **2**: p. 171.

in your 8 January speech and in your subsequent addresses. . . . I doubt whether any of the heads of the Governments with whom we have been dealing quite realise how far they are now committed to the proposed peace programme.

British Intelligence apparently intercepted this telegram, for it was shown to Lloyd George.[171] One is tempted to imagine a wry smile as he read it. In any case, the prime minister firmly believed that he was not committed to anything which was against British interests.

CONCLUSION

In its relations with President Wilson on questions of peace, Lloyd George's wartime government achieved its main goals without much difficulty. During the last few months of American neutrality, the prime minister quite easily parried the president's efforts to promote peace negotiations. Wilson's famous note of December, 1916, merely provoked British propaganda in the form of the Allies' reply and Balfour's commentary upon it. The famous "Peace without Victory" address was answered in a speech by Bonar Law in support of a new war loan to help win the war. As America's entry into the war drew nearer, Lloyd George allowed Wilson to attempt to bring about a separate peace with Austria-Hungary, but only after Britain's own approaches to Austria-Hungary had proved futile. Throughout this neutrality period, the British insistence upon decisively defeating Germany was not compromised.

After the president launched his own crusade against Germany and became an advocate of victory, the British gladly used his convenient public statements to turn aside pacifist criticism and peace moves from other quarters. Indeed, they were able to let the president's reply to the pope be taken as representative of their own attitude, despite some differences of opinion between Washington and London. For the duration of the war, the British avoided a breach with the president without binding themselves to the embarrassing points in his program.

In view of Britain's heavy dependence upon American supplies and assistance, the success which the Lloyd George government had in its wartime relations with the president seems noteworthy. Obviously the favorable results cannot be attributed merely to British diplomatic skill, though that played a part. Wilson himself contributed heavily to British success. During the years of American neutrality, his peace moves had generally been cautious. Actually, Britain's heavy dependence upon the United States for supplies tends to create an exaggerated impression of the president's power to shape events. Formidable complications inhibited Wilson's ambition to be a peacemaker. Berlin

---

[171] Telegram from House to Wilson, 5 Nov., 1918, Lloyd George Papers, F/60/1/8.

could only be decisively influenced, if at all, by military threats; yet, the United States was not well prepared for war. Moreover, it is doubtful that the president could have achieved significantly greater preparedness at that time. Even assuming greater preparedness, the strong pacifist sentiments in America during the latter part of 1916 would have made the use of military threats by the White House politically hazardous. Furthermore, German professions of moderation were not convincing. In these circumstances, threatening to cut off essential supplies to the Allies would have been difficult to justify, and if the Allies proved unreasonable, carrying out the threat would have been economically and politically expensive. Thus, after the House-Grey understanding of February, 1916, failed to produce results, the president limited himself to requests for statements of war aims and to appeals for moderation—moves which the British could handle without serious trouble.

Once Germany finally opted for unrestricted submarine warfare early in 1917, all the Lloyd George government had to do was to wait for American belligerency. Characteristically, Lloyd George was not content with a patient policy. In a public tribute to Abraham Lincoln he suggested that participation in the war was consistent with American ideals. The prime minister also dangled before the president's eyes the prospect of full participation in the eventual peace conference in return for joining the war. Though the German government's willingness to gamble on their U-boats undoubtedly deserves most of the credit for American military involvement, the prime minister's bait may have encouraged Wilson's full-scale belligerency.

After the United States entered the war and adopted a policy of victory, Wilson also had an interest in avoiding conflicts with his associates over war aims and was willing to smooth over differences of opinion. The British and Americans were under tremendous pressure to cooperate in the face of an enemy who remained continuously formidable until the latter part of 1918. Despite American mobilization, the German threat seemed to increase. Mobilization required about a year to yield significant results—a fact which Lloyd George found agonizing and outrageous. Moreover, America's contribution was offset to a considerable extent by the Russian collapse, which freed German troops for the western front. Meanwhile, both France and Italy were very seriously afflicted with war-weariness.

Fortunately for Wilson and the British government, their differences were few. The League of Nations idea was heavily endorsed on both sides of the Atlantic. This met a widespread conviction that some extraordinary political commitments would have to be made to reduce the possibility of future wars. In Washington especially, but also in London, this meant that deep-rooted isolationist impulses would have to be overcome. The League of Nations idea was particularly attractive to both governments because it could be presented as something distinct from a conventional peacetime alliance.

They also generally agreed on territorial terms. Neither power sought territory on the European continent. The British, of course, intended to have the lion's share of captured German colonies and wanted to control large parts of captured Turkish territory—especially Mesopotamia. These *desiderata* clearly posed some danger of Anglo-American disagreements. Two sources of acute embarrassment were readily apparent. Despite the tact of General Jan Smuts, the British Dominions in the southern hemisphere were inclined to be adamant about retaining German colonies. The outbursts of Prime Minister William Morris Hughes of Australia are famous in this regard. As for the captured Turkish territory, Wilson did not like Britain's involvement in secret agreements carving up that region. Yet London was willing to go very far to make British acquisitions palatable to Washington. Offering the Americans some of the territory was one obvious tactic. Invoking slogans associated with ideals of national self-determination was another. Despite the bizarre difficulties involved in ascertaining the wishes of various tribes in captured German colonies, Lloyd George's speeches went further in this direction than Wilson's. Furthermore, Wilson himself had assured Balfour that he would be flexible in applying the principle of self-determination. Thus, the notion that the president might accept British retention of captured territory under some formula like "trusteeship" was well founded. In fact, Wilson reinforced this view near the end of the war in a tactful conversation with Wiseman. He intimated that he himself would be content to see Britain administer the German colonies, but he suggested that, in order to avoid some of the international jealousy which this could arouse, they might be administered in trust for the League of Nations.[1]

The few disagreements which did surface concerning peace terms were all manageable. By its very nature, the question of a *post bellum* trade war was easy to postpone until hostilities ceased. In the meantime, even Wilson used threats of economic discrimination against Germany as a political weapon. This was an interesting aspect of his speech of 4 December, 1917. His Fourteen Points address of 8 January, 1918, also contained an economic threat.[2]

Another difference of opinion centered around the president's distinction between an autocratic German government and the German people. Various British leaders expressed qualms about this formula ranging

---

[1] "Notes of an Interview with the President at the White House, October 16th 1918," F.O. 800/214. Published in Fowler, 1969: pp. 283–290.

[2] See above pp. 70 and 74.

from a fear that it precluded negotiations with an un-reformed German government to the foreboding that a democratized Germany would be treated too leniently. The issue did not become a serious problem. Meaningful peace negotiations remained a mirage until the latter part of 1918, and the character of the government in Berlin did not change until Germany was defeated. At that time the president quickly dashed German hopes that he would be lenient.

Freedom of the seas was the most sensitive point of contention between Wilson and the British government. Yet, even during his neutrality the president had, while protesting, acquiesced in Britain's "blockade" measures which extensively interfered with neutral commerce. Furthermore, after the United States entered the war, the president cooperated with the Allies' "blockade." The freedom of the seas issue pertained to rights at sea during future wars. Consequently the disagreement did not come to a head until the pre-armistice negotiations. The president's views were still vague on the issue. He did not envision the abolition of blockades, though he wanted future maritime interference with trade to be linked to the League of Nations. This enabled the British to argue that they must reserve their freedom of action at least until the League could be effectively established, and eventually the president agreed to postpone the dispute indefinitely. The position of the United States remained ambiguous. On the one hand, the memory of British interference with American trade still smarted. On the other, America's enhanced status as a great naval power gave her some identity of interest with Great Britain in preserving a free hand. Perhaps this realization worked surreptitiously to confuse Washington's point of view. Wilson later dropped the issue of freedom of the seas at the Paris Peace Conference. His explanation was that since there would be no neutrals in the League of Nations, defining the maritime rights of neutrals during wartime was no longer a problem. America's naval building program turned out to be a more serious source of tension in 1919 than freedom of the seas.[3]

In any case, a basic theme which emerges from this study is that British and American views on peace terms harmonized to a striking degree. Obviously one must look beyond differences of opinion to explain the friction which developed from time to time. The president's political decision to maintain a demonstrably independent stance in his relations with the Allies hampered the development of genuine coordination on the diplomatic front.

Personality problems also contributed to the periodic irritations. Ironically, for instance, both Wilson and Lloyd George were personally inclined to act without mutual consultation, and both were very sensitive about not being consulted. British leaders, of course, generally resented the president's Olympian style. His tardiness about consulting his "associates" became the subject of bitter complaint in October, 1918, when he carried on his extraordinary correspondence with Germany. The British did not readily appreciate his skill and effectiveness during that exchange. Indeed, they privately criticized him for being merely a "rhetorician" who was incapable of skillfully drafting important documents in substantive negotiations. The political sagacity with which Wilson often used his glittering idealism was easily overlooked. The prime minister once entertained his colleagues with the observation that Wilson was "a curious mixture of old Bryce and Sir Arthur Yapp. . . ."[4] It must have been irritating to reflect that such a man had tremendous power. His aloof, selfrighteous style, no doubt, seemed all the more galling because the enormous influence which he claimed and enjoyed appeared to be out of all proportion to what the United States had sacrificed in the war effort. America had, in fact, prospered economically.

Commercial rivalry also caused friction in relations between Washington and London. Recent historians have drawn attention to the president's economic concerns—particularly his advocacy of open-door expansion of American trade. Yet, a broader political rivalry may have been a more serious irritant of Anglo-American relations. The basic similarity between British and American attitudes toward peace terms in one sense aggravated antagonism because it set the stage for a contest between two powers who wanted to preside over their common values. Occasionally the question of political dominance was actually articulated.[5] Moreover, the desire for dominance was reflected in the general feeling in Whitehall that British statesmanship was superior to Wilson's. The administration in Washington naturally assumed the reverse.

The British, of course, tried to avoid antagonizing the president, in view of the emerging wealth and power of the United States. They wanted to promote Anglo-American cooperation not only to win the war, but also to shape and secure the peace settlement in accordance with British interests. Though the British felt bound to uphold the Treaty of London if Italy proved adamant, Lloyd George and Balfour undoubtedly thought that Wilson might facilitate Britain's discreet evasion of some of its unsavory provisions. Harold Nicolson went so far as to suggest that in the settlement of Balkan questions only the president could cut through the tangle of conflicting claims and commit-

---

[3] Tillman, 1961: pp. 289–294.

[4] Jones, 1969: 1: pp. 69–70. See also Chamberlain to his wife, Ivy, 16 Oct., 1918, Austen Chamberlain Papers, AC 6/1/319. Viscount James Bryce was a scholarly Gladstonian liberal and former ambassador to Washington. Sir Arthur Yapp was the evangelical and teetotal national secretary of the Y.M.C.A.

[5] See above, for example, pp. 90 and 104. See also Chapter V, note 137.

ments. Lord Robert Cecil dreamed of general benefits to all mankind which might be achieved if Wilson could be induced to apply his influence upon peace terms in accordance with British views.

Balfour clearly shared this attitude, and he was particularly skillful in his pursuit of Anglo-American co-operation. His tact and charm during his mission to the United States in the spring of 1917 were impressive. He genuinely believed in the necessity of honest consultation. His frankness was not, to be sure, unqualified. Information about Britain's secret understanding with Japan concerning Shantung was not freely volunteered. Yet, he was apparently willing to provide copies of all of Britain's secret agreements when Wilson and House requested him to do so. Furthermore, Balfour frequently championed the cause of Anglo-American consultation in handling various peace moves. His opposition to Lloyd George's desire to conceal the overture which Germany made through Spain in the autumn of 1917 is a case in point. The foreign secretary's determined and successful advocacy of consultation qualifies his prevailing reputation for elegant indolence and patriotic deference to the prime minister's views.[6] Balfour could be effective when he felt strongly about a policy, and the need to promote Anglo-American harmony was one of his priorities.

The Foreign Office adapted to the president's preference for secrecy and informal negotiation. Balfour readily utilized the unusually close relationship which Wiseman cultivated with House and, to a lesser extent, with the president. This channel of communication probably more than compensated for the troubled ambassadorships of Page and Spring Rice. The former cut himself off from the administration by adopting outspoken Anglophile and pro-Ally views. Spring Rice was hampered by close associations with some of Wilson's Republican opponents and by his own excitable temperament. Lansing thought he was suited to be only a high-ranking clerk.[7] His exaggerated fear of enemy plots often made him seem ridiculous and mentally unbalanced. House observed that he saw "spooks everywhere."[8] Lord Reading was a more able ambassador, though he too irritated the president by the frequency of his requests to visit the White House in order to advocate his government's views.[9] The secretary of state was more accessible, but his influence upon Wilson was obviously questionable. As Spring Rice observed, Lansing was "treated as a clerk."[10] In this context, Wiseman played his hand very cleverly. Some of his work was perhaps of dubious benefit. For example, in ingratiating himself to House and Wilson, he described his own government as regrettably reactionary.[11] This may have enhanced his own position, but it probably reinforced an unfortunate prejudice of his hosts. On the other hand, considerable antagonism was mollified by his intimate, discreet work.

Balfour's and Wiseman's tactful style was ideally suited to the needs and assumptions of British diplomacy. The Lloyd George government clearly required good relations with the president in order to secure its war aims. Wilson obviously wanted to play a great role in peace negotiations, and he could conceivably put enormous pressure on the British to conform to his wishes. There was no need to compromise their main aims until the president actually did so, and it became unlikely that Wilson would disrupt his relations with Britain once he committed himself to victory; nevertheless, it was prudent not to antagonize him unnecessarily. The task was to smooth over differences of opinion and evade conflicts by exploiting the vagueness of Wilson's peace program and by stressing the basic similarities of view.

The situation at the end of the war appeared fully satisfactory. The Lloyd George government enjoyed good relations with the Wilson administration; it had, with America's help, won the war and could go on to the peace conference without being committed to carry out any of the president's general principles in a way which it considered harmful. Wilson may have scored a diplomatic victory in the pre-armistice negotiations, but the Lloyd George government had easily **avoided a defeat.**

---

[6] *Cf.,* Warman, 1972: pp. 150–151.

[7] See Lansing's character sketch of Spring Rice, dated May, 1917, Lansing Papers, Private Memoranda.

[8] House Diary, 5 Mar., 1917.

[9] See Lansing's character sketch of Lord Reading, dated Apr., 1918, Lansing Papers, Private Memoranda.

[10] Spring Rice to Balfour, 22 Dec., 1917, quoted in Gwynn, 1929: 2: p. 366.

[11] House Diary, 16 Sept., 1917.

SELECTED BIBLIOGRAPHY*

I. PRIMARY SOURCES

A. Unpublished Official Records

Cabinet Papers (Public Record Office).
Foreign Office Papers (Public Record Office).

B. Unpublished Private Papers

Balfour Papers (British Museum).
Balfour Papers, F.O. 800 (Public Record Office).
Robert Cecil Papers (British Museum).
Robert Cecil Papers, F.O. 800 (Public Record Office).
Austen Chamberlain Papers (Birmingham University Library).
Drummond Papers, F.O. 800 (Public Record Office).
Hardinge Papers (Cambridge University Library).
House Diary and Papers (Yale University Library).
Lansing Desk Diary, Diary and Papers (Library of Congress).
Lansing Papers (Princeton University Library).
Bonar Law Papers (Beaverbrook Library).
Lloyd George Papers (Beaverbrook Library).
Lothian Papers (Scottish Record Office).
Milner Papers (Bodleian Library).
Page Diary and Papers (Houghton Library, Harvard University).
Reading Papers, F.O. 800 (Public Record Office).
Spring Rice Papers, F.O. 800 (Public Record Office).
Wilson Papers (Library of Congress).
Wiseman Papers, F.O. 800 (Public Record Office).
Wiseman Papers (Yale University Library).

C. Published Official and Public Documents

BAKER, RAY STANNARD, and WILLIAM E. DODD, eds. 1926. *The Public Papers of Woodrow Wilson: The New Democracy* (2 v., New York) **2.**
BAKER, RAY STANNARD, and WILLIAM E. DODD, eds. 1927. *The Public Papers of Woodrow Wilson: War and Peace* (2 v., New York) **1.**
DEPARTMENT OF STATE. 1929. *Papers Relating to the Foreign Relations of the United States, 1916, Supplement, the World War* (Washington).
—— 1931. *Papers Relating to the Foreign Relations of the United States, 1917, Supplement 1, the World War* (Washington).
—— 1932. *Papers Relating to the Foreign Relations of the United States, 1917, Supplement 2, the World War* (2 v., Washington) **1.**
—— 1932. *Papers Relating to the Foreign Relations of the United States, 1918, Russia* (3 v., Washington) **2.**
—— 1933. *Papers Relating to the Foreign Relations of the United States, 1918, Supplement 1* (2 v., Washington) **1.**
—— 1940. *Papers Relating to the Foreign Relations of the United States, the Lansing Papers 1914–1920* (2 v., Washington) **2.**
DICKINSON, G. LOWES, ed. 1919. *Documents and Statements Relating to Peace Proposals and War Aims, December 1916–November 1918* (London).
Parliamentary Debates. 5th Series, 1916–1918.
Parliamentary Papers. Session 1917–18.
SCOTT, JAMES BROWN, ed. 1921. *Official Statements of War Aims and Peace Proposals, December 1916 to November 1918* (Washington).

———

* This bibliography does not contain all of the sources consulted. Only those which proved useful to this author are listed.

D. Memoirs, Diaries, Correspondence and Other Papers

AMERY, L. S. 1953–1955. *My Political Life* (3 v., London) **2.**
BAKER, RAY STANNARD. 1927–1939. *Woodrow Wilson: Life and Letters* (8 v., New York) **6–8.**
BEAVERBROOK, LORD. 1956. *Men and Power, 1917–1918* (London).
CALLWELL, SIR C. E. 1927. *Field-Marshall Sir Henry Wilson: His Life and Diaries* (London).
CECIL, VISCOUNT. 1949. *All the Way* (London).
CHURCHILL, WINSTON S. 1931. *The World Crisis, 1911–1918* (rev. ed., London).
—— 1937. *Great Contemporaries* (London).
GREY, VISCOUNT. 1925. *Twenty-Five Years, 1892–1916* (2 v., London) **2.**
GWYNN, STEPHEN, ed. 1929. *The Letters and Friendships of Sir Cecil Spring Rice: A Record* (2 v., London) **2.**
HANCOCK, W. K., and JEAN VAN DER POEL, eds. 1966. *Selections from the Smuts Papers* (4 v., Cambridge, England) **3.**
HANKEY, LORD. 1961. *The Supreme Command* (2 v., London) **2.**
HENDRICK, BURTON J. 1923. *The Life and Letters of Walter H. Page* (2 v., London) **2.**
HOUSE, COLONEL EDWARD MANDELL. See Seymour.
JAMES, ROBERT RHODES, ed. 1969. *Memoirs of a Conservative: J. C. C. Davidson's Memoirs and Papers* (London).
JONES, THOMAS. 1969–1971. *Whitehall Diary.* Edited by Keith Middlemas (3 v., London) **1.**
LANSING, ROBERT. 1935. *War Memoirs* (London).
LLOYD GEORGE, DAVID. 1933–1937. *War Memoirs* (6 v., Boston) **2–6.**
—— 1938. *The Truth about the Peace Treaties* (2 v., London) **1.**
MURRAY, ARTHUR C. (Viscount Elibank). 1946. *At Close Quarters: A Sidelight on Anglo-American Diplomatic Relations* (London).
RIDDELL, LORD. 1933. *Lord Riddell's War Diary, 1914–1918* (London).
ROSKILL, STEPHEN. 1970–1972. *Hankey: Man of Secrets* (2 v., London) **1.**
   This book has been listed here rather than with the secondary sources, because it was particularly useful as a source for those portions of Hankey's Diary which were not published in *The Supreme Command.*
SEYMOUR, CHARLES, ed. 1926–1928. *The Intimate Papers of Colonel House* (4 v., New York) **2–4.**
TAYLOR, A. J. P., ed. 1971. *Lloyd George: A Diary by Frances Stevenson* (New York).
WILLERT, ARTHUR. 1952. *The Road to Safety: A Study in Anglo-American Relations* (London).
WILSON, TREVOR, ed. 1970. *The Political Diaries of C. P. Scott, 1911–1928* (Ithaca).

E. Newspapers

London *Times,* 1916–1918.
Manchester Guardian, 1916–1917.
New York Times, 1916–1918.

II. SECONDARY SOURCES

BAKER, RAY STANNARD. 1923. *Woodrow Wilson and World Settlement* (3 v., New York) **1.**
BELOFF, MAX. 1969. *Imperial Sunset* (London).
BUTLER, J. R. M. 1960. *Lord Lothian (Philip Kerr) 1882–1940* (London).

COOPER, JOHN MILTON, JR. 1973. "The British Response to the House-Grey Memorandum: New Evidence and New Questions." *Jour. Amer. Hist.* **54**: pp. 958–971.
  The last five pages are devoted to the publication of several documents.
DUGDALE, BLANCHE E. C. 1936. *Arthur James Balfour* (2 v., London) **2**.
FEST, WILFRIED B. 1970. "The Habsburg Monarchy in British Policy, 1914–1918." (D. Phil. Dissertation, Oxford Univ.)
—— 1972. "British War Aims and German Peace Feelers during the First World War (December 1916–November 1918)" *Hist. Jour.* **15**: pp. 285–308.
FOWLER, W. B. 1969. *British-American Relations, 1917–1918: The Role of Sir William Wiseman* (Princeton).
Gelfand, Lawrence E. 1963. *The Inquiry: American Preparations for Peace, 1917–1919* (New Haven).
GEORGE, ALEXANDER L., and JULIETTE L. GEORGE. 1964. *Woodrow Wilson and Colonel House: A Personality Study* (New York).
GOLLIN, A. M. 1964. *Proconsul in Politics: A Study of Lord Milner in Opposition and Power* (London).
GREGORY, ROSS. 1970. *Walter Hines Page: Ambassador to the Court of St. James* (Louisville).
GUINN, PAUL. 1965. *British Strategy and Politics, 1914 to 1918* (Oxford).
HANCOCK, W. K. 1962–1968. *Smuts: The Sanguine Years, 1870–1919* (2 v., Cambridge, England) **1**.
HOELZLE, ERWIN. 1962. "Das Experiment des Friedens im Ersten Weltkrieg 1914–1917." *Geschicte in Wissenschaft und Unterricht* 13th year: pp. 465–522.
HYDE, MONTGOMERY. 1967. *Lord Reading: The Life of Rufus Isaacs, First Marquess of Reading* (London).
LANGER, WILLIAM L. 1957. "From Isolation to Mediation" and "Peace and the New World Order." *Woodrow Wilson and the World Today,* edited by Arthur P. Dudden (Philadelphia).
LEVIN, N. GORDON. 1968. *Woodrow Wilson and World Politics: America's Response to War and Revolution* (New York).
LINK, ARTHUR S. 1954. *Woodrow Wilson and the Progressive Era, 1910–1917* (New York).
—— 1956. *Wilson: The New Freedom* (Princeton).
—— 1959. *President Wilson and His English Critics* (Oxford).
  This essay has been reprinted in the collection of Link's essays published in 1971. See below.
—— 1964. *Wilson: Confusions and Crises, 1915–1916* (Princeton).
—— 1965. *Wilson: Campaigns for Progressivism and Peace, 1916–1917* (Princeton).
—— 1965a. *Wilson the Diplomatist: A Look at his Major Foreign Policies* (reprint edition, Chicago).
—— 1966. "Woodrow Wilson and Peace Moves." *The Listener* **75**: pp. 868–871.
  This article has also been reprinted in the collection of Link's essays cited immediately below.
—— 1971. *The Higher Realism of Woodrow Wilson and Other Essays* (Nashville).
—— 1973. Untitled essay. *Wilson's Diplomacy: An International Symposium.* Edited by J. Joseph Huthmacher and Warren I. Susman. (Cambridge, Mass.).
LOUIS, WILLIAM ROGER. 1967. *Great Britain and Germany's Lost Colonies, 1914–1919* (Oxford).
MAMATEY, VICTOR S. 1957. *The United States and East Central Europe, 1914–1918: A Study in Wilsonian Diplomacy and Propaganda* (Princeton).
MARTIN, LAURENCE. 1958. *Peace without Victory: Woodrow Wilson and the British Liberals* (New Haven).

MASON, CHRISTOPHER M. 1970. "British Policy on the Establishment of a League of Nations, 1914–1919." (Ph.D. Dissertation, Cambridge Univ.)
MAY, ERNEST R. 1959. *The World War and American Isolation, 1914–1917* (Cambridge, Mass.).
MAYER, ARNO J. 1959. *The Political Origins of the New Diplomacy, 1917–1918* (New Haven).
—— 1968. *Politics and Diplomacy of Peacemaking: Containment and Counterrevolution at Versailles, 1918–1919* (London).
MORGAN, KENNETH O. 1970. "Lloyd George's Premiership: A Study in 'Prime Ministerial Government'." *Hist. Jour.* **13**: pp. 130–157.
NELSON, HAROLD I. 1963. *Land and Power: British and Allied Policy on Germany's Frontiers, 1916–1919* (London).
NORTHEDGE, F. S. 1966. *The Troubled Giant: Britain Among the Great Powers, 1916–1939* (London).
NOTTER, HARLEY. 1937. *The Origins of the Foreign Policy of Woodrow Wilson* (Baltimore).
OSGOOD, ROBERT E. 1953. *Ideals and Self-Interest in America's Foreign Relations: The Great Transformation of the Twentieth Century* (Chicago).
OWEN, FRANK. 1955. *Tempestuous Journey: Lloyd George, His Life and Times* (New York).
PARRINI, CARL P. 1969. *Heir to Empire: United States Economic Diplomacy, 1916–1923* (Pittsburgh).
PELLING, HENRY. 1956. *America and the British Left: From Bright to Bevan* (London).
RAPPAPORT, ARMIN. 1951. *The British Press and Wilsonian Neutrality* (London).
RENOUVIN, PIERRE. 1968. *L'Armistice de Rethondes, 11 Novembre 1918* (Paris).
ROBBINS, KEITH. 1971. *Sir Edward Grey, A Biography of Lord Grey of Fallodon* (London).
ROSKILL, STEPHEN. 1968. *Naval Policy Between the Wars: The Period of Anglo-American Antagonism, 1919–1929* (London).
ROTHWELL, V. H. 1971. *British War Aims and Peace Diplomacy, 1914–1918* (Oxford).
RUDIN, HARRY R. 1944. *Armistice 1918* (New Haven).
SEYMOUR, CHARLES. 1942. *American Diplomacy During the World War* (Baltimore).
TAYLOR, A. J. P. 1957. *The Trouble Makers: Dissent over Foreign Policy, 1792–1939* (London).
—— 1964. *Politics in Wartime and other Essays* (London).
—— 1965. *English History, 1914–1945* (Oxford).
TILLMAN, SETH P. 1961. *Anglo-American Relations at the Paris Peace Conference of 1919* (Princeton).
TRASK, DAVID F. 1961. *The United States in the Supreme War Council: American War Aims and Inter-Allied Strategy, 1917–1918* (Middletown, Conn.).
—— 1973. *Captains and Cabinets: Anglo-American Naval Relations, 1917–1918* (Columbia, Mo.).
TREVELYAN, GEORGE MACAULAY. 1937. *Grey of Fallodon* (London).
TUCHMANN, BARBARA W. 1958. *The Zimmermann Telegram* (London).
WALTERS, F. P. 1952. *A History of the League of Nations* (2 v., London) **1**.
WARMAN, ROBERTA M. 1972. "The Erosion of Foreign Office Influence in the Making of Foreign Policy, 1916–1918." *Hist. Jour.* **15**: pp. 133–159.
WELLS, SAMUEL F., JR. 1972. "New Perspectives on Wilsonian Diplomacy: The Secular Evangelism of American Political Economy." *Perspectives in Amer. History* **6**: pp. 389–419.

WILLIAMS, WILLIAM APPLEMAN. 1962. *The Tragedy of American Diplomacy* (New York).

WINKLER, HENRY R. 1967. *The League of Nations Movement in Great Britain 1914–1919* (reprint edition, Meteuchen, N. J.).

WOODWARD, DAVID R. 1970. "Great Britain and President Wilson's Efforts to End World War I in 1916." *Maryland Historian* 1: pp. 45–58.

—— 1971. "David Lloyd George, A Negotiated Peace with Germany and the Kuhlmann Peace Kite of September, 1917." *Canadian Jour. History* 6: pp. 75–93.

—— 1971. "The Origins and Intent of David Lloyd George's January 5 War Aims Speech." *The Historian* 34: pp. 22–39.

YOUNG, KENNETH. 1963. *Arthur James Balfour: The Happy Life of the Politician, Prime Minister, Statesman and Philosopher, 1848–1930* (London).

ZEMAN, Z. A. B. 1971. *A Diplomatic History of the First World War* (London).

INDEX

The Resignation of George Washington as Commander-in-Chief
of the Continental Army, December 23, 1783

The Ratification of the Treaty of Paris, January 14, 1784

Bicentennial Celebrations

ANNAPOLIS, MARYLAND
December 23, 1983 – January 14, 1984

George Washington's Resignation

When General George Washington resigned as Commander-in-Chief of the Continental Army, he set a precedent that is still one of the most important principles of America's freedoms.

Washington understood clearly that he walked on untrodden ground and everything he did would set a precedent. He and the Congress agreed that the military must remain under civilian authority and he resolved to return his commission to the body that had appointed him Commander-in-Chief of the Continental Army on June 15, 1775.

Turning his commission over to the Continental Congress as it existed in those days was truly an act of faith. It was a Congress that had not paid its own soldiers for four years and had no power to raise money. Many of its delegates did not even show up for sessions. It was, in the words of one citizen of the day, "responsible for everything, unable to do anything, hated by the public creditors, insulted by the soldiery and unsupported by the citizens."

After an emotional farewell to his officers at Fraunces Tavern, General Washington left New York for Annapolis on December 4, 1783. At each major town along the way, including Philadelphia, Wilmington and Baltimore, he was feted with elegant dinners and balls. When he arrived at Annapolis on December 19, he was welcomed by a number of prominent Annapolitans at the town gates on West Street and cannons were fired to greet him. He lodged during his stay at the new Mann's Tavern on Conduit Street.

The Continental Congress did not, as usual, have even the minimum number of delegates needed to do business. But it was decided that the representatives of the seven states in attendance could receive the resignation and they issued the following Resolution: "Decided that His Excellency, the Commander-in-Chief, be admitted to a public audience the following Tuesday (23) at noon – a public entertainment be given Monday (22)."

Monday was, indeed, a day of celebration. A lavish dinner, capped by 13 toasts, was held in the afternoon and, in the evening, a dance was held in the State House. For the public not invited to the ball, Cornelius Mills was authorized to serve liquors at his tavern.

On the morning of December 23, General Washington made his way on foot through the streets of Annapolis in full military dress to the State House. At the State House, he was ushered into the Old Senate Chamber where the delegates awaited him, seated with their hats on in accordance with previously agreed protocol. Before speaking, Washington bowed both to the President of the Congress and to the delegates who removed their hats for a moment to recognize his presence but did not bow.

With shaking hands and a voice that was choked with emotion, Washington read an address to the Congress which ended with these words: ". . . commending the interests of our dearest country to the protection of Almighty God and those who have superintendence of them to his holy keeping . . . I here offer my commission and take my leave of all the employments of public life." By one account of the scene: "It was a solemn and affecting spectacle . . . The spectators all wept, and there was hardly a member of Congress who did not shed tears."

As soon as the ceremony was finished, Washington left for his beloved Mount Vernon where he would spend Christmas with his wife, Martha. He was accompanied on his journey home as far as the South River by Governor William Paca.

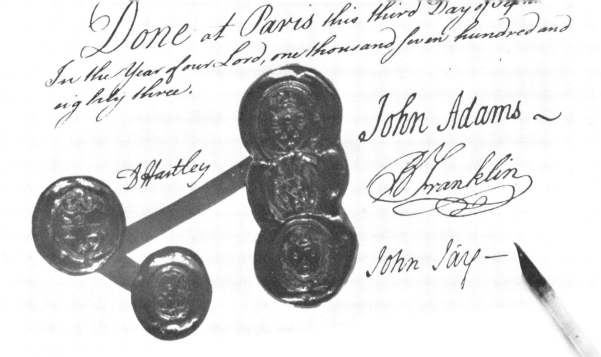

Done at Paris this third Day of Sep. In the Year of our Lord, one thousand seven hundred and eighty three.

B Hartley

John Adams

B Franklin

John Jay

The Treaty of Paris - The Work of Peace

The Declaration of Independence of July 1776 sounded the call for a free America but it took almost eight years of bloodshed to make freedom a reality. It finally came with the ratification of the Treaty of Paris in Annapolis on January 14, 1784.

The Treaty of Paris had been signed by British and American negotiators in Paris on September 3, 1783 but it still had to be ratified by the American Congress before the Revolutionary War would be officially over and America could become a full-fledged member of the community of nations.

As the United States' first peace treaty, the Treaty of Paris is one of the most important documents in American history. In it, Great Britain not only recognized the independence of her former colonies but also granted the new country's claim to all of the land south of Canada, east of the Mississippi, west of the Appalachians and north of Florida. This doubled the size of America at a single stroke.

These extraordinary provisions were the result of the work of a brilliant team of American negotiators in Paris – Benjamin Franklin, John Jay, John Adams and Henry Laurens. The achievement of these men in gaining these concessions from Great Britain was enormous as there were other countries, especially France and Spain, who could have laid claim to many of the territories. The negotiations were, in the words of Benjamin Franklin, "the best of all works, the work of peace."

The events and negotiations that led up to the ratification of the Treaty of Paris had gone on since 1779. In October 1781, General Cornwallis surrendered at Yorktown but it was not until November 1782 that the Preliminary Articles of Peace were signed in Paris and the following month King George III, in a speech to Parliament, finally recognized the independence of the colonies. On September 3, 1783, the definitive Treaty of Paris was signed.

The definitive treaty had to be quickly ratified so that copies of treaties signed by both sides could be exchanged by the deadline of March 3, 1784, six months after the signing. The American copy of the treaty reached the President of the Continental Congress, Thomas Mifflin of Pennsylvania, on November 22, and he immediately wrote to the governors of the 13 states asking them to send representatives to the Continental Congress as soon as possible. Congress was scheduled to meet in Annapolis on November 26, but it was not until December 13 that the first session was held.

While awaiting the necessary number of delegates to arrive to take action on the treaty, Congress witnessed another pivotal event in the founding of the country – the resignation of George Washington as Commander-in-Chief of the Continental Army on December 23, 1783.

During this wait, a controversy was raging in Congress. One faction wanted to go ahead and ratify the treaty without all of the delegates needed under the terms of the Articles of Confederation of 1781, arguing, in effect, that the British would never know the difference. The other side, led by Thomas Jefferson, insisted that it was important that they obey their own rules. This side prevailed and set another important precedent in the formation of the nation.

Finally, on the morning of January 14, 1784, the Congress was able to ratify the treaty. As the deadline for returning the ratified treaty to Paris was fast approaching, three separate copies were sent with three different messengers to ensure that at least one arrived safely.

The treaty did not, in fact, make it to Paris before the deadline and the British could have, technically, negated the entire treaty. They were, thankfully, not inclined to prolong the hostilities any longer and the ratifications were amicably exchanged on May 12, 1784, almost eight years after the Declaration of Independence.

The John Shaw Flags

The Shaw flags which will be flying in Annapolis during the Bicentennial celebrations are replicas of the original pair of flags ordered by the Governor and the Council of Maryland to welcome the President of Congress when Congress met in Annapolis from November 26, 1783 until June 3, 1784. The first official session of Congress in Annapolis was December 13, 1783.

When Congress passed a resolution in 1777 outlining what the flag of the United States should look like, it was not very precise and, therefore, left a lot of room for variation. While it gave a very sketchy description, "The flag . . . be 13 stripes alternate red and white . . . the union be 13 stars white on a field of blue representing a constellation," it did not specify size, arrangement or number of points on each star, nor which color of stripe, red or white, was to be used first. Without such guidelines, flags made by different flag makers varied widely. Some were quite large; others were small, narrow, or even triangular. It was not until 1818 that detailed instructions and drawings of the "Standard Flag of the United States" were drawn up and sent to all garrisons.

John Shaw was the chief mechanic, maintenance supervisor and carpenter of the present Maryland State House. Born in Glasgow, Scotland in 1745, he arrived in Annapolis in the early 1770s. Though best known as a cabinetmaker, having been a partner in a cabinet shop on Church Street, Shaw was also an inventor, state armourer, a local assessor, an undertaker, merchant and City Councilman. His principal concern was the State House, probably already under construction when he arrived in the city.

Upon discovery of a receipt in the Maryland Archives for the material Shaw used in making his flags, the advice of an expert on flags was sought in order to help reconstruct the original flags. Mrs. Grace Rogers Cooper, one of the country's foremost authorities on flags and the author of "Thirteen Star Flags," was asked to help with the reconstruction.

Mrs. Cooper was able to determine, from the amount of material ordered by the state in 1783, the design and size of each flag. With this information, Mrs. Cooper concluded that each flag measured nine feet, nine inches by twenty-three feet and that one flag began with a red stripe while the other began with a white stripe. Since eight-point stars were commonly used in 1783, they were selected for the replica flags.

The flags have been donated to the state by the Maryland State Society of the Daughters of the American Revolution and are being presented by Mrs. Charles A. Bloedorn, Regent of the Maryland DAR, in a dedication ceremony at St. John's College on December 13th.

Annapolis-America's First Peacetime Capital

Annapolis in the 1780s was a small town of about 1,200 people, described by a delegate to the Continental Congress as "pleasantly situated on a bason which forms the mouth of the River Severn. They count about 300 houses some of them Superb and Magnificent with corresponding Gardens and Improvements."

Annapolis was not a major city like New York, Philadelphia or Boston but it had been the capital of Maryland since 1694 and, in 1783-4, it was the focus of the nation and the world.

When George Washington came to Annapolis in December 1783, construction of the State House was not complete, though it had served the state legislature since 1779 and had been the seat of the Continental Congress for more than a month. That winter of 1783-4 was an extremely harsh one, the Bay was frozen for months and the delegates complained about the unreliability of stage and post and the high cost of firewood.

The city was the winter home of many of the landed gentry and was the center of the political and judicial life of the state as well as the county seat of Anne Arundel county. In 1783, it was a congested town where prices were high, lodgings scarce and goods from Europe hard to obtain.

Despite the problems of war debts, inflation and the needs of returning veterans, the fortunate elite of Annapolis were still able to enjoy much of the social life for which Annapolis was famous before the war. There were races and theatre in season and many dinners, teas and balls. One delegate raved about Annapolis cuisine, such as "the good fat turkie, the fine fish and Delightful Oysters."

George Washington had been a frequent visitor to the city and had many friends there; he especially enjoyed the theatre and horse racing, a favorite pastime for almost everyone. Many of the announcements in the local weekly newspaper, the Maryland Gazette, concerned horses. The Gazette was published every Thursday by the Green family and was, in effect, the town bulletin board.

Fifty of the 300 buildings in Annapolis in 1783 are still standing, or have been faithfully reconstructed, and they will be marked for the celebrations with replicas of the John Shaw flag. A self-guided walking tour of these buildings has been mapped out along with historical information and is available from the Visitors' Center in the State House.

ANNAPOLIS, *December 25.*

On Friday evening laſt his EXCELLENCY GENERAL WASHINGTON, with his ſuite, arrived here on his way to Mount Vernon. His Excellency was met, a few miles from this city, by the honourable generals Gates and Smallwood, and ſeveral of the principal inhabitants, who attended him to Mr. Mann's, where apartments had been prepared for his reception. His Excellency's arrival was announced by the diſcharge of cannon. After receiving the heart felt welcome of all who had the honour of knowing him—his Excellency waited on the Preſident of Congreſs, with whom he and the members of that body, together with the principal civil and military officers of this ſtate, dined on Saturday. On Sunday morning his Excellency returned the viſits of the citizens and others who had waited on him, after which he dined, with a number of other gentlemen, with Mr. Harford.

On Monday Congreſs gave his Excellency a public dinner at the Ball-room, where upwards of two hundred perſons of diſtinction were preſent; every thing being provided by Mr. Mann in the moſt elegant and profuſe ſtile. After dinner the following toaſts were drank, under the diſcharge of the artillery.

1. The United States.
2. The Army.
3. His Moſt Chriſtian Majeſty.
4. The United Netherlands.
5. The King of Sweden.
6. Our Commiſſioners abroad.
7. The Miniſter of France.
8. The Miniſter of the United Netherlands.
9. Harmony and a flouriſhing commerce throughout the union.
10. May virtue and wiſdom influence the councils of the United States, and may their conduct merit the bleſſings of Peace and Independence.
11. The virtuous daughters of America.
12. Governor and ſtate of Maryland.
13. Long health and happineſs to our illuſtrious general.

At night the ſtadt-houſe was beautifully illuminated, where a Ball was given by the General Aſſembly, at which a very numerous and brilliant appearance of ladies were preſent.

The following are the Addreſſes of the honourable the Governor and the Council, the General Aſſembly, and the Corporation, to his Excellency, with his Anſwers.

Annapolis, December 26, 1783.

Schedule of Bicentennial Events

Tuesday, December 13   Dedication of the John Shaw Flag.

1:00 pm   Dedication ceremony of the John Shaw Flag of 1783 at the flag pole, McDowell Hall, St. John's College. The flag will be presented to the state by Mrs. Charles A. Bloedorn, State Regent of the Daughters of the American Revolution, and will be accepted by the Maryland Hall of Records, the Maryland Historical Trust and St. John's College. The Westminster High School Marching Band from Carroll County will perform.

Thursday, December 22   Candlelight Receptions.

7:00 –
9:30 pm   Sponsored by the Mayor's Bicentennial Committee of Annapolis. The public may enjoy light refreshments by candlelight in six of the city's most historic buildings: William Paca House, Hammond-Harwood House, Chase-Lloyd House, Ogle Hall (Alumni House), John Callahan House and Lloyd Dulany House (the Masonic Temple). There will be a $3 charge to attend.

Friday, December 23   Resignation Day.

George Washington's resignation as Commander-in-Chief of the Continental Army will be re-enacted.

10:30 –
11:00 am   George Washington will walk from the site of Mann's Tavern on Conduit Street to the State House where he will be greeted by the Mayor of Annapolis. The public is invited to join him in his walk and there will be a gun salute while it is in progress.

11:00 am   Raising of the John Shaw Flag over the State House where it will fly during the Bicentennial celebrations. Ceremony will be accompanied by fife & drum music and a musket salute.

12:00 pm   George Washington will go into the Old Senate Chamber where he will resign his commission. To be televised live by the Maryland Center for Public Broadcasting and narrated by Roger Mudd.

Exhibits will open in the State House to the public in the

Shilling: The Baltimore Museum of Art; gift of Virginia P.B. White, Baltimore

Front cover: From the Collection of the Hammond-Harwood House Association. Photocopy courtesy of the Maryland Hall of Records Commission

Courtesy of Historic Annapolis, Inc.

Courtesy of David W. Harp

afternoon: "Annapolis the Capital," "The Road to Peace," "Washington Bowed" and "On The Map." These exhibits, arranged by the Maryland Hall of Records, will be on display in the State House.

January 3 – 14   County Observance Days.
Many of Maryland's counties will sponsor exhibits in Annapolis. These will be on display in the Treasury Building on Bladen Street. There will also be musical programs offered by a number of the counties.

Maryland Heritage Weekend, January 6 – 8.

Friday, January 6   Music in Colonial Annapolis.
8:15 pm   A program of music that was performed in Annapolis during the middle of the 1700s. Key Auditorium, St. John's College. Free tickets will be available after December 15th at various locations in Annapolis (see local press for details). Program arranged and directed by Dr. John Barry Talley, Director of Musical Activities, U.S. Naval Academy.

Saturday, January 7   Historic Properties Tour.
11:00 am
and
2:00 pm   Guides will conduct tours of seven historic buildings. The cost of the tour, which will last about two hours, will be $8 for adults and $6.50 for senior citizens and youths aged 6-18. Please call the Reservations Office at Historic Annapolis, Inc. for reservations (301) 267-8149, Baltimore area 269-1910.

3:00
and
7:30 pm   **Pageant of the Maryland Soldier.**
This colorful sound and light presentation will follow the history of the Maryland soldier for 350 years, using authentic uniforms and equipment. Halsey Field House, United States Naval Academy. Tickets are free and are available from the USNA Public Affairs Office, the State House Visitors' Center and other locations around the state (see local press for details).

Sunday, January 8   Historic Properties Tour.
11:00 am   Make reservations, see January 7.
and 2:00 pm

Friday, January 13   Lecture on the Treaty of Paris.
8:15 pm   *"How the Great Peace of 1783 was Made and Ratified."* By Professor Richard Morris, Gouverneur Morris Professor of History Emeritus, Columbia University. Key Auditorium, St. John's College.

Saturday, January 14   Treaty of Paris Ratification Day.
10:30 am   **Memorial Ceremony.**
At the French Monument, St. John's College.

11:00 am   Tactical demonstration with music and musketry of the American Revolution by the Annapolis Bicentennial Brigade.

1:30 pm   **Ratification of the Treaty of Paris.**
Program in the Old Senate Chamber of the State House. To be televised by the Maryland Center for Public Broadcasting.

1:30 pm   **18th Century Parade.**
Battalions of 1,200 American and French troops led by U.S. Army's ceremonial Commander-in-Chief's Guard and Fife & Drum Corp, and 18th Century field music. Beginning at St. John's College and ending at the State House. See map for parade route.

Feu de Joie.
Spectacular 18th Century military celebration with music, artillery and continuous volley of muskets, State Circle.

Ringing of Church Bells in City of Annapolis.

Mustering out of the First Maryland Regiment, Maryland's official Bicentennial troops, front lawn, St. John's College.

8:30 pm   **Fireworks over the Annapolis Harbor.**

9:00 pm –
1:00 am   **Treaty of Paris Ball.**
Sponsored by the Chamber of Commerce of Greater Annapolis, in the George Washington Room of the Hilton Hotel. For information call 268-7676.

For further information on Bicentennial events call
(301) 268-9080

Maryland's 350th Anniversary

This is a gala year for Maryland. Not only is the state celebrating its unique role in the birth of the American nation, but 1984 is Maryland's 350th anniversary.

In March 1634, some 140 travelers arrived at St. Clement's Island in the Potomac River and, shortly thereafter, established the first settlement, St. Mary's City, in southern Maryland. It had been four months since they had sailed on the Ark and the Dove from Cowes on the Isle of Wight off the south coast of England.

St. Mary's City was the first capital of Maryland, from 1634 to 1694, and during that time, Marylanders made some significant contributions to the traditions of American freedom.

To commemorate this proud heritage, the State of Maryland and her counties will be holding special celebrations throughout 1984. The events began on November 22 with a ceremony in Cowes to mark the sailing of the Ark and Dove.

On Maryland Day, March 25, celebrations will be held on St. Clement's Island and in St. Mary's City. On St. Clement's Island, the landing will be re-enacted and a Mass will be said using 17th century liturgy and vestments. Ecumenical services will also take place, commemorating Maryland's long tradition of religious toleration. In St. Mary's City a new museum and visitors' center will be officially opened. Also, a special commemorative session of the Maryland General Assembly will convene at the place it first met nearly 350 years ago.

On April 21, the 335th anniversary of the passage of the "Toleration Act," which was the first enactment into law of the Calvert policy of separation of Church and State, will be commemorated. June 20 has been designated Charter Day to mark the granting of the Charter of Maryland to Cecil Calvert, Second Lord Baltimore, in 1632 in England.

"Lord Baltimore's World" will be celebrated at St. Mary's City over eight consecutive weekends from May 19 to July 8 with skits, games, music, drama, story-tellings, arts & crafts and a food festival all blended together to make 17th century England and Maryland come to life.

On June 23-24, the official state celebration of the 350th anniversary will take place at St. Mary's City, with the dedication of the new St. Mary's museum and other events.

Another important milestone in the development of America's rights and freedoms is Margaret Brent Day on January 21. Widely regarded as America's first suffragette, Mistress Brent asked for two votes in the 1647/48 Maryland General Assembly, a request that was denied.

Maryland's Bicentennial and 350th anniversary celebrations are taking place under the auspices of the Maryland Heritage Committee. For further information, write to The Maryland Heritage Committee, Room H4, State House, Annapolis, MD 21404.

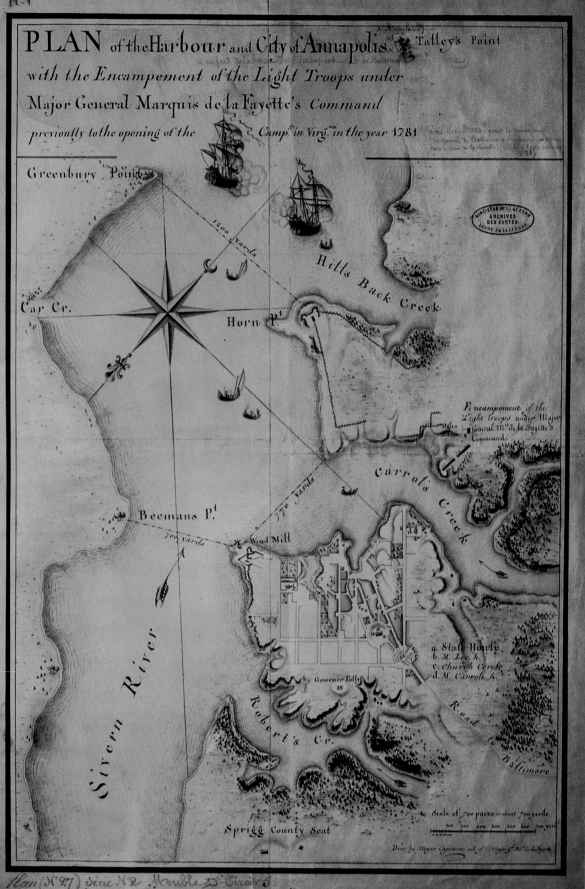

PLAN of the Harbour and City of Annapolis. Talley's Point

with the Encampement of the Light Troops under

Major General Marquis de la Fayette's Command

previously to the opening of the Camp. in Virg.ia in the year 1781

Greenbury Point

Car Cr.

Hills Back Creek

Horn Pt.

Encampement of the Light troops under Major General Mr. de la Fayette's Command.

Carrols Creek

Beemans Pt.

Wind Mill

Severn River

a. State House.
b. Mr. Lee. h.
c. Church Circle.
d. M. Carrols. h.

Governor Folly

Robert's Cr.

Road to Baltimore

Scale of 700 paces or about 700 yards

Sprigg County Seat

Courtesy of M.E. Warren